HEADWATERS

Walking to
British River Sources

HEADWATERS

Walking to British River Sources

F

FRANCES LINCOLN LIMITED
PUBLISHERS

PHIL CLAYTON

Frances Lincoln Limited
www.franceslincoln.com

Headwaters: Walking to British River Sources
Copyright © Frances Lincoln Limited 2012
Text copyright © Phil Clayton 2012
Illustrations copyright © Phil Clayton 2012
except for those listed on page 224
First Frances Lincoln edition 2012

A catalogue record for this book is available from the
British Library.

9780711233638
Printed and bound in China

1 2 3 4 5 6 7 8 9

A note on the maps:
The sketch maps in this book are indicative only of the
locations of rivers and their sources. Detailed Ordnance
Survey mapping should be used when in the field, or on
the hill, or in the swamp . . .
PAGE 2 On the Dyfi
PAGE 3 *Source of the Severn*, a nineteenth-century view.

**For Dot, Cathy, Kate, Ruby, Bella and
Marigold – the ladies in my life.**

KEY

 Sea

Urban areas

High ground

* Features of interest

▲ Summits

 Road

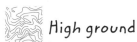 Direction of
river flow

CONTENTS

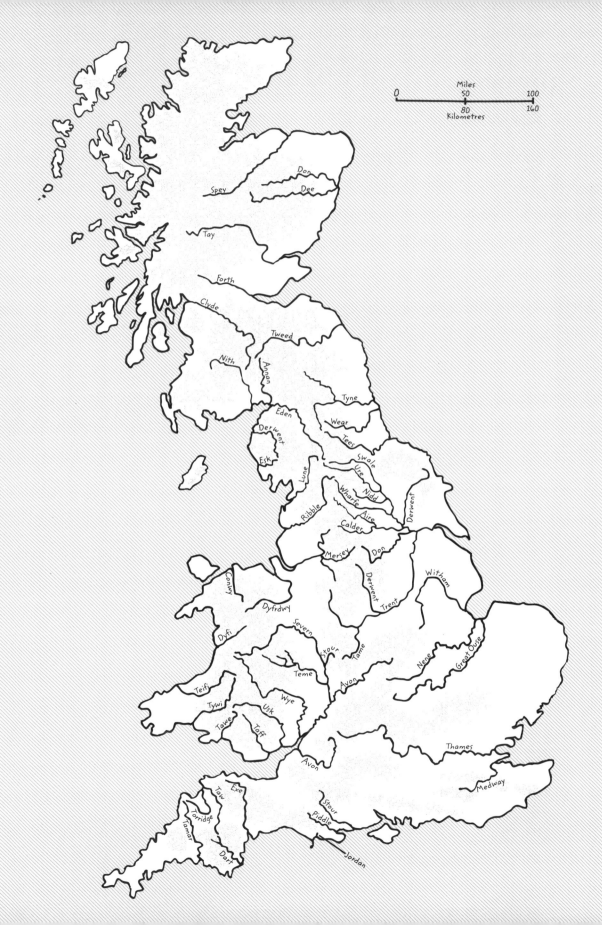

Miles
0
50
100
80
160
Kilometres

Spey
Don
Dee
Tay
Forth
Clyde
Tweed
Nith
Annan
Tyne
Eden
Wear
Derwent
Tees
Esk
Swale
Lune
Ure
Nidd
Wharfe
Ribble
Aire
Derwent
Calder
Don
Mersey
Derwent
Witham
Trent
Conwy
Dyfrdwy
Severn
Nene
Great Ouse
Dyfi
Stour
Tame
Teme
Avon
Teifi
Wye
Tywi
Usk
Thames
Tawe
Taff
Avon
Medway
Exe
Taw
Stour
Torridge
Piddle
Tamar
Jordan
Dart

INTRODUCTION:
WHY SOURCES?

Everyone knows that a source is where a river begins. To define it: 'the fountain-head or origin of a river or stream; the spring or place from which a flow of water takes its beginning'.[1] However, things are not as straightforward on the ground as they are in the dictionary. Although for a few rivers there is but one fountainhead, while others are reckoned to start from the confluence of a couple of headwaters, many rivers have a plethora of little streams, each making a bid to be the source. The dendritic pattern of many river systems means that looking for the source is rather like searching for the ultimate end of the uttermost twig of the furthermost branch of a convoluted tree.

A comparison with hilltops may be apt. A summit is a fixed and usually visible point. When you reach the top of a hill or mountain, you will normally find

a cairn or one of the Ordnance Survey's trig points. Although there are some exceptions to this rule – on certain lesser-known hills the true summit can be hard to find, the top just a slightly higher peat hag or one tussock among hundreds – but generally, with a bit of scurrying around, you can enjoy the satisfaction of having visited it.

The source of a river is a very different animal. According to season, it can fluctuate. In a dry spell it may move downstream. In winter it could well be frozen or hidden under snow. In a downpour it might be dripping off your chin. Maps are not quite as helpful as they are with summits either. If a top has a trig point, then it will be shown; failing that there is generally a little dot and altitude number of a spot height to help with location. In the case of rivers there will just be the end of a faint blue line (the beginning, really) and perhaps 'Tees Head' or some such printed over a fairly wide area.

1   *Oxford English Dictionary.*

The source road

One way of solving the problem would be to measure the various tributaries, giving the longest the honour of being the source, or the one with the strongest flow or the one that starts from the greatest altitude. However, making measurements in the field can be difficult or tedious, and those taken from maps may not always be absolutely reliable; anyway, it all seems a little too clinical. Searching out every last runnel, however honourable in intent, could be thought of as taking things a little too far and could even lead to accusations of – perish the thought – obsession. Let such calculations be left to the more scientifically minded; let the source be where landscape and emotion suggest it ought to be, and hang the bit of string and the ruler. Some might even argue that where the source actually is doesn't matter anyway – it's the idea of the source that fires the imagination and drives the seeker to look for it.

There is a challenge in looking for where rivers start. We usually see our rivers in the lowlands, when they are already broad and settled, but to discover one at its beginning and to follow its first, faltering trickles until it widens out and begins to flow confidently down its valley is to gain a different perspective. To cross that same river some time later knowing that you have seen it at source is like sharing a secret with an old friend. In the nineteenth century explorers spent fortunes, went mad and occasionally died seeking sources. Our rivers may not have the length and grandeur of the Amazon or the Zambezi, but the ones that rise in the uplands have their birthplaces in remote and sometimes wild areas. Merely being in such places is rewarding in itself, but to search for sources is really to get away from the beaten track. And if finding river sources in hills and mountains is difficult enough, then searching them out in urban areas is sometimes an impossibility, albeit one that can lead to Holmesian contemplation and much scratching around among old maps and documents, new streets and drain covers. Living as I do but a spit and a stride away from the English watershed, it behoves me to seek out the birthplaces of a couple of my nearest, urban rivers.

Hydronymy, the branch of linguistics dealing with the study of the names of water bodies like rivers, lakes and seas, is a fascinating subject. Many river names are very old: Nene, Tees, Tyne and Ure, for instance, are thought to date back to pre-Celtic times. Several names are from the same root. Exe, Axe, Esk and Usk come from the Old Celtic *isca*, meaning simply 'water' or 'fast flowing', while Tame, Teme, Taff, Tamar and Thames also share the same etymology, although the meaning is less clear; maybe 'dark water'. Trent is likely to be related to 'torrent' and Avon is simply another Celtic word, *afon*, for 'river', making river Avon the tautological 'river river'. It has increased my enjoyment and understanding of the landscape to learn a little about the meanings of Welsh and Gaelic place names and so, where thought not too dangerous for an Englishman, I have included a glossary with the entries for rivers in Wales and Scotland.

The Greek philosopher Heraclitus said 'You cannot step twice into the same river; for other waters are continually flowing in' and you'd be hard pressed to follow exactly some of the routes I've taken. In fact, I'd be hard pressed to, so this book is certainly not intended to be any kind of definitive guide. How can it be, when most sources themselves are not clearly defined? Indeed it is difficult to find consensus among different authorities even on the lengths of British rivers. That marvellous compendium of etymology, fact and fable *Brewer's Britain and Ireland* is at times at odds with the scholarly cornucopia that is the *Encyclopaedia Britannica*, while one of the best general books on the subject of the last few years, *Rivers and the British Landscape*,[2] quotes the *Guinness Book of Answers* as the reference for its table of river lengths. Uncannily, some books and websites confer precisely the same length, 70 miles (113km), on the rivers Tees, Medway, Mersey and Dyfrdwy

---

2 Owen, Pooley et al, Carnegie, 2005.

(Dee) and the Yorkshire Don. I contacted the Environment Agency, the UK government agency concerned mainly with rivers, and this resulted in a conversation with the extremely helpful Jonathan of the National Request Team who explained that, as the agency is more concerned with water quality and navigation and as it works across different regions which the same river may traverse, even it doesn't have a definitive list. So once more I say hang the bit of string and the ruler and concede that river lengths stated in this work are approximate.

I've been visiting sources for years, often without thinking about it, as when I walked the Pennine Way and splashed through several, but sometimes for that sole purpose, as when I took my excited four-year-old to Trewsbury Mead to look for the Thames in 1984 and found a dry field; but it has been only during the past three years that I've gone out specifically to find them. In that time I have visited sources during every month of the year and under many different meteorological conditions, and the accounts given here reflect that. I have had so much fun doing the groundwork, fieldwork and hackwork for this book that I would encourage anyone remotely interested to go out and find their nearest source. You may well be doing something unique, for while there is a defined number of mountains there is no end to the rivers, streams, becks, waters, sikes, gills, burns, streamlets, rills, brooks and bournes which can be traced back to their beginning, and the source you find on one day may not be the same as the one I found last year.

The fifty or so river sources described in this book have been included for a variety of reasons. Many of the rivers are among the longest in Great Britain. Others rise in the uplands and remote areas that attract my feet. Some have been chosen on a whim – who could resist the Piddle or the Jordan? The rivers are ordered in a broadly geographical pattern with a general trend from south to north.

It must be stressed that the walking, particularly in some areas of the Highlands of Scotland, the Pennines, Wales and Dartmoor, can sometimes be difficult and trying. The sources are often away from recognized paths and sometimes away from recognizable landmarks. Having spent half a lifetime and more tramping around such places I feel relatively inured to bogs, groughs, tussocks, bad weather and getting lost; anyway, has the person who's never been lost really been anywhere? Like another Blackburn lad, the great Lakeland guidebook author A. Wainwright, I like solitary walking and many of the jaunts described here have been on my own, but I have been lucky enough to have enjoyed the company of several friends who share my love of the remote places. They know who they are and I thank them.

When the indefatigable Victorian pedestrian George Borrow visited the source of the Severn, his guide encouraged him to drink the water and so 'take possession of the Holy Severn'. This is not a precedent that I have followed. Not because I have any objection to drinking wild water – indeed I've been known to lap out of puddles – but mainly because the 'here today, gone tomorrow' visitor can no more profess to capture the spirit of a river than can a mountaineer claim to conquer a summit.

I express no philosophical or spiritual reason for going out and looking for the starts of rivers; in my book source seeking is not soul searching, but it has been an immensely enjoyable experience that has taken me to parts of my country that I certainly would not otherwise have visited. It has taught me a great deal about the rivers themselves and about the landscapes where they rise. As the Scottish poet and novelist Nan Shepherd wrote: 'One cannot know the rivers till one has seen them at their sources; but this journey to the sources is not to be undertaken lightly.' I'm glad I didn't read that before I started!

PENINSULAR PERUSALS

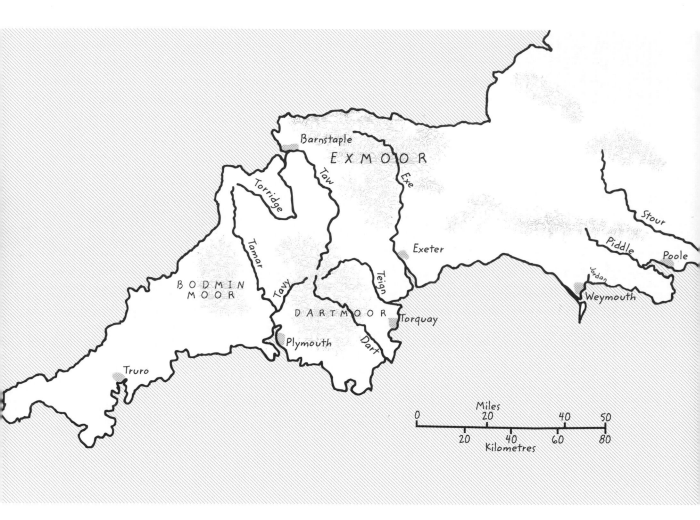

Britain's south-west peninsula – the traditional counties of Somerset, Dorset, Devon and Cornwall – juts defiantly into the Atlantic, narrowing westwards. This obviously restricts the length of rivers there but does not prevent two of them, the Exe and the Tamar, from taking virtually the longest possible course by rising almost on the north coast and ending on the south. Many of the south-west's rivers fan out from the high boss of Dartmoor and this chapter also includes the shortest river described in this book, the Dorset Jordan, and the one with the silliest name, the Piddle.

Exe
marks the spot

Shaped rather like a wedge of cheese, Exmoor rises precipitously from the sea, its sandstone strata dipping away more gently to the south. Thus it is that the Exe is born, a mere 5 miles (8km) from the Bristol Channel, to embark on a 54-mile (87km) journey to the English Channel. Like the other rivers rising on the moor, the Barle, the Bray, the East Lyn and the West Lyn, and lesser streams and waters, the Exe has cut a deep valley and it is these

EXE	
SOURCE	Exe Head, Devon
G.R.	SS 751 414
LENGTH	54 miles (87 kilometres)
TRIBUTARIES	Barle, Haddeo, Culm, Creedy
MOUTH	Exmouth

combes, with their steeply wooded sides, that characterize the local landscape. Just below the summit of the road between Simonsbath and Lynton, at Prayway Head, a lay-by is a good starting point for a visit to Exe Head. Here the Two Moors Way leaves the road and runs alongside a hedgebank before heading across collapsed-blancmange-shaped Dure Down. Exe Head stands in the broad col between Dure Down and Chains Barrow at the meeting point of tracks, paths, banks and fences. There are many of these banks and boundaries, leats and gutters, barrows and tumuli on Exmoor, reflecting a history reaching back to the Bronze Age, when people first cleared the higher land for farming.

A trickle of water crossing the track, marked as 'Ford' on the map, is the infant Exe. The tiny stream flows north for a couple of hundred yards, gaining more water from tricklets and drains, before swinging off to the east. After three-quarters of a mile (1.2km) the stream reaches the road at Exe Head Bridge, reconstructed in 1928, and flows on down its deepening valley through Exford and Exton, where it turns to the south, visiting Exbridge, Up Exe, Nether Exe, Exeter, Exwick, another Exton and Exmouth. There's no excuse for not knowing which river you're on. The walk from the lay-by to Exe Head and back via the bridge should take less than an hour.

It would be a shame to leave Exmoor without

Barle emerges

looking at some of its other features and a circular walk can include visits to several more of the sources found on the high moor. The first stretch, from the road to the source, is the route described above, across Dure Down. A signpost stands at Exe Head at the meeting of the Macmillan Way West, Two Moors Way and Tarka Trail. Fastened on to the post on a blustery March day, with a piece of elastic taken from someone's hair band, was a sad little faded message telling of lost rendezvous and missed meetings.

The path rises westerly alongside a barbed-wire entrenched ditch which carries a fair flow of water coming down from the Chains, the highest point on this stretch of Exmoor at almost 1,600 feet (488m). The actual summit of the moor is Dunkery Beacon, 100 feet (30.5m) higher and 9 miles (14.5km) further east. The ditch intercepts some of the little channels flowing down the moorland ridge and a spongy area just south of the trig point on Chains Barrow could well lay claim to be the Exe's source. Chains is a name reminiscent of chines, ravines in a cliff, and perhaps this is a reference to the steep little valleys on the north side of the ridge that feed West Lyn River and Hoaroak Water, a major tributary of the East Lyn. Chains Barrow itself, a grass-covered, circular, flat-topped mound about 30 yards (27.4m) in diameter and 5 feet (1.5m) high, stands in a little enclosure but a stile gives access to the trig point on top; it is described as a bowl barrow and probably dates from the Bronze Age. Returning to the track there is a gentle descent to Pinkworthy or Pinkery Pond.

Marks the spot

Appearing rather out of place on this lonely stretch of moor, the pond was created by damming the headwaters of the Barle. The earth dam was constructed around 1830 on the orders of John Knight, a Worcestershire ironmaster who had bought the former Royal Forest of Exmoor and its mineral rights from the Crown in 1818. The area had long been a royal hunting forest where deer and other animals were reserved for the monarch. Lying at about 1,445 feet (440.7m) above sea level, the pond has a surface area of about 7½ acres (3ha) and although its catchment area is limited the high annual rainfall more than compensates. Although the reason for its construction remains unknown, it is believed to have been part of a project to supply a leat to power a large waterwheel to be built near Simonsbath. The wheel would have assisted the working of an incline on a railway transporting iron ore from Exmoor to Porlock Weir. The scheme came to nothing and Knight retired to Rome. His son Frederick continued to improve the land and build farms on the moor. The little river Barle flows through the dam and emerges mysteriously from a cleft in the rock. Heather grows around it but the more common vegetation on this part of the moor, as anyone who follows the Barle upstream towards its source will discover, is blanket bog. Typical plants found here include cotton grass, deer sedge, bog asphodel, cross-leaved heath and even sundew and heath spotted orchid. At the end of a long winter it was a pale prairie of tussocky moor grass. Handy sheep tracks can be found crossing the squishy top of the broad col to the head of the West Lyn valley.

Looking down the peaceful and beautiful valley from the source of the West Lyn, it is difficult to imagine the day, in August 1952, when this calm was shattered. In just twenty-four hours, some 9 inches (228mm) of rain fell on an already saturated Exmoor from a depression that had stagnated in the south-west approaches for two days. As the water came off the moor it was channelled into the East and West Lyn rivers, which came together as a raging wall of floodwater in the restricted valley above Lynmouth. Buildings were battered by thousands of tons of rocks and debris carried along in the flood. Four main road bridges were destroyed and all the boats in the harbour were swept out to sea. The tragedy claimed 34 lives and 39 buildings collapsed. The amount of water pouring through Lynmouth at the time of the flood was four times the average flow of the Thames. Conspiracy theories about the flood being caused by RAF cloud seeding activities have been discounted by meteorologists, who affirm that the depression that brought the prolonged downpour was several hundred miles across, bringing heavy rain across the whole of the south-west and South Wales.

Exmoor can certainly be wet. It stands in the path of a south-westerly airflow from the Atlantic, and annual precipitation is over 80 inches (2,032 mm) on the Chains. Some of the rain soaks into the ground, a little is trapped in reservoirs, around a quarter evaporates and the rest runs off into the streams and rivers. Exmoor rivers are spate rivers which rise and fall rapidly and don't maintain an even flow. Interestingly the flow of the Barle inside the National Park is usually greater than that of the Exe, so the former could be thought of as Exmoor's main river.

From the head of the West Lyn valley, I followed a vague quad-bike track along the north side of the Chains and looked into the little valleys of the head-streams of Hoaroak Water, which feed the East Lyn River at Watersmeet. From Exe Head a path followed by the Macmillan Way West leads above

ON THE LYN, DEVON

A benign River Lyn

the river to the road by Exe Head Bridge. Looking along the broad valley towards Blackpitts Gate with its screen of conifers there is an oddly Scottish Southern Uplands feel to the scene.

During a walk when I saw more helicopters (two) than people (none), I failed to find the 'dreary string of quaking, bottomless bogs every bit as sinister as those found on Dartmoor', which one guide had promised, but I did enjoy a bracing walk across a small but perfectly formed moorland with broad tops, steep little valleys, much of historical interest and fine views both seaward and landward.

Tamar and Torridge

and Turner?

	TAMAR
SOURCE	Woolley Moor, Devon
G.R.	SS 270 166
LENGTH	60 miles (96.5 kilometres)
TRIBUTARIES	Inny, Ottery, Deer, Tavy
MOUTH	Plymouth Sound

Like the Exe on the other side of Devon, this West Country river is eccentric, rising near the north coast and flowing to the English Channel. The crashing breakers rolling in from the Atlantic are only about 4 miles (6.4km) to the west and 6½ miles (10.4km) to the north of the Tamar's source, yet the river flows 60 miles (96.5km) southwards to enter the English Channel at Plymouth Sound. Unlike the Exe, the Tamar marks the Devon county boundary for most of its length, virtually islanding Cornwall and its Celtic roots from the Anglo-Saxons, although you have to travel 10 miles (16km) or so downstream before meeting the Tre- and Pen-names of Kernewek, the ancient language.

There is a convenient lay-by, an abandoned meander of the road between Bude and Bideford, by Woolley Barrows. The road virtually follows the watershed with the Tamar and the Torridge rising to the east while the headstreams of Marsland Water emerge for their much shorter journey to the west. On a late March day before spring had even set off her green fuses, I crossed the main road and walked down the lane across mist-wreathed Woolley Moor, following a sign to a canine country club. The large mound in the field by the junction is Woolley Barrow, a neolithic long barrow partially excavated in 1976, when flint tools were found. The lane's verges were emblazoned with signs announcing that this was a Japanese Knotweed Control Site, with helpful pictures, for the local badgers presumably, as a deterrent against eating any hedgerow fruit.

The Source of the Tamar and the Torridge, by J.M.W. Turner, c.1813

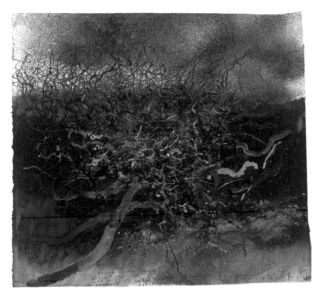

Wooley, the Source of the Tamar, Willow and Hazel Carr, by Kurt Jackson, May 2006

About 100 yards (91m) short of an old slate boundary stone engraved 'Bradworthy Moorwinstow', a little trickle of water by the south side of the road is the Tamar, heading southwards across a patch of boggy land into the hazel and willow of Woolley Wood. The river rises in a patch of marshy ground on the other side of the lane. A number of drains and ditches in the wood help boost its flow but the spring marked on the map between the lane and the wood proved to be less of a spring than a seep and then barely that. By the time the Tamar leaves the wood it is firmly established as the county boundary, a role it will play, with a few deviations, until it reaches the sea. A couple of miles downstream the little river has been dammed to form the two Tamar Lakes, Upper and Lower. The lower reservoir was formed in 1820 as a water supply for the Bude Canal and is now used for coarse fishing while there is fly-fishing on Upper Tamar Lake, which was constructed in 1973. Sport imitating class?

There is a work by J. M. W. Turner entitled *The Source of the Tamar and the Torridge*. The artist visited the area while engaged on his first tour of the West Country in 1811, during which he carried a map of Devonshire by John Carey, which denoted the head of the Torridge and Tamar Rivers. Turner's painting shows a stream in a valley with a figure kneeling by a pool while a dog looks on. Three packhorses and their driver walk along a track above the stream and a woman is seen further down. A group of men are minding fires giving off contrasting coloured smoke on the fairly steep hillside above. The stream flows away into the distance past low hills topped with some kind of outcrop or structure. An engraving of the work, started by W. B. Cooke in 1816 but not published for thirty-four years, shows these hilltop stones more clearly. Also in the engraving a man has joined the dog to look at the kneeling figure and a child accompanies the woman. Eric Shanes, in his *Turner's England 1810–1838*,[3] expands on the work:

> On the hillside two bonfires give off clouds of smoke whose opposed dark and light tones and differing directions respectively denote and parallel the rising and divergence of the two rivers. Below these clouds the Tamar winds away to the left, a course that is amplified by the left-hand pall of smoke, while the Torridge passes out of the front of the image in the direction repeated by the white smoke.

Oddly though, if, as the author states, the distant mounds are Woolley Barrows, then the Tamar is flowing in the wrong direction as, in reality, it flows away from them. I have also seen the title of the painting given as *Dartmoor: The Source of the Tamar and the Torridge*, which raises a few questions. Dartmoor is without question the source of neither the Tamar nor the Torridge, but the landscape in the painting certainly looks more like Dartmoor than this corner of Devon and Cornwall. Could the Woolley Barrows of the picture actually be a Dartmoor tor? It is certainly an intriguing work

3   Cassell, 1990.

where the willing suspension of disbelief, a concept coined by Devonian Samuel Taylor Coleridge, is called into play.

More recently (2006) Cornwall-based artist Kurt Jackson, whose work often features rivers, has produced a series of works under the title *The Tamar Dowr Tamer*. The latter is the Cornish name for the river. His atmospheric, mixed-media study *Wooley, the Source of the Tamar, Willow and Hazel Carr* shows the tangled branches, yellow as if lit from below and twisting like the river itself, standing out against the dark and moody background of the moor and the storm-tinged clouds above.

The Tamar and Torridge have been described as rising on either side of a clump of rushes and this is not so far from the truth. North of the Woolley Moor lane a rough area of sedge and tussock slopes down to a boggy depression in the bottom corner of a large enclosure. Here the Torridge escapes from the moor and, joined by a couple of drains and ditches, flows in a shallow valley to reach its first bridge at Brimford. It then turns north-east through a steep-sided little valley before another change of direction takes it to a confluence with the longer Clifford Water and its 40-mile (64km) journey to Bideford Bay.

On my return up the lane the mist had lifted somewhat and I could look out across the quiet rolling countryside that makes up this part of the south-west. In an area that seems proud of its isolation, Hartland, 5 miles (8km) north of the source, once claimed it was further from a railway than anywhere else in England. Having neither met nor seen anyone else during my cogitations around the source, I could vouch for the continued solitude of the spot.

Dartmoor Days: Dart, Taw, Teign, Tavy and West Okement
sound of slow trickling

There are few places better suited to giving birth to rivers than Dartmoor. A swelling, shallow-sloping

DART	
SOURCE	West Dart Head, Devon
	East Dart Head, Devon
G.R.	SX 601 815
	SX 608 854
LENGTH	46 miles (74 kilometres)
TRIBUTARIES	Webburn, Mardle, Hems,
	Harbourne
MOUTH	Dartmouth

dome of impervious granite, topped with a layer of extremely absorbent peat standing in the path of a moist south-westerly airstream, can hardly fail. And Dartmoor doesn't. The rivers Teign, Tavy, Taw, Avon, Erme, Okement, Yealm, Webburn, Bovey, Blackabrook, Walkham, Meavy, Swincombe, Burn, Harbourne, Lyd, Mardle, Ashburn, Sig, Lemon and Plym, as well as the Dart itself, all flow off the moor. Added to these, and the numerous streams, burns, brooks, lakes and waters, are the miles of artificial leats conducting water for drinking and domestic use and used as a power supply for mines and industry. Drake's Leat, finished in 1591, was the first and took water from the Meavy, carrying it 17 miles (27km) to Plymouth. In 1793 the Devonport Leat took water from the Cowsic, a headwater of the West Dart, and the Blackabrook and took it 21 miles (33.7km) to the coast. Although many of the leats are now dry, their courses can still be explored as they contour their way around the hillsides.

A great dome of granite, thrust up into the overlying sedimentary rocks, searing, melting and baking them, has been eroded for aeons by water and weather. The rock has split and rotted; the vertical and horizontal joints are visible in the hilltop tors that give this landscape its personality, and the loose, shattered chunks of clitter litter the slopes. Freshly cut granite glitters with the feldspar crystals it contains but this sparkle dulls with exposure to the air. Beneath the plants and soil, the rock is broken down to form the growan, which, together with the peat mass it supports, acts as a reservoir, slowly releasing the water into the rivers and streams. Unlike many other upland areas where the rivers fall quickly from the high land, on Dartmoor the upper courses are fairly gentle. The peaty water tumbles over little cascades connected by shallow pools and slow-moving streams. The valleys are often shallow and wide, spreading out to form boggy expanses such as Broad Marsh on the East Dart and Taw Marsh.

Most of the major rivers rising on Dartmoor have their sources in the northern half of the moor, on the high fen roof north of the road between Tavistock and Moretonhampstead. The Ordnance Survey map is littered with the confident promise of sources – Taw Head, Teign Head, East and West Dart Heads – so let's see if the promise is kept.

Postbridge, a hamlet consisting of a few houses, a shop, the East Dart Hotel and a National Park Information Centre, makes a good starting point for visiting several sources. Mid-March and mid-week the centre was giving little information but was being spruced up for the season. The clapper bridge crossing the East Dart 20-odd yards (18.2-odd m) downstream from the 1780s turnpike road bridge is the largest on the moor with four massive granite slabs, up to 15 feet (4.5m) long and 7 feet (2m) wide, each weighing over 8 tons. The three pillars have cutwaters on the upstream side and the bridge was probably built by local tin miners in the thirteenth or fourteenth century. A path leads from the east side of the road bridge across fields towards Ringhill Farm before heading down to the river again and through a patch of bamboo by Hartyland House. This house was built in the early nineteenth century by John and Thomas Hullett, brothers who, tradition states, founded a starch works in the area. They were 'improvers' who believed the moor could be tamed and made to turn out a range of agricultural products.

Potatoes were to be grown to provide starch, which was to be used for stiffening boat sails. Up on the moor beyond Hartland Tor is a well-preserved enclosure called 'The Sheepfold' on the map and known locally as Scotch Sheepfold, covering about three-quarters of an acre (0.3ha). Some authorities say it was built originally by the Hullett brothers and was where starch was manufactured. With the failure of the business in the 1830s, the structure was taken over by a Scottish shepherd, who used it for lambing. It is extremely well built of drystone walling with integral vertical pillars; a series of standing stones inside the wall perhaps supported a roof. At the southern end there was a building, a cottage that was subsequently burnt down in a fire in which a small girl lost her life. Her ghost is said

Post Bridge CDC26653   Chapman and Son, Dawlish

Postbridge bridges

Tracking East Dart

to haunt the area. Of the many fanciful attempts to make money out of the moor, the starch works must be one of the most futile.

Back down by the East Dart, the hounds of spring were only just on winter's traces and the northwards-leading path meandered past boulders and little pools which were still rimed with ice. The river soon swings away to the west at a point where it is joined by Ladehill Brook running down from Sittaford Tor and where a leat ran off it. The leat supplied water to the Powder Mills in the Cherry Brook valley a couple of miles to the south-south-west. The gunpowder mills worked for over half a century, closing just before the end of the nineteenth century.

From this point it is possible to follow the East Dart to its source, with the path climbing south-east through a wall gate and staying high above the river, eventually contouring round towards a fine waterfall. Passing through the intriguing Sandy

Hole Pass, you reach Broad Marsh but you can bypass it by walking through the drier grassland to the north. Kit Rocks, beside the river, is the next landmark and one of the few exposures of granite in this remote bit of Dartmoor. Further upstream, just after the Artillery Range Boundary Posts, the remains of a tinner's hut can be found on the west bank. The river is now so narrow it is easy to step from one side to the other. Ahead are Black Hill and Whitehorse Hill with East Dart Head lying in the boggy depression between the two, about 1½ miles (2.4km) further upstream. You pass another hut vestige, this time on the east side, by a little confluence. This is one of the less easily accessible parts of Dartmoor and the large, boggy, saucer-like depression around East Dart Head holds several head-streams which join at its southern end, where the tricklets coalesce by a low outcrop of granite and head off down the valley, the river's reed-marked course standing out as a khaki slash through the pale green surroundings. Within a mile (1.6km) of here will be found Taw, Teign and West Okement Heads – but it's a tough mile; and tougher still are the 2½ miles (4km) to West Dart Head away to the south-south-west. There are places where a slight rewrite of the Blues Brothers song 'Everybody Needs Somebody' springs to mind – 'You know people, when you do find a path, hold that path, hold that track, love it, please it, squeeze it, give it all your love. Signify your feelings with every gentle footstep, because it's so important to have that special path!'

As an alternative to tracking the East Dart to its source, you can follow Ladehill Brook north from its confluence for about 50 yards (45m) to the Beehive Hut. This horseshoe-shaped low stone wall, more igloo than beehive, is thought to be a store, a cache in which the tinners kept their tools and equipment when they were away on the moor. Covered in turf, the hut would have blended in with the generally gruffy nature of the ground. Medieval tinners were searching for cassiterite, specks and granules of tin ore weathered from the actual lodes and washed down and deposited by the streams. Being heavy, the cassiterite sank to the bottom, and the ground around the streams and rivers has been disturbed and dug over by the miners with their shovels, wooden pans and buckets. These streamers, who also dammed and diverted watercourses in order to provide a sudden flush to strip away vegetation

East Dart Head

and surface material, were responsible for leaving behind heaps of rubble and waste – the gruffy ground – throwing them up along the banks as they went. Now overgrown by bilberry, grass and heather, they are found beside most Dartmoor streams. Later operations, including opencast and deep mining, although this was more concentrated around the edge of the moor than its central granite core.

Speaking of caches, a mention should be made of the compulsively popular hide-and-seek game of geocaching, where items are hidden in containers and searched for using GPS technology. On Dartmoor it is pre-dated by about 150 years by letterboxing. The idea for this was initiated by James Perrott, a moorland guide from Chagford, in 1854 when he left a bottle containing his calling card by Cranmere Pool in the heart of the moor. In 1888 a metal box replaced the bottle and visitors left self-addressed postcards. The idea was that the next visitor collected the mail and put it in a postbox when he or she had regained civilization. By 1905 there was a logbook and two years later it was suggested that a rubber stamp be provided to prove that people had actually made it to the fairly inaccessible spot. In 1894 a second letterbox appeared, at Belstone Tor, and forty-four years later another was created at Ducks' Pool. Forty years ago there were a few dozen letterboxes on the moor. The idea has grown immensely since then and there are now thousands of letterboxes – in reality nowadays mostly plastic screw-top containers holding the all-important stamp – all over the moor.

A path leads north from above the Beehive Hut, following the east side of Ladehill Brook and staying above the marshy area. You can see Sittaford Tor ahead and at the end of the stream valley you may or may not see a group of hut circle remains, depending largely on the flexibility of your imagination. They are, to say the least, not in the best state of preservation. Continuing north you reach a much more visible antiquity but before that you can

Grey Wethers

make a visit to the boggy headwaters of the South Teign. The source lies in an extensive, shallow bowl above Fernworthy Forest, between the scant stones of a couple of ancient pounds. It is as confusing on the map as the ground, for as well as the natural stream channel, part of the leat which carried water on a meandering 7 miles (11.2km) from the East Dart to the crushing and dressing machines of the Birch Tor and Vitifer mines complex around Warren House crosses the area. Returning to the well-trodden path, you soon reach Grey Wethers. Two stone circles, each about 100 feet (30.5m) in diameter, stand 5 yards (4.5m) apart on the grassy plateau between the headwaters of the South and· North Teign, east of Sittaford Tor. The northern circle has twenty stones and the southern twenty-nine, all around 4 feet (1.2m) high. The circles were restored and many fallen stones raised in 1909.

Wether is an old name for a castrated ram, and local stories tell of a drunken farmer at Warren House Inn being convinced from a hazy distance that the stones were a grazing flock and buying them, only to return sober and no doubt a sadder and a wiser man on discovering his mistake. The circles are impressive from the inside but are better viewed from a distance, and the climb to Sittaford Tor, beside a superb stretch of drystone wall, gives good opportunities to look back to Grey Wethers and south Teign Head. The tor is a good viewpoint on a fine day and is the meeting point of several walls and fences. The walls surround newtakes, large areas of the moor that were enclosed by eighteenth- and early nineteenth-century improvers, often to the detriment of the commoners, whose land this had been. They stand in mute testimony to the skill of the wallers who built them.

Much of northern Dartmoor falls inside military firing ranges, clearly marked on the map and widely publicized. There are three ranges: Okehampton, Merrivale and Willsworthy. On one visit the red flag indicating activity on the Okehampton Range was flying on Quintin's Man, a spur top marked by an ancient cairn and a military observation post; the head of the North Teign would have to wait for another day. From Quintin's Man I decided to follow the range boundary posts round to Cut Hill and the source of the Tavy.

I'd been listening to someone talking on the radio about natural navigation – leave your compass at home and use the sun or moss on trees to find your way about – and decided that in thick weather the red-and-white-striped poles could be included, after all, they're as much part of the moorland scene as the sheep. In really poor conditions they can be a godsend, if you know where you are when you come across one. There is quite a good path following the markers around parts of the range boundaries and one led me down from Quintin's Man, crossing the North Teign at the head of Little Varracombe, to turn west and cross the East Dart just above Kit Rocks. Another two sharp changes of direction (feeling the wind on my face to maintain natural navigation) took me to the North West Passage. No, my route finding is not that bad! The said passage is a peat pass, one of several on Dartmoor. Passes had been created by moormen for centuries to make easier routes through the peat and blanket bog. Many were systematically cut by teams of men around the turn of the twentieth century at the bidding of Frank Philpotts, a keen huntsman who had them marked, at first by stakes. These were later replaced by granite blocks commemorating Philpotts and his work. Cut Hill,

Dartmoor souvenir

fourth-highest of Dartmoor's tops, lies in an area of blanket bog pierced here and there on the hill summits by granite tors. It is a letterboxing mecca, with hundreds of boxes in this remote area where the Ordnance Survey map shows a rare error: the brook indicated as Cut Hill Stream is actually Cut Lane Stream and the unnamed channel to the south, running west to east and joining the East Dart south of the confluence of the wrongly named Cut Hill Stream, is the real Cut Hill Stream or, possibly, Hangman's Stream. There, I'm glad that's cleared up. Talking of navigation, the Polynesian people of the Pacific had a completely different take on it. When island hopping in their canoes, they considered themselves the fixed point and believed that everything else – stars, clouds, atolls, the destination – moved towards them. I could go for that philosophy on parts of Dartmoor.

On a broad and wet shelf south of Cut Hill is Tavy Head, sometimes given the prefix 'North' to differentiate it from another southern one. Water dripping from a thick layer of peat starts a streamlet which, after collecting several unnamed tributaries as well as Fur Tor Brook, Amicombe Brook, the Red Lakes and Rattle Brook, runs off the moor through the steep-sided valley of Tavy Cleave, much romanticized in paint and print, before reaching Tavistock and the last 14 or so miles (22.5km) of its journey to the Tamar and the sea. The upper river is reckoned to be the fastest in England and second in Britain only to the Spey, falling 1,000 feet (305m) in just over 7 miles (11.2km). From its source the baby Tavy meanders through tussock and bog to its confluence with the other headstream coming from the south. At the junction stands another pile of stones, a tinner's hut which has marked this spot for maybe half a millennium. It is but a little way southwards to where the South Tavy emerges and scours a greener line through the bleached-looking tussocks of moor grass.

A gentle climb over Cut Hill's boggy southern shoulder brings you to the source of the West Dart. This has the look of a real source about it. The water emerges from what is almost a peaty cavern to trickle away down a gentle, broad valley. The existence of a slightly higher streamlet shouldn't detract from the obvious source – a river flowing from a niche is far more romantic. A walk across the watershed between the West and East Dart leads to Flat Tor, its rocky crest so flat as to be barely noticeable above the rushy grass. A descent past yet another tinner's hut and the glimpse of a substantial pool not marked on the map brought me down to Sandy Hole Pass. Here the East Dart passes through an artificially narrowed little gorge, a lovely spot. By building up the riverbanks with large granite blocks and narrowing the channel, the tinners increased its flow. The water was used for streaming. Further downstream is the start of the Vitifer Mine leat and an impressive waterfall. It would have to be a very tight schedule or a very vile day to make a walker visit Sandy Hole Pass and the waterfall without stopping at least once. It is often possible to cross the East Dart on large slabs above the falls and this gives the option of returning to the confluence of Ladehill Brook and the river to return past Hartyland and Ringhill to Postbridge. Alternatively a good path can be followed across Broad Down to a stile. From there the path descends to cross Braddon Lake before passing Roundy Park, site of a Bronze Age settlement, to a well-trodden track back to the National Park Centre at Postbridge.

On a day when the clouds were brushing the tops and tors, I set off from Observation Post 22 above East Okement Farm and headed off south along the Artillery Range Loop Road, feeling a bit of a cheat as I had driven a couple of miles on to the moor to take advantage of this parking spot, busy with vans and mini-buses. It had been possible, since the mid-1950s, to drive even further, to OP15, which is within easy striking distance of most of the main sources, but following a policy of benign neglect and more recently managed decline over the last twenty years, parts of the road had deteriorated to a very poor condition. The aim of the Duchy of Cornwall, the landowner, was to close most of the road to civilian traffic and despite a vigorous campaign by many locals, this happened in September 2009. The tarmac has been stripped from the first couple of hundred yards of the road beyond OP22 and a barrier installed. As I walked along the peaceful Sunday morning road I noticed a herd of black and white cows from East Okement Farm, grazing on the slopes of East Mill Tor. A National Park Ranger Land Rover passed me as I walked up the zig in the road, echoing the contours of East Okement Head, to OP15 but all was deserted at a spot which, as recently as May 2006, had been described as resembling 'a village car park with civilian vehicles sprawled besides the military observation posts'.

During the rest of the day I met several groups of generally genial young people in training for the forthcoming Ten Tors Expedition, due to take place in a couple of weeks' time. It was pleasing to see that one immutable law of expeditioning hadn't changed in decades: the scrawniest kid still seemed to carry the biggest pack. The challenge was founded in 1960, when around 200 youngsters took part. It has grown over the years and the entries are now limited to 2,400, made up of 400 teams of 6 teenagers, who have to visit 10 nominated tors out of 19, which are manned as checkpoints. Using one of 26 different routes ranging from 35 to 55 miles (56 to 88km) over the period of 34 hours the event includes an overnight camp. Although it is not a race, rather a test of navigation and endurance, natural adolescent competitiveness means that the record stands at just over 8¼ hours.

Today I was less interested in tors than trickles

and was in search of the sources of the Taw, East Dart and Teign, which lie close together in the heart of the moor. From Okement Hill the road descends to a ford and, above the boggy valley bottom, I contoured along a vague path heading towards the head of the Taw valley. Looking down, I noticed a stone on a little grassy knoll on the other side of the stream. Neither looked entirely natural, the hillock probably being a medieval spoil heap, while the stone proved to be a memorial to Ted Hughes. The Poet Laureate had moved to Dartmoor in 1961 and died in 1998. He had wished to have a slab of granite simply inscribed and sited near the head of the Taw, Teign, East Okement and Dart, his favourite place on the moor. The stone was reputedly flown in by helicopter in 2001, permission having been given by the Prince of Wales, a friend of the poet, as well as English Nature and the National Park Authority. Beyond the memorial the little valley narrows and steepens until the Taw is seen running over a thick bed of peat from the broad marshy col above. Soaked with the cold rain this is a bleak place, on the watershed of southern England; from here the Taw flows north to join the Bristol Channel at Bideford Bay, while East Dart heads south for 46 miles (74km) to Dartmouth. The upper stages of these two rivers present quite a contrast, the former running down a steep little valley while the latter flows through a broad basin.

As you follow the East Dart downstream for a

Sandy Hole Pass

half mile (800m) or so to the tinner's hut south-east of Black Hill, the low ridge to the east is the watershed, marked by many pale, angular quartzy rocks, between the East Dart and the Teign. Up here, with only the hiss of rain falling on the grass for company, it is easy to feel the remoteness of the moor. Above Teign Head stands a clump of boundary stones and markers, including a concrete one. Interestingly the stream with the more southerly source (North Teign) starts off flowing north and the northernmost one (East Dart) runs south. Both rivers eventually end up in the English Channel after collecting their major tributaries, North Teign being joined by South Teign near Chagford and East Dart meeting West Dart at, of course, Dartmeet.

Anyone wishing to experience a good Dartmoor valley bog could do worse than cross the Teign a few hundred yards downstream of the source, on a line between Kit Rocks and Quintin's Man. Here you will find patches of bright green sphagnum moss between tussocks and benty rushes, with the stream meandering through the middle. Some of the mire quivers when walked on, some will be far more accommodating and the unwary visitor may go in to the waist. The Dartmoor source searcher will find many more examples and will treat them with caution for, although they are rarely Grimpenlike, they can be irksome. Anyway, with patience it is always possible to find a way around them.

The Teign, first mentioned in AD 739 as 'Teng', is said to have inspired John Keats's epic poem *Endymion*, but finding Teign Head on a bare, open hillside it is hard to think that the poet actually visited its 'hidden source'. Having looked down the unchanging Upper Teign valley and recalling that a thing of beauty is a joy forever, I decided that my easiest way back to the start at OP22 was to take to the high land. A fair path climbs Whitehorse Hill from Quintin's Man, and near the summit, a deep peat pass heads eastwards. This was enhanced by an army bulldozer in 1963. The path contours

Cranmere Pool

around the east side of Hangingstone Hill to its summit, marked by the inevitable army observation hut, this one a tastefully stone built one as opposed to the steel cube on Quintin's Man. It is easier to follow the pass, for the direct route between the two hilltops is very wet. From here a good path descends to the Taw by Knack Mine, where there is a spoil heap and the remains of a building, which had two rooms and a fireplace. A ford crosses the river, which has certainly grown in 1½ miles (2.4km) from its source, and the track doubles back to rejoin the loop road. As an alternative it is easy to carry on to Oke Tor before dropping down to rejoin the road. The East Okement Farm cows had munched their way across from East Mill Tor and were now grazing the slopes of Oke Tor, having travelled at the rate of about an eighth of a mile an hour. I'd certainly done better than that but nowhere near as well as some of the Ten Tors teams. When I reached OP22 all the vehicles of four hours earlier had gone except mine and one other. I spoke to the driver of the mini-bus. Gazing out over the moor he was stoically waiting for his team of walkers to return from their practice hike.

There are as many other ways of reaching the Dartmoor sources as map coupled with imagination can devise and most of them can be found by following the river upstream. West Dart Head can be visited by tracking the river from Two Bridges,

passing the atmospheric Wistman's Wood, one of England's finest examples of high-altitude oak woodland, on the way. West Okement River, ascended from Meldon Reservoir, has a particularly fine, steep-sided valley, straight for much of the way and passing Black-a-Tor Copse, another upland wood, before ending with a capital-M-shaped flourish as it curves around Kneeset Nose, and almost ventures into Jackman's Bottom before swinging around again to West Okement Head by Cranmere Pool. The first thing to be said about Cranmere Pool is that it isn't really a pool. It may have been at one time and at wet times it holds any number of little pools, but the nearest proper pool is at Ockerton Court, half a mile (0.8km) to the north across the bog. Traditionally thought of as the central point of the wildest part of the moor, Cranmere Pool has long been a magnet for visitors. It stands in the middle of a large area of blanket bog and mire, its water dark-stained and almost stagnant. Reaching it gives you an odd sense of achievement and few can resist stamping something – map, notebook, back of hand – with the rubber stamp contained in the stone box. The stamp, circular and containing the message 'THE ORIGINAL DARTMOOR LETTER BOX', had changed from the hexagonal one of earlier visits and was now self-inking. Ah, the march of technology.

Approaching from the north, on another day when the sky was bright and the larks were singing and I'd had an interesting chat with an army officer, who had stopped me at the junction of the loop road and the track from Knack Mine in his Land Rover, having spotted me earlier crossing Oke Tor on my way from Belstone, and asked me if I'd noticed a smoke grenade on a rock as someone had reported seeing one, I decided to ignore all the guidebook advice about following the peat pass down to the West Okement to avoid the worst of the mire and instead went direct for Cranmere Pool. A faint and intermittent path – sheep, badger or human I cannot say – meandered across the boggy plateau. You can walk for a good 1½ miles (2.5km) here without crossing a single contour line and the plateau gave a good taste of proper Dartmoor walking, not to mention occasional wallowing. The blanket bog covering this part of the moor consists of about 85 per cent water, a fact that is soon readily apparent. Although Cranmere Pool is not reckoned directly to be West Okement's source, there are several little trickles in the vicinity, which head off in the right direction and join that stream for its 5-mile (8km) descent to Meldon Reservoir. Henry Williamson's *Tarka the Otter* followed the Torridge and then the Okement, one of its major tributaries, to this wilderness.

The Taw is another river that can be followed directly up to its source. Starting at Belstone, the route passes the old village stocks and heads south along a road and then track as far as the great bowl of Taw Marsh. When the track runs out you can follow the stream to the west of Steeperton Tor to climb steeply through narrow Steeperton Gorge to Knack Mine. From here the dedicated source seeker will stick with the river all the way to Taw Head, although it is also possible to use a length of the track climbing the lower slopes of Hangingstone Hill before descending to the river again at a ford.

The two dozen rivers rising on Dartmoor have a total length, in their moorland reaches, of around 140 miles (225km) and can be guaranteed to give the source searcher many days of fruitful exploration.

Of course, all this walking can be avoided by the simple expedient of visiting the honeypot that is Dartmeet, reckoned by some to be the real start of the Dart. Here, as well as the confluence, is found Pixieland, 'the home of the Dartmoor pixie and Dartmoor's most famous gift shop'. At least you are guaranteed to see piskies here. I'm not sure if I saw one on the moor, but something must have put that smoke grenade on the rock at Oke Tor!

Source seekers scouring their maps may be surprised to find 'Source of the River Dart' 15 miles (24km) north-east of the twin sources on Dartmoor. There is another river Dart in Devon. This one rises near Holmead Cross, 4½ miles (7.2km) west-nor'-west of Tiverton, and flows half a dozen miles to join the Exe at Bickleigh Bridge. Perhaps some eager cartographer seeing the head of a famously named stream put two and two together and made three. Rising near by is the Little Dart River, a tributary of the Taw.

Jordan
what did I see?

JORDAN	
SOURCE	Spring Bottom, Dorset
G.R.	SY 707 845
LENGTH	1½ miles (3.2 kilometres)
TRIBUTARIES	Osmington Brook
MOUTH	Bowleaze Cove

There are at least three river Jordans in England: in Northamptonshire, Cornwall and Dorset. One of them has certainly been deep and wide on more than one occasion but all of them may be chilly and cold depending on the season.

The Cornish version is the main tributary of the Valency and was a major contributor to the 10-foot (3m) wall of water that swept through Boscastle in 2004, causing huge damage and leading to the evacuation of scores of people from rooftops. Eight hours of torrential rain over the high ground just inland of the village on 16 August resulted in 2 million tonnes of water crashing through Boscastle, sweeping 115 vehicles away and destroying four properties as well as damaging many more. At the height of the downpour, almost 1 inch (25.4mm) of rain fell in fifteen minutes at Lesnewth, 2½ miles (4km) up the Valency valley. Since then, as part of Boscastle's flood defences, a scheme on the River Jordan, involving a flood relief culvert and a dissipation chamber, has been installed. The river, just over a mile (1.6km) long, rises from springs on the hillside above Boscastle, in the fields between Polrunny Farm and Tredorn Farm.

The Northamptonshire Jordan, also known as the Jordan Brook, a name perhaps more appropriate to its size, is about 3½ miles (5.6km) long. It rises from springs in fields to the south and east of Braybrooke before flowing through the village and entering Leicestershire at Little Bowden, a hamlet of Market Harborough. There was once a castle, probably a fortified and moated manor house, in Braybrooke and the river fed fishponds near by. In the village the river is crossed by a thirteenth-century bridge. The Jordan joins the Welland by a railway bridge near to Market Harborough station.

There is a lot to be said for following a river all the way upstream from sea to source. As mentioned elsewhere, William Henry Mounsey walked the length of the Eden in 1850 and several rivers now have long-distance paths all the way along them. However, most people don't have the time or inclination to track one of the longer rivers or are too busy (possibly visiting lots of other sources!) to achieve this full-length appreciation of a single watercourse. The Dorset Jordan provides a perfect opportunity to carry through this ambition. What's more, it can be done in half a day, as this Jordan is less than 2 miles (3.2km) long.

I parked the van in solitary splendour on the road above Bowleaze Cove and walked down to the beach. Across the cove, where the eastern end of the great sweep of Weymouth Bay comes up against Redcliff Point, stands the Riviera Hotel, a vast white curve of a building with a central tower, built in a Spanish style in the 1940s and expanded thirty years later. The rest of the lower valley floor is covered by Waterside Holiday Park with its funfair, café and amusement complex giving on to a hinterland of holiday homes and static caravans. In the middle of this the Jordan, straightened and chanelled, emerges from under a steel girder bridge between the Self Service Family Restaurant and the concrete retaining wall of the funfair, to dash, freely, across 50 yards (45m) of sandy beach into the sea. The river has to make the most of such opportunities; it doesn't get many nowadays. Photos of Bowleaze Cove in the 1930s show a little wooden footbridge crossing the river and a few huts and tents on the headland beyond. An even earlier visitor, John Constable, spent his honeymoon at nearby Osmington vicarage in 1816 and painted *Weymouth Bay, Bowleaze Cove and Jordon Hill*, now in the National Gallery. Beneath Constable's towering cumulus clouds, Jordan Hill, now topped with large houses and luxury apartments, appears bare, the river runs across the sands and quietly joins the sea and apart from a single figure on the beach there is little sign of humanity apart from tiny buildings in distant Weymouth.

Walking to the end of a pier that juts 30 yards (27m) out into the bay and looking inland, I caught a glimpse, between the restaurant conservatory and the helter-skelter, of the chalk ridge through which seeps the water that becomes the Jordan. Crossing the few yards of sand and pebbles, I scrambled under the rusty girders of the bridge and followed the river upstream along a littered grassy bank beside a multi-coloured wall before emerging in a car park and crossing a pergola-covered bridge overlooking a duck house on a little mid-stream island. I couldn't help thinking about ex-MP Sir Peter Viggers and his infamous example, a much more commodious affair than this one, which now stands at Hilton Park, a business park near the M6 in Staffordshire. Entering the Waterside Holiday Park and Spa I wandered about, catching glimpses of the river at the end of rows of holiday homes and passing the time of day with the workmen readying the place for the season, before escaping along a muddy litter-strewn path beside the meandering Jordan. This led into a low-lying scrubby no-man's-land before the next holiday park, divided into sections named after race courses and with a sign pointing to 'Ascot, Goodwood, Epsom, Sandown, Cheltenham, Launderette'.

A noticeboard informed me that 'the river acts as a wildlife corridor for many wildlife species' and if I were a frog I certainly wouldn't fancy my chances of crossing two holiday parks without its help. Leaving Ascot with its serried rows of apparently immobile homes you are suddenly confronted by the fourteenth-century church of St Andrew. A bizarre little passage. I walked down the main road to

the bridge over the Jordan and followed a little lane past the Bridge Inn. A sign on a wall proclaimed that this was a Neighbourhood Dog Watch area, which probably accounted for the way the bloke with the spaniel in front of me was furtively glancing about. Past Mill Cottage I followed a ginnel or snicket or whatever it's called in Dorset to rejoin the road, Puddledock Lane, where a pond had been made on a tributary of the Jordan that starts at a spring beneath Green Hill. The pond had an island and a pair each of ducks, geese and swans. I passed Willowbank Farm, home of the award-winning Weymouth Beach Donkeys, but they appeared to be away; perhaps like Premier League footballers they were relaxing on an Abu Dhabi beach before the season began.

Puddledock Lane swings round to the east, tracking the river at a distance, to Sutton Poyntz and giving glimpses across well-kept fields to the houses on Sutton Road. On the corner of the lane with the road is the confluence of the Jordan and its

Mouth of the Jordan

Sutton Poyntz mill pond

major, mile (1.6km) long, tributary running in from Osmington to the east. Earlier maps appear to show this stream as the main river but the one rising at Springhead now seems to be accepted as the one currently being Jordan. Just up Sutton Road, where it meets Plaisters Lane, is another confluence. As always the rocks beneath control the water above and Sutton Poyntz lies on a succession of bands of clays and shales, with occasional layers of cement-stone, known as the Kimmeridge Clay, which was formed around 143–138 million years ago. About three million years' worth of shallow-water sand-stones and limestones, the Portland Beds, were then laid down on top. Great earth movements around 110 million years ago folded all these rocks into a ridge, an anticline striking approximately east–west, and this was subsequently eroded, ex-posing the Kimmeridge Clay. Around 94–71 million years ago the whole area was again under the sea and the great beds of chalk now forming the hills to the north were laid down. Further faulting and fold-ing occurred to complicate the picture but wherever water percolating down through the porous chalk meets the Kimmeridge Clay, springs rise.

The signpost at the fork points to Springhead and the river flows alongside the road. Houses are reached over little bridges, some with concrete am-monites embossed on them. Sutton Mill, brick built

with a hipped roof and a lucam, dates from around 1815 and has been tastefully converted, while Silver Street behind the mill is worth exploring. The mill pond is the village centrepiece, overhung by willows and edged with thatched cottages, some dating from the eighteenth century and some sur-prisingly modern in everything but looks.

The solidly Victorian Springhead restaurant and pub was built as a hotel around 1890 and its sign shows a carter struggling with a pair of horses pulling a waggon on which rests a massive metal pipe. It recollects a tale that unites the most vision-ary and the most practical ends of the engineering spectrum. In September 1859, Isambard Kingdom Brunel's revolutionary leviathan, the iron paddle steamship *Great Eastern*, twice as long as any other vessel afloat, designed to carry 4,000 passen-gers to Australia without the need to re-fuel and double-hulled to be unsinkable, was undergoing sea trials in the Channel. From the first the ship had been dogged by misfortune, including rumours of entombed rivetters and a protracted launch saga lasting for nearly three months, which broke both the company's finances and Brunel's health. At five past six on the evening of 9 September the *Great Eastern* was in sight of Hastings when a huge ex-plosion ripped open the deck and the massive for-ward funnel was launched into the air on a great cloud of steam. Six stokers were killed but it was a tribute to her engineer that the ship survived an explosion that would have destroyed any other and that she could hold her course to Weymouth. The news was too much for Brunel, who died less than a week later. A coroner's inquest on the ac-cident was held after the ship docked in Portland Harbour. Upon inspection it was discovered that the upper section of the 7-foot (2.1m) diameter, ½-inch (12mm) wrought-iron plate funnel was relatively undamaged. A 5-foot (1.5m) length was salvaged, bought by the Weymouth Waterworks Company and installed by their engineers during the construction of a new dam at the Springhead pumping station, where it was converted to act as a filter. Serving this purpose from 1860 until 2003, it is the last surviving piece of ironwork from the ship and was presented to the SS *Great Britain* Trust in Bristol by Wessex Water the following year.

From the top end of the millpond I found a track leading up Fox Lane and past Springfield Cottage which led into a field by the side of the waterworks with its rusty wrought-iron fence manufactured by Hill and Smith of Brierley Hill. Through another gate and a path, the Millennium Oak Walk, runs parallel to the infant Jordan here, through woodland of sallow and hazel, oak and ash. At the next fence the path veers off up the scarp slope but it was possible, in early March at least, to descend to find the stream in the damp little valley bottom and follow it up to where it emerged through a pipe in the dam, only to go stealing away like Time. A tangled mass of vegetation – brambles, branches, roots and rushes – as well as a couple of semi-derelict barbed-wire fences hindered progress and it

might well be impossible to reach in the summer. Beyond the thicket the slope climbs steeply up from the combe, Spring Bottom, much of which is now enclosed by the waterworks fence. This tight little valley was caused by the same faults that account for the springs.

I followed the fence steeply up the hillside while pairs of buzzards and crows circled warily around each other overhead. Glancing into the enclosure, I looked in vain for the bubbling spring, whose waters never failed or lessened, seeing instead only a reedy depression at its foot. This is the site of a lake shown on the maps but no longer visible on the ground while a series of what appear to be inspection chamber covers march up the dry valley floor. The Jordan has its moments of beauty and freedom but few would claim that its beginning or end are lovely and untramelled.

The river had served the locals for centuries before the pumping station was built and excavations have revealed a dam built in the thirteenth or

SUTTON POYNTZ, PRESTON, WEYMOUTH

fourteenth century to feed a manorial pond beneath the fields west of the waterworks, which itself was constructed on the site of an earlier Upper Mill.

Reaching the ridge top I turned east, crossing a landscape pimpled with round barrows and striped by lynchets, towards White Horse Hill. I sat for a while on a barrow near the trig point on East Hill, looking out through the anticyclonic haze landward over pylons towards Maiden Castle. I'd walked around Maiden Castle a couple of nights before while staying on a little campsite – one tap, one hole in ground – at its foot. I was as amazed at the sheer size of the place as I had been forty years ago when I'd spent a night in a sleeping bag in one of its defensive ditches. I watched the sun disappear behind the Hardy Monument (as in 'Kiss me, Hardy' rather than *Casterbridge* Hardy) on Black Down and walked back to the van, refreshed by the sheer continuity of it all.

Looking seaward across the broad expanse of Weymouth Bay to Portland with its crab-claw-like breakwaters, I could see several tankers stationed offshore, waiting for another Arab dictator to fall and the price of oil to rise. Following the South Dorset Ridgeway down towards Osmington I walked through one of the muddiest stretches of track I've ever encountered, where the local bullocks had been holding a rave by the look of things. Seepages along the path were followed by a stream emerging from Hall's Farm by Osmington. This is the source of the main tributary, known locally as Osmington Brook, running along a broad valley parallel to the coast, which joins Jordan in Sutton Poyntz. I followed the brook across meadows, glancing across to White Horse Hill and passing a couple of metal detectorists working a recently ploughed field. The Osmington White Horse was carved in 1808 into the downs above the village in gratitude and loyalty to George III, who had visited Weymouth regularly during the previous couple of decades for the sake of his health. 280 feet (85m) long and 323 feet (98m) high, it portrays the King

on horseback riding away from the town and is the only mounted equestrian hill carving and one of only four to face to the right, of the couple of dozen existing or known about in the country. George III has been credited with starting Weymouth off as the first seaside resort. Were he to return and see what has become of Bowleaze Cove, he might well go mad.

By the time I returned to the cove the tide had retreated and the Jordan had eroded a little, braided channel across the sand, exposing the pebbles beneath, while a digger and concrete mixer were busy at work with half a dozen blokes, strengthening the foundations of the pier. I walked back across the grass to the van, which was now in the middle of a long line of parked vehicles. It must be fun here in the summer.

Piddle

tiny streams in a land of giants

	PIDDLE
SOURCE	Alton Pancras, Dorset
G.R.	ST 695 023
LENGTH	24 miles (38 kilometres)
TRIBUTARIES	Devil's Brook, Bere Stream
MOUTH	Poole Harbour

Fresh from playing the Wicked Wizard in our church production of *Jack and the Beanstalk*, how could I resist the pantomimic belly laugh that is the river Piddle? Tales of riverside villages changing their names to avoid embarrassment prior to a visit by Queen Victoria seem to be apocryphal and the fact that most names these days contain 'puddle' rather than 'piddle' seems to have come about phonologically during the Middle Ages. Local pronunciation, even of 'puddle' names, is 'piddle' anyway. The name of the river comes from the Old English word *pidele*, meaning 'a marsh or a fen'. It is also known as the Trent or North River. The river is a couple of dozen miles (38km) long, flowing south and then south-east to its mouth at Poole Harbour.

The little Dorset village of Alton Pancras is generally considered to house the source, but a study of the map suggests a series of springs in the surrounding valleys and linking them up makes for an interesting walk.

I decided to start at Piddletrenthide, a fine place for linguists and mathematicians, for not only was it the 'Piddle manor of thirty hides', the 'trent' coming from French and a 'hide' being a piece of land capable of supporting a family at the time of the Domesday survey, but its church bears an inscription of the date 1487 in Arabic numerals, a very early use of them in England. Most dates were still carved in Latin numerals for another century.

The parish provoked a flurry of correspondence in the letters column of *The Times* in the 1970s, when it was announced that the Revd J. E. B. Cattell, Vicar of Piddletrenthide with Alton Pancras and Plush, was to become priest-in-charge of Buckhorn Weston and Kington Magna. Following expressions of disbelief that such places could exist, other contributors sent in their own ecclesiastical transfers including these two from Yorkshire: the Revd G. D. Beaglehole, Vicar of Kexby with Wilberfoss, to be Vicar of Bossall with Buttercrambe; and the Revd G. Christie, Rector of Roos with Tunstall-in-Holderness, Vicar of Garton with Grimston and Hilston and Rural Dean of South Holderness, to be Vicar of Pocklington with Yapham-cum-Meltonby and Owsthorpe with Kilnwick Percy, and Millington with Great Givendale, and Rural Dean of Pocklington.

I followed a flinty footpath past a chalk quarry on East Hill and across a large field to the top of West Hill, which is actually east of East Hill. Anyone

Equine equipoise – White Horse Hill

gazing out across the upper Piddle valley will see how the dry valley of Navvy Shovel got its name. From West Hill I descended on a track etched into the hillside and garlanded by hart's-tongue fern, past fields of short-cropped grass like green velvet to Plush. A scatter of thatched cottages, Regency manor house, the little church of St John the Baptist and the Brace of Pheasants make up the tiny place, while the signpost at the road junction bears the grid reference 714022. I've also seen this helpful, pre-sat-nav practice on signs in the old West Riding of Yorkshire. The stream running through Plush is Piddle's first tributary, rising in fields just south of Folly Farmhouse a mile to the north-east and joining the river by Piddletrenthide Manor, thus reversing a naval maxim that plush often leads to folly.

A convoy of muck spreaders was trundling along as I left the road to climb steeply up on to Plush Hill. The paths and bridleways shown on my map had been recently ploughed out and not yet re-established, so it was easier to edge the field across the top of Firland Wood before following the top of the scarp along Higher Hill with its vague traces of 'Cross Dykes' and trig point. As I looked out over the valley head to Blackmore Vale beyond, a shaft of sunlight lit up the rushy patch in a meadow where the stream I had crossed at Plush rises. Here at the watershed between the Piddle and the Lydden, a tributary of the Stour, the seven dykes running down from Lyscombe Hill are just one part

Plush surroundings

of the rich history forged into this landscape. Field systems, tumuli, hill forts, deserted villages, earthworks and trackways all testify to a human presence from neolithic times. The Dorsetshire Gap, a crossing point of five ancient tracks which intersect at a narrow saddle on the hills above the house platforms and alleyways of the erstwhile village of Melcombe Horsey, is just a mile (1.6km) to the east.

Descending a track now followed by the Wessex Ridgeway long-distance footpath, I passed Folly Farmhouse and crossed the road to pass another cottage, which was once a drovers' inn called the Fox. Here I was passed at speed by a walker, who asked cryptically, 'Are you on the Giant's Daughter Marshals?' I replied that I was just ambling and he jogged off up the hill. Thinking about him later I wondered if this was an LDWA jaunt. The Long Distance Walkers' Association organizes, well, long-distance walks and I discovered that this was an event for marshals only who, presumably, were getting to know the 30-mile (48km) route prior to the real walk the following month. Starting at 8.00 a.m., the marshals were advised to carry torches. Well, it was still early March. The 150 entrants for the real event were promised light refreshments at all checkpoints and hot food and even showers at the finish. This would be looked on as a mere stroll by some LDWA members, who tackle 62 miles (100km) in 26 hours or even 100 miles (160km) in 48 hours. Although not enjoying such organized events (possibly because my brother Peter and I were disqualified from a Karrimor International Mountain Marathon once for straying 'out of bounds': we'd been nattering so much we forgot to look at the map and a marshal copped us), I am a member of the LDWA. This is merely out of vanity, to see if I'm still up there on the honours board of those who've climbed all the 2,000-footers in England and Wales. I followed the Wessex Ridgeway path up a hollow way 10 feet (3m) deep in places on to the springy turf of Ball Hill, where the markers on a post informed me that I was on the 212-mile (341km) Hardy Way as well as the 136-mile (218km) Wessex Ridgeway. Fertile ground for the LDWA, three more of whom zoomed past me as I descended into the Piddle valley. Mind, in 1975 the artist Richard Long produced a work, in black and white photos, map and collage, based on *A Six Day Walk over all the Roads, Lanes and Double Tracks inside a Six Mile Wide Circle centred on the Giant of Cerne Abbas*, so he had certainly walked this way too. In homage I laid half a dozen stones end to end on the path.

An article I had come across in *Hydrology: Science and Practice for the 21st Century*[4] led me to believe that the Piddle had five major sources stretching along the valley from beyond Alton Pancras to Piddletrenthide. The first was at Holcombe Dairy, a sequestered farm nestling under the dip slope of the ridge, which throws out the spur into which is carved that symbol of masculinity the Cerne Abbas Giant. The dairy was one of the last in Dorset to make its own butter and cheese, into the late 1920s. Beside a hipped-roofed barn stands a pond, out of which was flowing a lusty little stream. Behind the pond, in a tangled spinney, rose the spring, highest and furthest of the Piddle's sources. As I walked back down the lane, though, it was obvious that the little stream was intermittent, disappearing at intervals before returning to the surface. Once by the valley road it was continuous and was soon augmented by water emerging from a spring at Barcombe Farm, the combined flow rushing down a little artificial waterfall. It runs alongside the road all the way through Alton Pancras, where houses have their own miniature bridges, to its confluence with another, equally lively stream. Awultune is the village at the source and Pancras the patron saint of the church that stands on the bank of this next claimant, the one considered by most to be *the* source. The flint grey church was restored in the nineteenth century following the near collapse of the earlier Norman building.

There seemed to be no legal access from the church to the spring feeding this clear, cold stream and so, unlike the Victorian naturalist or the pure of heart who may have no compunction about boldly knocking on the manor house door, I resorted to (rearrange these words to make a comprehensible phrase) 'under wire hedge in squeezing a barbed'. I emerged into a delightful combe, Rake Bottom below Navvy Shovel, where within the space of 5 yards (4.5m) a dry track running along its foot became a bourne. Oozing out of an aquifer originating near the Cerne Giant it flowed away through the remnants of medieval carp ponds and Soggy Wood to become the stream running through the concrete pipe just above the church.

Back on the road down the valley, Thomas Hardy's Pydel Vale, I reckoned that the next source, called Sheepdip by the British Hydrologists, was in the watermeadows below a pumping station, and to my delight a stile gave access to the field and spring bubbling up through a flinty bed to flow away through bright green watercress.

At a spot where the Ordnance Survey graces the river with its name for the first time, a bridleway, 'Piddle Valley Local Agenda 21 Nature Conservation Area Bridleway 35' to be precise, crosses the Piddle on stepping stones before climbing steeply up a recently ploughed field. It was so flinty that I could have been walking across a pebble beach and my footsteps rang out as I crossed to a track leading to my final source, above Piddletrenthide. Where the lane fords the stream a gate leads into an area of woodland. This is Morningwell, once the watering place for the livestock of the village, where a series of springs feeds a lake surrounded by beech and yew trees. A spring trickles out from the very roots of a gnarled, mossy giant at the far end of the pond. Across a little bridge are old watercress beds and then the track leads past cottages and All Saints Church to a bridge over the Piddle, the first of a dozen or so to span the river as it runs through the village, which is as long and thin as its name suggests.

---

4   The Proceedings of the British Hydrological Society International Conference, 2004.

Morningwell

Stour

genius of the place

STOUR	
SOURCE	Stourhead, Wiltshire
G.R.	ST 761 353
LENGTH	60 miles (96.5 kilometres)
TRIBUTARIES	Lydden, Allen, Avon
MOUTH	Mudeford

Local pronunciation – what a joy, what a pitfall. I live near Brewood, which rhymes with 'food'. This Stour, like the West Midlands one, generally rhymes with 'hour', though several settlements along it are prefaced by 'Stur'. The Suffolk and Essex version and the Kentish one favour rhyming with 'tour', while the Oxfordshire and Warwickshire river can be pronounced like 'mower'. Local terms and conditions apply. Don't even start on 'Nene'.

Dorset's longest river, at almost 60 miles (96.5 km), rises just inside Wiltshire, where, dammed in a series of lakes, it supplies the setting for the splendour of Stourhead. Flowing through the Blackmore Vale, skirting Blandford Forum and the northern fringes of Bournemouth, it is joined by the Hampshire Avon before being besalted in Christchurch Harbour. Deflected by Hengistbury Head, it meets open sea at Mudeford, by the far western reaches of the Solent.

A touch of serendipity brought me here one Saturday afternoon in early March. Planning to drive down to Dorset to seek the sources of the Piddle and the Jordan, I noticed the National Trust symbol on the map indicating the house and gardens at Stourhead. I hadn't been there for maybe thirty years but recalled the lakes and surmised that it wasn't called Stourhead for nothing. Perusal of the OS map showed a series of springs in the area, so I drove into the car park, which was so full that I was guided into the staff section.

The chalklands of Wessex throw out a wedge-shaped western plateau, the watershed of the Brue, Wylye and Stour. From before the Norman Conquest the land was occupied by the manor of Stourton and the eponymous family whose coat of arms showed six springs. In the mid-fifteenth century Sir John Stourton was granted a licence to make a park. This allowed him to enclose 1,000 acres (404.6ha) of pasture and woodland including the combe holding the Stour's sources. The valley was dammed and a series of ponds formed. The family being staunchly Royalist – Sir John had been treasurer of Henry VI's household – the house was sacked by Parliamentary soldiers during the Civil War and the estate saddled with debt. By 1717 it had come into the possession of Henry Hoare, second generation of a famous banking family, who had the house rebuilt, in the Palladian style, and renamed it Stourhead. On his death in 1724, his son, another Henry, later known modestly as 'the magnificent', inherited the estate but did not make it his chief residence until after his mother's death in 1741. Becoming a widower himself for the second time in 1743, Henry set about creating the Stourhead we see today. Those were the days when men of vision with money and the foresight to plan, as well as the possibility of cheap labour, could create private worlds to which they could escape and indulge their imaginations.

A 60 foot (18.3m) high dam was constructed to transform two ponds into the Garden Lake and the classical structures that adorn the estate were built. Trees were planted and walks were made, one of which I followed, through banks of snowdrops and a few brave primroses and daffodils, past Henry's first garden building, the Temple of Flora, built

over a spring called Paradise Well, to the Grotto. Approached through a rock archway the mossy, tufa-clad walls shelter a nymph and a river god in two niches leading off a circular, domed chamber. The Nymph of the Grot is a copy, in white-painted lead, of the statue of the sleeping Ariadne in the Vatican Gardens. In Greek mythology Ariadne was the daughter of King Minos, who assisted Theseus in escaping the Minotaur in the labyrinth. Here she rests peacefully, the water running over a cascade and fed by springs, Stour sources, which are said never to run dry. The river god, also of painted lead, perches on his rocky islet, pointing towards the Pantheon. He is said to be modelled on Salvator Rosa's painting of Tiber and Aeneas. With his left hand gripping an urn, from which pours a constant fountain of water, and with his right foot planted firmly in the stream he may be based on Pater Tiberi, but here he is decidedly Father Stour.

From the nearby Iron Bridge I could see the river cascading down from the Garden or Great Lake to a lower one, which then feeds into New Lake on its journey to the sea. Having noted half a dozen other springs dotted about the woods on the greensand slopes above the lake, I left Stourhead's manicured gardens and headed to the west. I also left the people. Stourhead attracts around 350,000 visitors a year and a helpful National Trust lady in reception told me of 9,000 coming over three days last summer

Father Stour

but, away from the immediate vicinity of house and gardens, I had the place virtually to myself.

As I entered the woods at Baker's Copse, a multitude of forest roads and tracks meant that finding the various springs marked on the map was an interesting exercise. I've never really been one for orienteering and in the days of helping my friend Paul with his Mountain Leadership Certificate courses, whenever the subject of micro-navigation cropped up – find this sheepfold, find this boulder – I always used to aver that I was more comfortable with macro-navigation. If I was on the right mountain I was happy enough. Here it was a case of diversions down shady green glades off forest rides and thrashing about in thickets. I must admit that

I used my compass more in Stourhead's woods than during any other walk in this book. At times I could have done with Ariadne's thread. In Perfect's Copse I startled a pair of roe deer, who flashed their white rumps at me before vanishing. I thought about them later when seeing an advert at the Farm Shop for Stourhead Sizzler Sausages – 'Do your bit to manage the deer population on the estate. Pork is added to the venison to keep it moist. Port and juniper berries complete a sophisticated sausage.' I'm not surprised they ran so fast.

I gained height, springs and photos, eventually emerging from the trees at the head of Great Combe, a few hundred yards down the road from Alfred's Tower on Kingsettle Hill. One of the finest

Stourhead: The Lake from Six Wells Bottom, by Francis Nicholson, c.1812

St Peter's Pump

triangular follies in the land, the 160 foot (48m) high plain brick structure was the crowning glory of Henry Hoare's pattern of perfection. Marking the place where King Alfred raised his standard against the Danes in AD 879, it also commemorated peace with France at the end of the Seven Years War in 1763, presumably of great interest to a banker, and the accession of George III three years earlier.

I made my way along to the Terrace at the head of Six Wells Bottom, where Alfred is reputed to have rested with his army, his prayers for water being answered by the appearance of six pure springs. The almost dry valley leads down between belts of trees, Sunny Hanging to the east, Shady Hanging westwards – definitely one for the natural navigator – and back to the ponds, lake and gardens below. Near its head stands St Peter's Pump, given by most

authorities as the source of the Stour. Standing atop a limestone rubble grotto, the market cross of 1474 was brought here from Bristol by Henry Hoare in 1768 and erected over what was presumably the highest spring, though the one in Great Combe runs it close. A curved recess on the southern side holds a round dry well, site of the former spring. This is one British source that, like that of the Seine emerging from its statue-topped grotto, is properly dealt with. On the day of my visit water was emerging 75 yards (68m) further down the valley, only to sink again a little distance later. It reappeared, for good this time, to feed three ponds at the foot of the valley, which in turn flow into the Garden Lake.

On my return to the car park by way of visitor reception, the National Trust lady reckoned it had been a quiet day; it certainly had been in the woods.

VALLEYS BROAD AND FAIR

Most of the river sources described in this book rise in the uplands and highlands, but several of our longest rivers have lowland sources and they are portrayed here. Although I have mostly tramped across moor and mountain, I have found that there is something rather strange yet pleasing about searching meadows and pastures for streams and springs, while even the most apparently tamed places can still hold pockets of wildness. The walking also tends to be easier, though it was while following the Thames to its source that my feet were consistently wetter and colder than on any other expedition recounted here.

Thames

in paradise

	THAMES
SOURCE	Thames Head, Gloucestershire
G.R.	SO 976 000
LENGTH	215 miles (346 kilometres)
TRIBUTARIES	Churn, Windrush, Evenlode, Cherwell, Thame, Colne, Lea, Kennet, Wey, Mole, Medway
MOUTH	the Nore

The longest river entirely in England is reckoned to have a length of 215 miles (346km), only 5 (8) less than the Severn. The meaning of the name is uncertain but it may be 'dark river'. There are similar names up and down the country, such as Tame in Manchester and Birmingham, Team in County Durham, Teme which flows through Tenbury to join the Severn, and Tamar which separates the Cornish from the rest of us. The roots of the name may even stretch back to before the Tower of Babel; Tamasa is a tributary of Mother Ganges. The 'h' in Thames was apparently added in the seventeenth century to make the name more classical in appearance; the letter has certainly never been pronounced. It is ironic that in our one classical reference, Julius Caesar's account of his British expedition, the river is Tamesis.

'Water is rarely seen', 'A dry dip in the meadow', 'Frequent lack of water', 'For most of the year it remains dry ground', 'Very little or no water': so state various authorities stretching back as far as sixteenth-century antiquarian John Leland. The summer Thames rarely shows water at its source, as I noticed in 1984 when I walked across a bone-dry field known as Trewsbury Mead to a granite block inscribed:

```
THE CONSERVATORS OF THE RIVER THAMES
               1857—1974
THIS STONE WAS PLACED HERE TO MARK THE
        SOURCE OF THE RIVER THAMES
```

The stone replaced a statue of Father Thames, which stood, or rather lounged, here for fourteen years but was removed to St John's Lock below Lechlade to protect him from vandal attacks. There is even dispute about whether this well-marked spot actually is the fountainhead. The claims of Seven Springs, source of the Churn, 350 feet (106m) higher and 12 miles (19km) further from the sea, have often been put forward, even in such exalted though less elevated Thameside surroundings as the House of Commons, and the spot has its own inscription:

```
       HIC TUUS
   O TAMESINE PATER
SEPTEMGEMINUS FONS
```

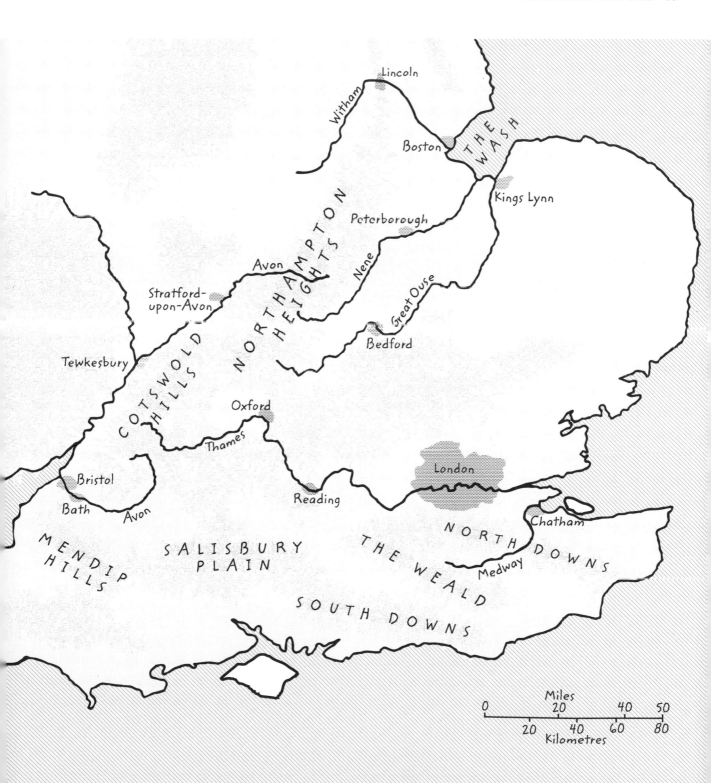

Which means 'Here, O Father Thames, Is Your Seven Sourced Fountain'. However, as far as anyone knows, the Churn has always carried the name from Seven Springs to its confluence with the Thames at Cricklade, while the Thames is called the Thames from Thames Head. The source seeker will, of course, visit both places and will be impressed, in different ways, by both.

Many visitors have emphasized the claims of Seven Springs as the true source of the Thames and for much of the year it has the stronger flow. Indeed there are some who claim that Thames Head itself only appeared as a source after the construction of the Thames and Severn Canal in the late eighteenth century. Seven Springs stands near the meeting of six roads and lanes a couple of miles south of Cheltenham. Here, above the Cotswolds scarp, rises the river Churn, which flows down the dip slope to join the Thames near Cricklade. At about 15 miles (24km), its length from source to confluence is actually greater than that of the Thames from Thames Head to the confluence, but the Churn has historically been considered the tributary. Seven Springs is certainly an imposing place, for the springs are found, shaded by beech trees, at the foot of a little cliff in a quarry-like angular dell. A flight of stone steps leads down from a handy lay-by off the A436 road. There are two stone plaques, both with the inscription referred to above, one on the retaining wall above the culvert that takes the little stream under the road and the other on the wall at right angles to it. The stream quickly flows beneath the road and into a lake in the grounds of the walker-friendly Seven Springs Inn. The last time I was there some of the trees in the dell had been cleared, giving a more open aspect, and the first daffodil of the year was in bloom. At least it was the first I had seen, late after a cold winter, on 6 March. There was also a litterbin and a concrete public footpath sign, both of which had presumably been helped down from the road above.

The originators of the Thames Path National Trail were in no doubt about where the true source lay and so, on a bright, clear, crisp and cold first day of December, with frost on the ground and hoar on the branches, I walked the 10 or so miles (16ish km) from Neigh Bridge to Thames Head and back. Neigh Bridge forms part of the Cotswold Water Park, 40 square miles (103.6 sq. km) of country-side containing 140 lakes formed by gravel extraction. There was certainly plenty of water flowing under Neigh Bridge and I started to become hopeful that there might even be water at the source. The Thames Path National Trail, a 184-mile (296km) walk, follows the river closely along these last few miles and meanders alongside the stream, which here was chattering and gurgling with a sound reminiscent of the one you get when you stop paddling a canoe and lie back to enjoy the effort and listen to the water.

I thought back to when we had cruised up the navigable river, watching the Thames Path walkers taking short cuts across the necks of meanders while our narrowboat boxed the compass. Following the path across the meadows, I walked in parallel with the sheep walking the opposite bank above the flooded field. A path leads off to cross the river by a footbridge next to the sixteenth-century Kemble Mill. This couple-of-mile stretch of the river between Neigh Bridge and Parker's Bridge, itself less than 2 miles from the source, passes Kemble Mill, Old Mill Farm, Upper Mill Farm and Mill Farm. This seems to be a remarkable number of water-mill place names in such a short distance on a stream that doesn't hold a great deal of water at the best of times and, nowadays at least, is often dry. Not today, however. Approaching Old Mill Farm I found the path marker stake standing in the middle of a vast swamp. Water was pouring off the fields into the river and there was no way of avoiding it. I rolled up my trousers and off I splashed, emerging happy that it had only come up to my ankles. By the time I was nearing Upper Mill Farm, the ground was even more flooded. The stile and gate to the next field stood marooned in a lake and a bridge over a ditch looked more like a diving board. My confidence in there being water at the source was increasing but my confidence in actually reaching it wasn't. Things improved for the next couple of fields, as the path follows the former millstream, until, as I reached power lines, the flood returned and I was wading again. This time it was over my knees. The next stretch, where the path runs through trees on the riverbank, was a simple paddle. Emerging on to the road at Ewen, I knew that for the next few hundred yards at least I'd be dry. Ewen, a village which carries the Old English name for 'source', is an attractive Cotswold stone place with several new houses. Mill Farm was having a facelift. It was the highest mill on the Thames, with just enough water to turn a wheel. Although the river hereabouts is often virtually dry now, this wasn't always the case, for before gravel extraction downstream and the building of the Thames and Severn Canal in 1789 interrupted drainage patterns there was a more consistent flow.

Just before the path leaves the road to follow a riverside route through trees, there is a millennium seat, given by Kemble and Ewen Women's Institute, for Thames walkers. I sat gratefully and wrung the water out of my socks, a process I would repeat an hour or so later on my return. At Parker's Bridge the path heads up through the fields once

Thames Path starts here!

more, soon reaching another flooded section before emerging on to the A429. Across the road stands an information board, and the path crosses a foot-bridge over a tributary, often dry, but in spate and the bridge certainly necessary today. There was still a strong flow on the Thames by Lyd Well, an ancient spring where the first waters of the river are often seen bubbling up to the surface. Lying behind a wall, the well was subsumed in the general aqueosity of the scene. (In drier times Lyd Well is accessible from the concrete farm track by way of an insulated section of electrified fence.) Of the tumble of stones marking a former footbridge mentioned in the guidebook there was no sign and a lake occupied much of the meadow below the steps leading up to the road. This is a fascinating place, for here the Thames is crossed by the Fosse Way, built two millennia ago to link the Roman centre of Cirencester with Exeter, Bath and Lincoln. A couple of hundred yards north-east along the road stands a lowered bridge where the road crosses the route of the Thames and Severn Canal, a waterway intimately connected with the river and its water supply. You will also be conscious of a later transport route, for the trains on the former Cheltenham and Great Western Union Railway line of 1844 can be heard across the fields as the Thames path nears the source, while the Thames Head Inn stands on the road next to the site of Tetbury Road station.

Having crossed the erstwhile frontier between Britannia and the barbarians, the Thames Path continues very much as before, across green meadows. In this case Trewsbury Mead, site of the Thames Conservators' stone. On this occasion I put up a flock of several dozen gulls which had taken to the water. The last two stiles on the Thames Path were each standing in the middle of their own lakes, so by the time I had waded to the stone, I felt I'd made up for the dry disappointment of a quarter century ago. As I paused by the monolith to watch the water streaming past it was clearly evident that, today at least, this wasn't the source, so I followed the water through another couple of fields to the embankment along which once ran the canal. A climb up on to the bank revealed the dry course of the cut at Trewsbury Bridge and I was able to follow the old towpath for a couple of hundred yards to the west to where I could see the highest surface water, rising by a wall. A few years ago, on the hottest summer's day of the twenty-first century so far, we had cruised our boat through London, gazing in awe at Tower Bridge, the Houses of Parliament, the London Eye and all the other glories that make up the metropolitan Thames as viewed from a stance 18 inches above the river's surface. It seemed odd to think of all that 'liquid history' starting in the corner of a field adorned with a dozen or so blue-plastic-sheeted straw bales.

If you follow the canal towpath for a further half mile or so, you will reach the east portal of Sapperton Tunnel. This 3,817 yard (3,490m) long bore opened in April 1789 and was the longest in England until 1811, when Standedge on the Huddersfield Narrow Canal opened. Sapperton, like most early canal tunnels, was built without towpaths and boats were legged through by men lying on their backs and walking along the walls. Presumably the excavations tapped underground springs, so the tunnel can also lay claim to be the true source. If the Cotswold Canals Trust has its way, some day the tunnel, which was abandoned in 1927 (but had seen its last fully loaded boat sixteen years earlier), may once more be fully navigable and further investigations may be carried out. The canal, which had a pumping engine east of the road at Thames Head, is said to have disturbed the water supply in the area. Indeed, Hilaire Belloc considered that the gods of the Thames deserted the river after the pumping station had been set up and the stream pumped dry. The Great Well, which was sunk to a depth of 63 feet (19m), can still be seen, 200 yards (182.8m)

Seven Springs

'liquid history'

Avon
smooth runs the water

	AVON
SOURCE	Manor Farm, Naseby, Northamptonshire
G.R.	SP 688 782
LENGTH	95 miles (154 kilometres)
TRIBUTARIES	Sowe, Leam, Dene, Arrow
MOUTH	confluence with Severn at Tewkesbury

east of the old road bridge. The pumphouse itself is no more, though the keeper's house is now a private residence.

Wading back to Trewsbury Mead from the highest spring, I decided not to follow the largely submerged Thames Path all the way back to Neigh Bridge and so took to the roads from Ewen. I was walking down a quiet lane when I discovered it was a Quiet Lane. Wooden posts planted in the verge told me so. Quiet Lanes, apparently, are minor rural roads, which are suitable for walkers, cyclists and horse-riders to share with motorized vehicles. They seem to spring from the common-sense-free-zone values of the health-and-safety planner community and have been developed solely to encourage the promulgation of vast amounts of blindingly obvious supporting documentary evidence. I, pedestrian, shared this particular stretch of tarmac quite amicably with a cyclist and a couple of motorists, and I dare say we could have done it without even knowing it was a designated Quiet Lane.

The numerous authors who describe the Thames as rising in a 'remote Gloucestershire meadow' have obviously never visited the source of the Severn, or Don (Yorkshire or Aberdeen version), or Eden or Tywi, or Spey or Dee or Dyfrdwy or . . . !

The Upper or Warwickshire Avon runs for 95 miles (154km) to its confluence with the Severn at Tewkesbury. Of all the sources in this book, that of Shakespeare's Avon is the easiest to visit. Marked by a sugar-loaf-shaped, cast-iron monument standing in a slight depression, it is to be found in the front garden of Manor Farm in the Northamptonshire village of Naseby. The farm, built in 1720 at the junction of Church Street, Newlands and Welford Road, is a Grade II listed building.

However, as the land rises slightly to the northeast, to where a memorial obelisk stands overlooking the site of the decisive Civil War Battle of Naseby, the pedant may feel obliged to make further exploration. This mound, on which the memorial stands, the former site of a windmill, is a fitting place to visit, as it is the highest ground for a couple of miles around along this particular stretch of the English watershed. Any rain falling on its southwestern slopes, therefore, ought to end up in the Bristol Channel via Avon and Severn. Water draining off in other directions, though, will find its way to the North Sea, for headwaters of the Welland, Nene and Ise all rise near by. A couple of springs in nearby fields can certainly put forward a claim to be the sources of the Ise and one of the first tributaries of Avon itself.

After an examination of the source, an exploration of the village and its vicinity will reveal many places of interest. Naseby is the starting point for Shakespeare's Avon Way, an 88-mile (142km) long-distance path, inaugurated in April 2008, which uses rights of way to follow the river as closely as possible from the source to its confluence with the Severn.

Although a small village now, in the Middle Ages Naseby was a flourishing market town, granted its charter by King John in 1203. The shaft of the old market cross can be found on Church Street near the end of Carvells Lane. The Black Death of 1349 took its toll on the village and the population decreased. Some parts of the settlement were abandoned and the outlines of small lanes, enclosures and buildings can be seen in surrounding fields.

Were it not for the Civil War battle, Naseby's name would be as well known outside the area as those of other little local villages such as Yelvertoft, Arthingworth and Lubenham. The fighting took place north-west of the village, in the then open fields of Broad Moor, which lies between two of Avon's small upper tributaries. By the end of the day King Charles had lost his infantry, his artillery, his baggage train, his private papers, the battle and, to all intents and purposes, his throne and, ultimately, his head. The appearance of the area today, well viewed from the monument by the Sibbertoft road, which is seen as a patchwork of straight-sided fields, was brought about by enclosure in 1828.

On leaving the village, the infant Avon itself is directed around a couple of fields before passing under Carvells Lane, a track that leads down past Naseby Reservoir, where the river is also heading on a roughly parallel course. Constructed around the end of the eighteenth century, the 95-acre (38.5ha) reservoir is a popular fishing and sailing venue. Perhaps the most dramatic event in the reservoir's history was in July 1939, when a Fairey Battle aircraft of 40 Squadron ditched after engine failure. The crew members were rescued by the reservoir superintendent in his rowing boat.

A 4 mile (6.4km) long feeder flows from the reservoir to top up the Leicester Section of the Grand Union Canal and the last mile and three-quarters (2.8km) of the channel was made navigable in 1814 as the Welford Arm. A public footpath follows the river and canal feeder for about three-quarters of a mile (1.2km) from Welford to Sulby Abbey and it is interesting to compare the meandering course of

Manor Farm, Naseby

Young Avon

the Avon with the straighter, artificial watercourse. Although the waterways intersect, they do not intermingle, as a siphon takes the Naseby Reservoir feeder water underneath the river and a tributary. The Premonstratensian Sulby Abbey itself, founded in 1155 and dissolved in 1538, was obviously sited to take advantage of the proximity of the Avon, and among earthworks discernible on the site are the remains of fishponds and a watermill.

Also worth mentioning is a small stream whose headwaters converge with the Avon just below Naseby Reservoir. It is less worth mentioning for the fact of the stream itself but for the hill on which it rises on the north side. The Cold Ashby trig point at the east end of Honey Hill carries a plaque stating 'ORDNANCE SURVEY COLD ASHBY The first observations for the retriangulation of Great Britain were made at this trigonometrical station by Sergeant G. F. Mullinger, Royal Engineers on 18th April 1936. There are 11,678 such stations and the last observations were made at Thorney Gale in Westmorland on 4th June 1962.'

Beyond Welford the river, now acting as the boundary between Leicestershire and Northamptonshire, parallels the canal before turning south-westwards to flow through Stanford Reservoir and beyond to Rugby, Warwick, Stratford, Evesham and the Severn at Tewkesbury, site of the decisive Wars of the Roses battle of 1471, when Edward IV of York completely defeated the forces loyal to the House of Lancaster. This Avon is a river bracketed by battles.

Great Ouse

Say it. Ouse. Slowly.

One of the most altered rivers in Britain, the Great Ouse flows for about 160 miles (257km) north-eastwards from the Northamptonshire Heights to The Wash. The Heights, part of a great line of Jurassic limestone hills stretching from Yorkshire to Dorset, reach about 500 feet (153m), where they form that

GREAT OUSE	
SOURCE	nr. Syresham, Northamptonshire
G.R.	SP 637 446
LENGTH	160 miles (257 kilometres)
TRIBUTARIES	Ouzel, Ivel, Cam, Lark, Little Ouse, Wissey
MOUTH	The Wash nr. King's Lynn

part of the English watershed that gives rise to the Great Ouse.

Different authorities give vague and various locations for the source of the river. 'The River Great Ouse rises near Brackley in Northamptonshire.' 'In a field near Brackley.' 'Rises near Silverstone.' 'The river has several sources close to the villages of Syresham and Sulgrave in Northamptonshire.' 'A field south of Farthinghoe.'

One to investigate, then. The highest naming of the Great Ouse on the 1:25 000 Ordnance Survey map is on the branch rising north of Syresham, while the highly suggestive Ouse Well appears half a mile (0.8km) south-east of Farthinghoe. A further study of the map shows that the many headwaters rising around Sulgrave coalesce near Wappenham to form the Tove, which flows through Towcester to join the Great Ouse north-west of Milton Keynes.

A gentle walk of 1½ miles (2.4km) in the vicinity of Farthinghoe will bring you to Ouse Well, a contender for head source. Farthinghoe, a small ironstone village bisected by the busy A422 Banbury–Brackley road, provides parking at the village hall, past the school on Cockley Road. A route, which if not entirely strictly legal, at least has the benefit of avoiding the main road except for two crossings of it, can be followed from here. At a sharp bend on Cockley Road, a bridleway leads eastwards until, after a couple of fields, a path heads off towards Glebe Farm on the main road. The farm now serves a variety of purposes, with various firms making bespoke furniture, framing pictures, servicing vehicles and even selling eggs. One of the Great Ouse's headstreams dips under the main road here and, although there is no right of way, a path has been trodden out along the edge of the fields, tracking the little stream past Ouse Well to a minor road. The well is a forceful little spring with pennywort floating in the clear water. At the time of my visit its water was flowing into a little stream in a shallow, wooded dell. This occasion coincided with a wet spell and the spring may well be the headwater in time of drought. Further up the stream divides, with one branch starting at a rubbish-strewn hollow on the edge of a wood just off the minor road running south from the main road. The other was seemingly causing some difficulties, as roadworks and ground clearance were being undertaken at just the spot where it passes under the road. On this occasion, at least, this Ouse source was a muddy puddle in the field just beyond the road. The minor road can be followed back to cross the A422 on to a bridleway that leads back to Cockley Road and the village hall. The water from the Farthinghoe sources, joined by streams rising just east of Greatworth, flows to the south-east to join the Syresham branch just south of Brackley.

Syresham is a fascinating little spot. There can be few villages with so many intriguing place names in such a small area: Kingshill Farm, King Richard's Copse, the King's Head, Abbey Way House, Priesthaywood Farm, Magdalen Spring, Old Mountains and Old Park Farm. A place with a past. Starting from the church of St James the Great, a road leads to a stile and a path crosses a paddock, occupied by a flock of black sheep, and then a field. To the south the young Great Ouse flows past a little sewage works, while the path follows a hedge and gets ever closer to the stream before leaving it, where it was gushing with gusto from a pipe beneath the track leading to the road by Park Manor Farm. There were drifts of snowdrops, fair maids of February, madly bobbing on the verges as I made my way along the quiet road. The weather vane on the roof of Wild House Farm confirmed the westerly direction of the gale while my hat blowing across the road confirmed its strength. As I turned off the road into regenerated woodland, the green plastic sapling protectors had certainly proved their worth but didn't look as if they were going to biodegrade any time soon. After crossing a footbridge over a milky Ouse, you soon reach Priesthaywood Farm. The priest or monk who lived by this enclosed wood or woodland clearing would hardly recognize the upmarket premises it currently is. A bit of poor navigation took me off the path and I met a fox in a field by Priesthaywood. We stood and stared at each other for the best part of a minute, he obviously unconcerned that this is Grafton Hunt country. The hunt was named after its founder, Charles FitzRoy, the 2nd Duke of Grafton, who started it following his appointment by Queen Anne as Lord Warden and Chief Ranger of Whittlewood Forest in 1712; the hounds meet every Tuesday and Saturday during the season, which lasts from September to March. Perhaps my fox knew this was Friday or was aware of the terms of the Hunting Act (2004). He soon ran off when a nearby bird-scarer fired.

The Great Ouse, hardly great here, is dammed to form four modern-looking ponds before the path arrives at Wappenham Lodge Farm, a fine Georgian farmhouse complete with bricked-up

The first bridge

BEDFORD, A PEEP ON THE OUSE.

tax-avoidance window and a semi-fossilized Albion lorry. The track heading to the watershed, source and ultimately Abthorpe is technically a byway open to all traffic but, as the gates at both ends are chained and the by-way sign by Wappenham Lodge has been dug up, it would be a brave driver who ventured along it. When I went along the track, it was so muddy that I soon felt I was walking in those elevator shoes once said to be worn by actors of restricted height. A triangular route around the last field on the map with a blue line in it takes you across the two highest bridges on the Great Ouse, though it is open to debate as to whether a concrete pipe really classes as a bridge. Standing on the last, or first, crossing over the little stream, I recalled some of the bridges we had cruised beneath while on the river the previous summer, the fifteenth-century bridge at St Ives, one of only five in England to incorporate a chapel, and the even earlier old

bridge in Huntingdon, being two memorable ones.

Back at Priesthaywood Farm, a byway runs off to the south-east, clipping the edge of King Richard's Copse, part of the one-time royal hunting ground of Whittlewood Forest. Large areas of the former forest survive as woods, partly as a result of the clay-loaded soil that underlies them. In medieval times, Northamptonshire was dominated by royal forests. This does not mean that the area was necessarily totally covered in woodland but it was the area covered by Forest Law, a largely Norman introduction designed to protect the King's hunting. At their greatest extent, Whittlewood, Salcey and Rockingham stretched in an unbroken band from the Welland in the north to the Great Ouse in the south, covering about half the county.

A bridleway heads off south-west towards Kingshill Farm, joining the farm track to run down to the road by Syresham Pocket Park, an open space owned and managed by locals on a site which was formerly being used for fly-tipping. New paths and ramps have been created and wildlife encouraged in an area by the side of the Great Ouse by King's Hill Bridge. A short walk along the road, now by-passed by the A43, leads back to the village.

South of King's Hill Bridge was Biddlesden Abbey, which owned much of the land around here and accounts for many of the monastic names in the vicinity. There was another abbey at Luffield, now buried beneath the Silverstone motor-racing circuit, a couple of miles to the east. Following the dissolution of the monasteries, the Biddlesden estate passed to Magdalen College, Oxford, accounting for the College Farm passed on the way back to Syresham as well as Magdalen Spring, source of another Great Ouse headwater, which lies south of the large main road junction south-west of the village.

The Ouse Valley Way starts at Syresham, outside the King's Head, but again, like several other river walks, it doesn't visit the source. It doesn't visit the river much in its first few miles, crossing it just once in the 9½ miles (15km) to Buckingham. The way was formally opened in May 2004. South of Syresham the Great Ouse forms the county boundary between Northamptonshire and Buckinghamshire.

A mile or so to the north-west of Syresham, the Old Mountains is a listed scheduled ancient monument, probably built between 1250 and 1350, either as a park keeper's lodge or as a guest house for Astwell Manor. The site was moated, though this was more likely to have been for status or to collect water for fish rearing than defence. The earthwork remains of a large fishpond have been identified in the fields to the south. It is thought that the pond, made by damming yet another of the Great Ouse's headwaters, once covered the entire field, which was called Pool Meadow on early maps. Some of the Old Mountains are the remnants of rabbit warrens reaching a height of about 6 feet (1.8m). Fish and rabbit meat were important in the medieval manorial diet. Local superstition credits the Old Mountains with an eerie character, for it is said that often no birds are heard singing in the trees growing on the remains of the moated site, even though it is surrounded by open land. The stream flowing from Old Mountains joins the main channel by Kingshill Farm after flowing through Syresham.

Nene

royal road

	NENE
SOURCE	nr. Arbury Hill, Northamptonshire
G.R.	SP 536 590
LENGTH	105 miles (169 kilometres)
TRIBUTARIES	Wooton Brook, Ise, Harpers Brook
MOUTH	Crab's Hole, The Wash

I went to find some of the sources of the Nene on a spring morning when the Meteorological Office had omitted to inform this corner of Northamptonshire that the showers were supposed to be isolated, not prolonged and continuous. A bad day for walking but a good day for source searching in an area whose history is visible in its many earthworks.

The Nene, variously pronounced 'nene' or 'nen' – you're bound to get the wrong one and a wry smile when you say the name in front of a local – is one of Britain's lesser-known rivers. The sixth longest in Great Britain, it flows for about 105 miles (169km) from the limestone uplands of the eastern Midlands to The Wash through predominantly agricultural surroundings, except where it passes through Northampton, Peterborough and Wisbech. It is navigable for its last 91 miles (146km), below Northampton, with thirty-seven locks to Peterborough, below which its course has been greatly altered and the river largely loses itself in the Middle Level Navigations of the Fens.

A good walk, visiting various sources, begins in the pretty brownstone and thatch village of Badby, where the long-distance Nene Valley Way starts. The good folk of the village were looking forward to their annual Bluebell Sunday when I was there, for the display of the flowers in the local woods is special. Over the A361, a minor road soon descends to cross one of Nene's headwaters and on a very wet morning, I soon noticed several others. One spring up on the slopes of Arbury Hill was particularly vigorous and was pouring water over the road. At Staverton Lodge there is an archetypal duck pond and a couple of hundred yards down the road a strong flow was emerging from a large pond below the hill, one of the Nene's recognised sources. Ridge and furrow earthworks in the field point to former arable farming. There is no direct approach to Arbury Hill, Northamptonshire's County Top, from this side but a track leads diagonally back across a series of fields along the west side of the hill. This track soon meets another, which you can follow eastwards through trees along the south side of the hill. A pond in the field to the south, in the col between Arbury and Sharman's Hills, is another Nene source. This stream, which later flows down through attractive parkland around Fawsley Hall before it joins the main river itself, can be found at the foot of the field and a track leads down past the oddly named – for Northamptonshire at least – Konigsee Farm to the main road. The student of agricultural relics will look into the field behind the signpost whence the stream issues and you can follow the hedge back to where a double fence prevents access to the pond but gives a view of it.

It seems remiss to visit this corner of the county without walking up to its highest point and you can easily reach the flat summit of Arbury Hill from the south via a gate and various bits of a motocross route, along which the bikes have carved gashes in the ground. Earthworks of a different nature mark the top, for here are the rectangular remains of a prehistoric camp. The view from the summit is rather tree-blocked, apart from northwards where the large pond west of Staverton Lodge shows up well, but the exercise is worthwhile. When you return to the bridleway, you can follow it west across the fields south of Highfields Farm and through a belt, braces and string gate to a patch of shady woodland, where a pond might well lay claim to be the source of the Cherwell at the start of its journey south to Oxford and the Thames. The next earthworks to be crossed are the remains of the excavations and one of the four air shafts above Catesby Tunnel. This 2,997-yard (2,740m) bore was built on the Great Central Railway's main line to London and was dug in 1897, apparently because the owner of Catesby House wanted the view from the back of his house to remain unsullied. As the railway was constructed within a hundred yards of the place you can quite see his point of view, though such a request never seems to have been agreed to in most places where railways passed.

The path emerges on to a minor road, which you can follow to the quiet village of Hellidon. Here you will find the Red Lion with its range of locally brewed Hook Norton ales, a welcome resting place. Here also the weather started to brighten up. Here furthermore will be seen the source of a third river, for the Leam is said to rise in the cellars of Leam House just below the pub. Behind the house you can glimpse Leam Pool, one of a series of lakes and

Staverton duck pond

fishponds along the upper course of the river.

The way is now north, following the little Leam for a couple of miles. Stockwell Lane leads through the pleasant village and meets the gated road to Lower Catesby. I'm not usually one for road walking, but the lane to Lower Catesby is a delight, giving long-ranging views over the rolling uplands that here form the English watershed and particularly fine glimpses of Catesby House and the more distant Shuckburgh Park. The latter, not usually open to the public, is built on the site of the deserted village of Upper Shuckborough, whose twelfth-century church was much altered by the Shuckburgh family in the late nineteenth century. Here I was following a part of the Jurassic Way, a long-distance route running over 88 miles (142km) from Banbury in Oxfordshire to the Lincolnshire town of Stamford. For most of its course it follows the limestone heights of Northamptonshire and this is part of its Rivers and Railway section. Soon the road crosses the Leam and enters Lower Catesby, where the rather jolly red-brick Old Coach House is now a guesthouse.

There was a Cistercian Priory here and further earthworks and fishponds show its position in the fields to the west of the present tiny settlement. Founded in 1175, the nunnery seems to have been a well-run place, beneficial to and respected in the neighbourhood. Our common view of religious houses, before Henry VIII dissolved them, as places of ill repute may stem at least partly from sixteenth-century spin and propaganda. Dr John Tregonnell, who visited the priory in September 1535, reported to Thomas Cromwell, the King's vicar-general, that 'the prioress and sisters are free from suspicion'. The local commissioners, when they visited Catesby on 12 May the following year, were so impressed by what they saw that they wrote, 'The house of Catesby we founde in very perfect order, the prioress a sure, wyse, discrete, and very religious woman with ix nunnys under her obedyencye, as religious and devoute and as good obedyencye as we have in tyme

past seen or be lyke shall see.' They went on to report on the good works the nuns did for the 'kynges people' and made a plea that if any religious house should be spared dissolution it should be Catesby. It was all to no avail and the Prioress Joyce, 'a right sad matron' who was granted a pension of £20, her nine nuns and twenty-six dependants were all ejected. Vestments, furniture and other goods and ornaments of the church and associated buildings raised £400, lead from the roof £110; the priory's plate fetched £29 4s. and the broken metal of two hand bells £3. The present chapel dates from the nineteenth century.

As you continue on the gravelled track ahead, a Jurassic Way signpost on the right points the way diagonally across fields, which were full of sheep when I crossed them. It was a chorus of bleating that was partly responsible for some of the earthworks hereabouts, for many medieval villages were deserted when their landowners changed from arable farming to sheep rearing and this led at least in part to the delicious open nature of this part of Northamptonshire. The lost medieval village of Newbold lay almost directly beneath the impressive twelve-arched Catesby viaduct, which you soon see crossing the Leam valley.

A pair of blue-brick Great Central Railway bridge abutments led me through the abandoned railway and across broad arable fields towards Bates Farm and Staverton. The earthworks of the former GCR are very impressive, which is only right on this the last main line of the high days of the Victorian railways. In the early 1840s a railway was built linking Manchester and Sheffield and this grew into the Manchester, Sheffield and Lincolnshire Railway, working over an area between Liverpool and the east coast. Under the leadership of Sir Edward Watkin, one of the most able railway administrators and politicians of his day, the MS&LR had an ambitious management, who embarked on a scheme to reach London, renaming the company the Great Central as a result. The line opened for coal traffic in July 1898 and eight months later, on 15 March 1899, the Great Central's first passenger express left its new Marylebone terminus. Although the GCR gained a reputation for fast running and luxury, it never really paid its way, for the construction costs had been so great. It became part of the London and North Eastern Railway in 1923 and British Railways in 1948, and its Johnny-come-lately status and the fact that its major centres were served by other lines meant that the line was a prime candidate for closure when road competition began to bite. The run-down started in 1960, long lengths of the line closed in 1966 and the last reach from Rugby to Nottingham in 1969. Built to Continental loading gauge standards, the Great Central would have been handy, if it still existed, as part of the projected high-speed rail line between London and the north, currently being mooted at

a cost of around £32 billion. The words 'metaphor', 'government', 'transport', 'policy', 'brewery' and 'organize' spring to mind. A section of the former line, between Loughborough and Leicester, has been preserved.

The walk continues across fields to Bates Farm and into Staverton, crossing three of the little Leam's tributaries on the way. It's good to know that, the walk being on the Jurassic Way, well-drained limestone is somewhere beneath your feet, but this didn't seem to fit with the fact that by the time I'd crossed the fields between the railway and the first stream I was walking about 4 inches taller from all the mud collected on my trainers. Staverton is a prosperous little village on the main road from Daventry to Leamington Spa but you won't have to cross it, unless you want to visit the Countryman. As

A Nene headwater

you turn right along the road and past the garage, a footpath sign points into a field opposite the church. This leads to a path through conifers and, crossing a stony track, descends across a field into a very attractive valley where high fences and tracks indicate sporting country. Just past a large pond through the trees to the right, you encounter a ditch, yet another of the Nene's headwaters, and this is soon joined by another, which the contours suggest is the outflow from the large pond below Arbury Hill. The path follows the stream for a further field before, in the next one, it bifurcates, one way going over a plank bridge to cross more fields and stiles, the other remaining with the channel before crossing it and cutting diagonally across the last field. Both paths end up on the main road, which you must cross before reaching Badby village again.

Witham

haunts of coot and hern

WITHAM	
SOURCE	Cribb's Lodge, Leicestershire
G.R.	SK 884 183
LENGTH	82 miles (132 kilometres)
TRIBUTARIES	Brant, Till, Bain
MOUTH	The Haven, The Wash

One of the many managed rivers in eastern England, Witham starts its 82-mile (132km) journey just inside Leicestershire but on entering Lincolnshire a mile (1.6km) from its source, it never deserts the county again until it enters the Wash. As it does so it flows through that fine trio of Lincolnshire settlements Grantham, Lincoln and Boston and, after the county city, is navigable and much altered. The river heads determinedly north until it reaches Lincoln and is then deflected southeastwards by the Wolds.

A gentle stroll around fields and meadows,

lasting a couple of hours, introduced us to several of Witham's headstreams. Cribb's Meadow, bisected by the little river, is about 3 miles (4.8km) east of Wymondham and 2 miles (3.2km) west of South Witham. It is a Site of Special Scientific Interest and a National Nature Reserve. Covering about 12 acres (4.8ha), it is mainly grassland over calcareous boulder clay, resulting in a neutral soil which encourages a rich range of species. A variety of meadow plants including cowslip, twayblade, adder's-tongue fern and common spotted orchid grow here in the spring and summer; common and great crested newts are found in the two ponds on the site, and there are many varieties of butterfly. I always thought you'd be more likely to see Grizzled Skippers and Dingy Skippers at the other end of the Witham, where it joins the sea beyond Boston, but they thrive here.

A path leads from a gate beside a former railway embankment, now covered by scrub as well as large oak and ash trees that have grown since the railway line was closed in 1959. Built by the Midland Railway in 1893, the route was operated by the Midland and Great Northern Joint Railway. Knocking railways is no new thing; the M&GR was known locally as the Muddle and Get Nowhere. More up to date are a couple of Cathodic Protection Ground Bed Location concrete posts just before where the bridleway crosses from the right to the left of the hedge. Mostly blackthorn so far, with a fine array of ripe sloes on a late October day, the hedge becomes predominantly hawthorn as it bounds a large field. Recently ploughed and harrowed, the many nodules of flint showed the calcareous nature of the soil. The clay was to come later.

You soon pass Cribb's Lodge. The place names here commemorate the boxer Tom Cribb, who fought a black American former slave, Tom Molineaux, for the heavyweight championship of England at nearby Thistleton Gap in 1811. A huge crowd of up to 20,000 watched the prizefight, which resulted in victory for Cribb after eleven bloody

Tom Cribb

rounds. A previous bout, the year before, had lasted a gruelling thirty-three rounds before Cribb seized the victory amid accusations of cheating. Why drag thousands of people to this middle-of-nowhere spot to watch a boxing bout? The counties of Leicestershire, Lincolnshire and Rutland met here, so if the magistrates arrived to halt the illegal fight, the contestants and crowd could escape across the county boundary and carry on.

At a field corner you leave the Rutland Round, which you have been following from the start and is surely the shortest county circumambulation in England, and follow a bridleway to a narrowing of the field and a crossing of the ditch along which flows the infant Witham. Where the bridleway crosses the ditch, large-scale Ordnance maps indicate 'Issues' and sure enough water seeping out of the ground marks one of the major sources of the river. The bridleway broadens out between new hawthorn hedges, which are a welcome sight after decades when hedges were grubbed out and fields turned into prairies. Any vestige of a watershed is barely perceptible but water flowing west from here coalesces to become the river Eye, a tributary of the Wreake, before joining the Soar and eventually the Trent, nearly doubling the distance it takes to reach the North Sea compared with Witham water.

When you return along the bridleway, a footpath crosses it and dives through the hedge near an electricity pole. We walked down the path to a bridge over this tiny southern branch of the Witham, disturbing a hare that skitted off across the field, and made our way past the very select-looking Pasture Farm. A tarmac drive, crossing another Witham headstream, leads to the Wymondham road,

which you follow past Highfield Farm to a further bridleway heading north alongside a large field. A headwater, shown on the 1:25 000 map but not on the 1:50 000, barely appears on the ground either, apart from a damp patch on the path. At a kissing gate, where the bridleway continues forwards as a footpath, we turned right between hedges to where a depression in the field and a slight flow through a pipe beneath the hedge mark the Witham's second major source.

At the end of the field a byway runs south across fields towards Crown Point Farm and a crossing of the by now yard-wide northern branch of the Witham. This is where you will appreciate the clay part of the calcareous clay that is beneath the feet around here. The byway is well churned up by the passage of vehicles and the collecting power of boot soles results in the walker walking tall. On reaching the road again, we followed the Viking Way, Rutland Round and the E2 European Long Distance Route for a while before arriving back at Cribb's Meadow. If we'd decided that this little Rutland and Leicestershire stroll wasn't enough, we could simply have carried on to Nice and the Mediterranean, where we could have tasted a glass or two of Château de Cremat rather than the sloe gin 'de Cribb's Meadow' which we enjoyed that Christmas.

Medway
a mere trickle still

MEDWAY	
SOURCE	Turners Hill, West Sussex
G.R.	TQ 336 356
LENGTH	75 miles (120 kilometres)
TRIBUTARIES	Eden, Bourne, Beult, Len
MOUTH	Sheerness, Thames Estuary

Around 75 miles (120km) long, the Medway is the longest river in Kent, though it rises in the Weald of West Sussex close to the village of Turners Hill. It flows mainly north-east and then north, passing through Tonbridge, Maidstone and Rochester before joining the Thames estuary by Sheerness. The river was used for transport as far back as Roman times and is still navigable as far as Tonbridge.

Although only a couple of miles from Crawley and the M23, the area is still heavily wooded and a search for the source goes a long way to prove that you don't need to go to the wilderness to find wild places. I parked opposite St Leonard's Church in a little pull-in where some previous visitor had dropped a plastic bag full of rubbish, and set off down the road before doubling back along a footpath leading to Butcher's Wood. The path descended an ingrained chalky path through dappled sunlight to a wooden footbridge. Water was just about trickling beneath and I tracked it uphill to its source, a tiny spring rising in a tangle of roots and branches beneath a holly tree and within sight of the church tower. Several streamlets dribble out of the ground near by and coalesce to form the little Medway. Today at least it was rising a couple of hundred yards higher than where it's indicated on the map. Like several others of these lowland sources which appear in fairly dense woodland, you'd probably be hard pressed to reach the spot in summer, and there mightn't be any water there anyway.

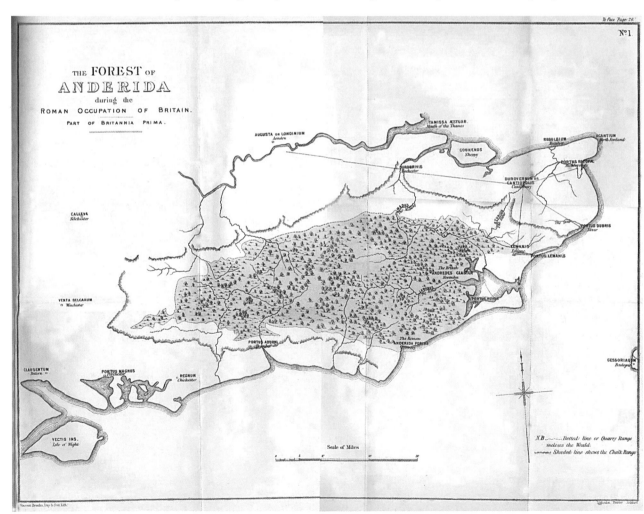

The Forest of Anderida from *A History of The Weald of Kent* by Robert Furley, FSA, 1871

Back to the bridge and I decided to follow the Medway downstream for a while to see if I could locate another spring, shown on the map as rising on the edge of Miswell Wood. A slender beech grew tall from the rotting lower trunk and root system of its tumbled former self and I wondered if this was an orphan of the Great Storm of October 1987, when 15,000 trees were felled overnight in the Royal Botanic Gardens at nearby Wakehurst Place. In Butcher's Wood it looked as if many of the trees had once been coppiced, while large patches of ground were beginning to be covered with the green shoots of bluebells, the annual promise that winter was, at last, passing. Where the map showed the Medway rising like three or four little blue eyelashes, the gently sloping hillside was live with water seeping out to flow down and join the main channel.

Lines of power cables ran through a clearing with the Medway's first tributary beneath them and when I turned into a field to track the stream a pair of fallow deer ran across in front of me. Mis Well, as I suppose this second source is called, stands by another holly tree on the edge of Miswell Wood and a field, beneath the power lines. As I stood and watched the clear water rising from the earth, I heard a woodpecker at work in the thicket and became aware of other birds – chaffinch, blackbird and tits – singing and calling the start of spring. These patches of woodland are the remnants of the great Weald of Sussex, Surrey and Kent, known to the Romans as Sylva Anderida and to the Saxons as Andredswald. It stretched 120 miles (193km) from east to west and 30 miles (48km) from north to south, a dense belt of dark, sombre forest which held deer, boar and wolves. Truly the Wild Wood.

I wandered back to the footbridge and made my way through beechwoods and then by field paths and alongside trim allotments to Turners Hill. During the hour and a quarter of my stroll I had met no one. As I walked past the village school a football landed in the road and started bouncing down the hill towards – who knows, Crawley Down or Caterham or Croydon. I retrieved it with a last-ditch effort and at some risk to life and limb, and then played a long ball back over the high wire fence incarcerating the likes of your local Lampards and Terrys, who were enjoying their break from Literacy Hour. I walked up to my van with the eyes of a local – 'Hmmm, lay-by, camper van, bag of rubbish.' So I did my bit for Turners Hill, picked it up and popped it into my bin when I got home.

Avon (Bristol)
all my worries far behind

AVON (BRISTOL)	
SOURCE	Tetbury branch
	Wor Well, Gloucestershire
	Sherston branch
	Joyce's Pool, Gloucestershire
G.R.	ST 901 939
	ST 824 877
LENGTH	75 miles (120 kilometres)
TRIBUTARIES	Marden, Frome, Boyd, Chew, Frome
MOUTH	Avonmouth, Bristol Channel

Rising from several sources in the Cotswolds fed by springs from the Great Oolite limestone, the two main headwaters of the Bristol Avon, the Tetbury and Sherston branches, meet at Malmesbury. The river, also known as the Lower Avon, then runs generally southwards through Chippenham and Melksham before swinging to the west and then north-west, flowing through Bradford-on-Avon, Bath and Bristol to join the Bristol Channel at Avonmouth after a journey of about 75 miles (120km). Having cruised the length between Bath and Bristol harbour, a fine stretch of river, I was interested to see where it all began.

The 7 miles (11km) long Tetbury Avon, also known as Ingleburn – 'English river' – rises at Wor

Well, two-thirds of a mile (1km) north-east of the town, just across the Cirencester Road from a trading estate. With a name more suited to the north-east than the south-west, Wor Well should really be a source of the Tyne. The Ordnance Survey has no doubts about recognizing it and 'Wor Well (source of River Avon)' is printed boldly across the map. A new public footpath follows a new tarmac drive leading to the new Worwell Farmhouse, a superior residence built of local stone in traditional style. Although no right of way is marked on the map, a sign proclaims there to be one and the helpful lady in the Tetbury Tourist Information centre indicated that some *quid pro quo* arrangement had been struck. Before the drive swings round to make its grand entrance to the farmhouse, Wor Well may, or may not, depending on the state of the undergrowth, be seen on the right. One time I visited all had been cleared and the water appeared, live and limpid, beneath a low limestone wall. A number of saplings had been planted next to the well, which is guarded by a couple of carved wooden ducks, and an old stone, sculpted with a lion's head gushing water, lay on wooden blocks a little way up the track. Is it to become a feature in the future?

Close inspection of the map shows a further little blue circle to the west and on another visit I could hear water emanating from a small, fenced hollow surrounded by blackthorn and maple, nearer to the top of the drive. It was silent and dry on another occasion and this higher spring doesn't seem to flow with the constancy of the lower Wor Well.

Where the tarmac heads away to the house a grassy path runs parallels to the stream, already strong and clear, to its confluence with another feeder flowing in the bottom of the valley. This is crossed by a wooden bridge, after which the path rises to cross a track, part of the route of the former railway which connected the town with the main line at Kemble between 1889 and 1963. Here was the site of a tragedy in 1891 when a deaf and elderly farm labourer was struck and killed by a train.

Following the old railway up the valley to the left, you soon cross a fine brick-built culvert, dry when we visited. The line curves into a wooded cutting below Little Larkhill Farm and in wet weather another headstream runs parallel to the railway on its east side, as shown by a rather rickety, wooden bridge. Returning to the confluence the path crosses a stone clapper bridge over the combined Tetbury Avon headstreams and, after half a mile or so, reaches the site of Tetbury station with its car park and preserved goods shed.

Several other springs are shown on the map in the Tetbury area, the most westerly one appearing to rise by a bridleway known as Chavenage Lane a few hundred yards east of the small village of Beverston. This was dry when we visited but a two-strand barbed-wire fence indicated the route that the stream, rising in the fields east of Beverston, follows in wetter times. Also of note, a spring in Magdalen Meadow was given as a source of the Avon too and was once famous as a healing and petrifying well. It can still be seen but Magdalen Meadow is now the Tetbury Tesco car park and the spring is in a walled enclosure. The well was granted to the people of Tetbury in 1357 by John de Breuse who, according to an accompanying plaque, was 'an ancestor of the town's original owner'. Yes, I know.

Longer than the Tetbury branch, the Sherston Avon has several sources, stretching along the Cotswolds between Didmarton and Old Sodbury. Joyce's Pool, by the quiet village of Didmarton, is the most obvious but not undisputed source of the Sherston Branch. The Ordnance Survey gives the stream emerging from the pool the label 'River Avon (Sherston Branch)', even though several of the more southerly headstreams, rising around Badminton and converging near Luckington, are longer. In earlier times local farmers would have watered their livestock here and in 1856 it was the scene of a tragedy when a local lad fell through the ice on the frozen pool and drowned. This melancholy aspect seems to be reflected in Kurt Jackson's

Magdalen Well

dark and atmospheric paintings of the source in his 2006 Avon exhibition. Joyce's Pool is now a pleasant roadside pond, surrounded by trees and grass with a couple of benches. An ideal spot to sit and think or, indeed, just sit. In early February I thought, I bet there'll be daffodils here in a month or so. The stream flowing from the pool goes under the A433 to run down the gentle Cotswold dip slope to Sherston and its Malmesbury meeting with the Tetbury arm.

Another stream head is marked on the map just north of Little Badminton and the journey to it from Didmarton, passing lodges, follies, ha-has and manicured woodland, leaves you in little doubt that you are entering 'Beaufortshire', the Badminton estate with its grand house, the principal home of the Duke of Beaufort for the last three centuries. This is the landscape of English idyll, of honey-coloured limestone cottages, drystone walls, rolling sheep

pasture and rich cropland, of clumps, coverts and copses. Just below a tight bend on the road, where the cement-rounded top of the wall was decorated with the detritus of a recent collision including sundry bits of metal and plastic and an unbroken wing mirror mirror, a depression in the field marked where, in wet weather at least, another Avon spring emerges from the rock beneath. I had to be content with a tiny trickle further down, beside the road just inside the park from Shepherd's Lodge.

Having determined to visit some other Avon sources on foot, I parked at Great Badminton village hall and walked beside a strong stream up to the road heading to Acton Turville. Leaving Badminton past golden Cotswold stone cottages, I became aware of the dull roar of the M4 only a mile or so to the south but this was soon drowned by shrieks of laughter and the clip-clop of hoofs on tarmac, a sound more appropriate to the surroundings. Over the Easter weekend up to a quarter of a million people per day swarm to Badminton for the annual Horse Trials while the Duke of Beaufort's Hunt has been chasing foxes in the surrounding countryside since 1762; well, it did until February 2005 and, I daresay, will do so again. Another stream, running beside the railway bridge by the disused Badminton station, was little more than damp. Also here is an old Buffer Depot, an intriguing name in the heart of traditional Toryland but actually a throwback to the Second World War. Such depots were set up by the government as strategic stores, holding a variety of foodstuffs, and were maintained throughout the Cold War. During the 1980s they contained such items as fat, known as Ministry Marge, which had an expected shelf life of twenty years, and sweet biscuits that had been baked during the 1960s. All the Buffer Depots and their food stocks had been disposed of by the end of 1995.

I walked westwards along the B4040, in parallel to a little valley across the railway line here descending from Chipping Sodbury tunnel. The 2½ mile (4km) long bore cuts through the Cotswold crest and is prone to flooding, proving that there's water in them thar hills. In fact it is closed on average twenty-four times a year, resulting in the diversion or cancellation of around fifty passenger and forty goods trains. An aqueduct was built to carry a little Avon headstream over the railway east of the tunnel mouth. The meticulous nature of Ordnance Survey mapping is well shown here, where a scant line of trees between the road and railway is actually named 'Oaks'. The early map engravers certainly had much practice with their little tree symbols around Badminton. I have always loved Ordnance Survey maps. A map is a constant delight for the source seeker, an inspiration before, a reassurance during and a souvenir after a visit. The 1:25 000-scale Explorer Maps, or 'two-and-a-half inch series' as some still think of them, provide a wealth of detail, even down to features such as walls and fences. On the top of a Pennine fell in driving rain and 20 yards visibility, this can be a great comfort. I have few regrets but one of them is to do with the OS's Explorers. When first issued these orange-sleeved sheets had a photo on the front cover with a brief description; for example, sheet 155, Bristol and Bath, had a picture of the River Avon just below Pulteney Bridge with the simple caption 'River Avon Bath'. My home sheet, 219, Wolverhampton and Dudley, came out with a photo of one of the

Sherston Avon

local canal tunnels and the engine house that stands besides it. There was a slight mistake in the caption – they'd named the wrong canal and put it in the next town – so I wrote to the OS to point out the error. Some time afterwards the OS changed its policy for Explorer Map covers and although there is still a photo on the front, it remains anonymous. Now, on the inside of the cover, there is one of the most mealy-mouthed, back-covering paragraphs I've ever read. I hope it wasn't my letter that made them change. Say it ain't so, OS.

The B4040 is fairly busy but it has a verge which, though not especially easy to walk along, partly because of the uneven nature of the grass and partly because of the amount of rubbish strewn along it, you can hop up on to. Past Newhouse Farm I deserted it northwards along a lane leading to Lime Avenue. The lane passes over the railway tunnel and is flanked by a pair of round, castellated, tower-like structures surrounded by trees. Now acting as ventilation shafts, these were originally two of the six construction shafts used during the driving of the railway tunnel and the trees grow on the spoil that came up them. Their medieval appearance is no doubt a nod to the near neighbours, for the twin domes and flagpole of Badminton House can be seen across the fields.

The cottage at the end of Lime Avenue bears the date stone 1902, which makes it a near contemporary of the tunnel. Like many of the tracks in the vicinity, Lime Avenue is a permissive path and is obviously popular, especially with horse riders. It is no doubt at its most splendid in early summer, but then the water table is likely to be lower and the chances of finding surface water less. You can't have it all ways always. At a crossroads I turned left into Seven Mile Plantation, a shelter belt planted by Capability Brown, which runs in a semi-circle around the northern side of the estate, and my nose indicated they were muck spreading before I heard the noise of the tractor in an adjacent field. I passed a Badminton estate boundary stone, dated 1783 (incidentally the year Brown died), and turned off on to a bridleway following a tumbled stone wall around ploughed fields. Large cornfields are now a feature of the Cotswolds, replacing the sheep pasture of former years. A footpath took me through belts of conifers separated by a junior ash grove to Grickstone Farm.

This is one of those places that speak of continuity. A cluster of houses and farm buildings, including a listed mid-eighteenth-century barn, huddle in a tight little valley just below the scarp edge. Down the valley a slight rise in the ground marks the scant remains of a three-chambered neolithic long barrow, now virtually ploughed away. It was excavated in 1844, when many skeletons were found, and several stones could still be seen during the 1960s. The Grickstone itself stands just above the farm that bears its name. A standing, or rather leaning, stone some 6 feet (1.8m) long, it is found by the corner of a wood and some speculate that it may once have been part of a burial chamber long since destroyed. Local historians H. O'Neil and L. V. Grinsell reported that their source had told them that it dated from 'when the Greek wars were in England' and that a Greek officer was supposed to be buried beneath it. For the source seeker it is the spring, buried away in a dense little copse besides the farm road, that is the real spirit of the place. One of Avon's headstreams, probably the highest constant one, bursts into daylight to run away beneath the ivy-covered trees. Next to it is a circular depression, the remains of the well, the reason for Grickstone and its long, long history.

I followed the tiny stream that joins the spring's water in the thicket, up to where it petered out in a sedgey ditch just south of the A46. Cutting up to Hall Lane I could see Crowshall Barn Farm and the dry valley, which is wet when the water table is higher and is then Avon's highest source. I visited the scarp edge before returning to Badminton, walking through horsey paddocks before crossing the road to perch on a stile and look out over the Vale

of Berkeley and across the Severn to the Forest of Dean. A couple of miles north along the escarpment rises the 100 foot (30m) high Somerset Monument, erected in 1846 in memory of Robert Edward Henry Somerset, nephew of the 6th Duke of Beaufort. He was one of Wellington's generals at Waterloo and died in 1842. Further afield the Tyndale Monument at North Nibley, built in 1866, 350 years after his martyrdom, to honour local lad and biblical translator William Tyndale, can also be seen.

Before returning to Badminton, I climbed back over the stile and noticed a Monarch's Way sign. I'm a great fan of contrived routes and some of my peak-bagging ones have been epic. I recall a crossing of the Lake District from Shap to Cleator Moor which I planned so that I could visit three widely scattered tops I had somehow managed to miss over the years. I remember it chiefly as one of the wettest walks I've ever undertaken and for a night spent under a bench in Little Langdale, but that's another story. Most long-distance paths are contrived to a greater or lesser extent. The Pennine Way doesn't always follow the Pennine watershed and abandons the range altogether once past Cross Fell, while the Offa's Dyke Path can't follow the dyke where Offa didn't build it, but the Monarch's Way is the most wonderful contrivance. Living less than a mile from the Way as it passes between Boscobel House, where Charles II hid in the oak tree, and Moseley Old Hall, where he was given dry clothes, food and a sleep in a proper bed for the first time in a week, I'm always happy when I bump into one of its far-flung stretches. Anyone wishing to follow the entire approximate escape route of the King will need to be prepared for 615 quirky miles (990km) of paths, bridleways, country lanes, canal towpaths and disused railway lines. Indeed, in the heart of the Black Country, which was pre-industrial when Charles crossed it, the Monarch's Way follows the towpath through the nearly 1¾ mile (2,768m) long Netherton Tunnel – the very one pictured on my conscience-stirring Explorer map.

A WELCOME IN THE HILLSIDE

The Valleys of South Wales. Male voice choirs and coal mines, head-frames and heritage, terraced housing, Keir Hardy and Max Boyce, bulldozed steelworks, Felinfoel Best Bitter. But it needs to be remembered that the common image is a recent one. Especially recent in the timescale of the rivers that dissect the region, that is. Less than two hundred years ago the Valleys were still fairly lightly peopled; it was the decades between 1850 and the First World War that saw the explosion of population as the coal seams, exposed by the rivers flowing down from the high land of Black Mountain and the Brecon Beacons, were exploited. Two of the longest of the twenty or so valleys slicing through the landscape are those of the Taff and the Tawe, whose sources are described in this chapter. The Usk is also included here, as it flows through a south Wales valley, even though it isn't really a South Wales Valley.

Taff

at the top

	TAFF
SOURCE	Taf Fawr – Y Gyrn, Powys
	Taf fechan – Pen y Fan, Powys
G.R.	SN 991 220
	SO 012 212
LENGTH	40 miles (64 kilometres)
TRIBUTARIES	Nant Morlais, Taf Bargoed,
	Cynon, Rhondda
MOUTH	Cardiff Bay

Taf in Welsh, the river rises in the Brecon Beacons and flows for about 40 miles (64km) southwards through Merthyr Tydfil and Pontypridd, gaining its main tributaries, the Rhondda and Cynon, to join

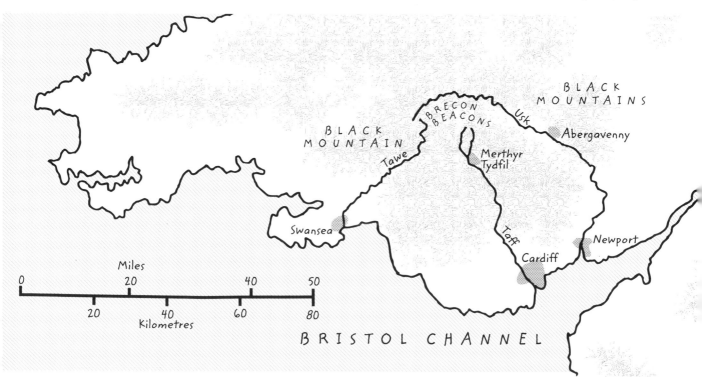

the Bristol Channel at Cardiff. The Welsh capital is named after the river; Caerdydd means 'fort on the Taff'. The name probably comes from the same pre-Celtic root as Thames and Tamar, maybe meaning 'dark water' or simply 'to flow'. Another Tâf, rising on the Prescelly Mountains in Ceredigion, joins the Twyi to flow into Carmarthen Bay.

Two headstreams, Taf Fawr and Taf Fechan, rise 1½ miles (2.4km) apart on the dip slopes of Pen y Fan and Corn Du, the highest summits in the Brecon Beacons, and flow separately for about 10 miles (16km) before merging at the wooded confluence, north of Merthyr, which gives Cefn Coed-y-Cymer its name. Fawr and Fechan flow down either side of a broad ridge and you can have a good walk by following the northern part of it – the southern section becomes broader and less defined – from the Taf Fechan valley. There is plenty of car parking in the upper reaches of Taf Fechan Forest, from where you can follow the road to near the dam of the Lower Neuadd Reservoir, which was virtually empty the last time I passed. From the end of the dam a stiff climb gains the ridge near the trig point on Twyn Mwyalchod, where there were no blackbirds. This carries a flush bracket plate numbered S2166 as well as a plaque in memory of Tony Swierzy, who died on an SAS Everest expedition in 1984. It is unlikely that you will go far around the Beacons without meeting a few of his successors.

There follows a steady ascent along the top of Graig Fan Ddu and across the narrow ridge of Rhiw yr Ysgafarnog, where there were no hares, to Bwlch Duwynt, from where there are excellent views of Corn Du and Pen y Fan. All along this stretch the ground falls away steeply into Blaen Taf Fechan, 700 feet (213m) below. On one visit the initial climb was in cold, thick mist, which started to clear when I reached the trig point and had all but disappeared within twenty minutes. Mind, it was twenty minutes of Brocken spectres and glories as the winter sun slanted across the ridge, casting my giant shadow on to the top of the cloud bank.

From Bwlch Duwynt, the sources of Taf Fawr

Corn Du and Pen y Fan

and Taf Fechan can be seen, Fawr in the col between Corn Du and Y Gyrn and Fechan from a line of springs seaming across the southern slopes of Corn Du and Pen y Fan. Come here on a day when a southerly or south-easterly gale is blowing up the valley, funnelling the wind and clouds over the col, truly to appreciate the name.

It is an easy matter to follow the path to the north-west above Craig Cwm Llwch and down past Tommy Jones's obelisk to the Taf Fawr source. Tommy was five when his father, a miner, brought him to visit his grandfather at the farm of Cwm Llwch, which stands in a pleasant wooded valley to the north of Corn Du. They had walked up from Brecon station to a place called the Login, only a few hundred yards from their destination. There Mr Jones and Tommy were met by the grandfather and Tommy's thirteen-year-old cousin, William. The boys were sent on to the farm but for some reason Tommy caught fright and ran off to find his father. He never found him and when William arrived back at the Login a short time later without the boy, the alarm was raised. With the help of some soldiers, Tommy's father and grandfather searched the area for most of the night and for many days afterwards. It was not until almost a month later, at the beginning of September 1900, that the boy's body was found. Tommy had somehow managed to lose his way and climb 1,300 feet (397m) up on to the ridge before dying of exhaustion.

Taf Fawr rises on the broad, boggy ridge

connecting the high tops of the Beacons to the decidedly lesser summit of Y Gyrn. Where sheep and quad-bike tracks cross the gently sloping col, a series of muddy and stony depressions marks the source. The top few feet of Fan Fawr just peep over the blancmange sprawl of Y Gyrn to the south-west, while Corn Du and Pen y Fan rise invitingly to the east.

An easy approach to Taf Fawr's source simply follows the broad track up from the Storey Arms on the A470 road between Brecon and Merthyr to where it crosses Blaen Taf Fawr and then tracks the declining stream to its source. It should be noted that care is needed when following the upper reaches of the stream as it runs, often invisibly, through potentially ankle-breaking gullies and grass-covered slits. A path runs parallel to the stream a few yards away on its western side anyway.

On one visit I walked up from the Storey Arms, once an inn and now an outdoor centre, following the well-built path to the top of its crest before striking off along a path leading north to meet the fence and broken wall that lead to Y Gyrn's summit. Just before the top a stile crosses the fence and it is an

easy descent to the col and Taf Fawr's source. From here I picked up the path leading to the foot of the track up to Corn Du, a long climb where some of the stones of the staircase are scratched with the initials of the weary. From the summit are fine views down the Taf Fechan valley and across to the 2,907-foot (886m) Pen y Fan. Another finely engineered path leads you to this, the highest summit in the Brecon Beacons and south Wales and the site of another excavated Bronze Age cairn. The men from the National Trust were just cementing a metal plaque on to a freshly constructed cairn and the builder's spaniel kept bringing him pieces of rock. The first time I was here there was a trig point with a neatly stencilled 'ENGLISH GO HOME' on the side. On a later visit the pillar had vanished, pushed over the edge by Nationalists I always imagined, but probably removed during the archaeology. The top of Pen y Fan has seen some strange sights, including a parking meter which once appeared on the summit, although there is no record of any beacons on the Beacons until Victorian times, when the Queen's Golden and Diamond Jubilees were celebrated with

TAFF FECHAN AND BEACONS   NEAR MERTHYR TYDFIL

Taf Fawr source

bonfires. One was even lit in December 1992 to celebrate the advent of the European Market. Wow.

On my latest visit, apart from the cairn constructors and dog, there was the usual collection of walkers admiring the view and a group of soldiers enjoying a rest. The aptly named Fan Dance is part of the Fitness and Navigation part of the selection course for the Special Air Service and Special Boat Service. The 15-mile (24km) course involves two groups, one starting from the Storey Arms and the other from the site of Torpantau station above Pentwyn Reservoir on the opposite side of the mountain. Each initiate carries a 40lb backpack, rifle and water bottle as they climb Pen y Fan and descend the other side. Then they turn round and reverse the route.

The path down Pen y Fan's south-east ridge,

above sharply etched Craig Cwm Sere, passes one of Taf Fechan's highest sources. It must be everyone's idea of the classic source: a bubbling spring high on a mountain side; shattered rock and trickling water a mere 200 yards (183m) away from the highest point in a 60-mile (96.5km) radius. A well-walked path passes close by. This used to be a horrible descent but rebuilding works have improved the situation. The spring lies between the old, abandoned scar and its successor, and a well-constructed stone channel now carries the tiny stream across the new path. This path leads down to the col between Pen y Fan and Cribyn, whose summit can be visited or avoided before you reach Bwlch ar y Fan, before descending gently and straight above Neuadd reservoirs to join the tarmac road in the Taf Fechan Forest.

Contouring back from the spring across the hillside below Pen y Fan leads you to any number of further little springs and boggy hollows, one of which is just below a crescent-shaped sheep bivvy giving views down Blaen Taf Fechan to its string of reservoirs. From here a sheep track leads to the col between Pen y Fan and Corn Du, where you pass a couple more springs. The strongest of Taf Fechan's springs emerges from a little tunnel of rocks above the path crossing Corn Du's southern flank. Back to Bwlch Duwynt and it is an easy matter to pick up the path across Blaen Taf Fawr to the Storey Arms.

The valleys of both Taf Fawr and Fechan are used for water storage. The high rainfall, glaciated valleys and absorbent nature of the Old Red Sandstone make the area ideal for reservoir construction. The Neuadd, Pentwyn and Pontsticill Reservoirs of the Faf Fechan and Beacons, Cantref and Llwyn-on along the Taf Fawr supply much of South Wales. Something to contemplate while walking the Beacons in a downpour.

Glossary

Bwlch ar y Fan: pass on the crest
Bwlch Duwynt: pass of the black or foul-weather wind
Cefn Coed-y-Cymer: ridge of the source wood

Old Storey Arms Inn, demolished 1924

Corn Du: black horn

Craig Cwm Llwch: dust valley crag

Cribyn: crest

Fan Fawr: big top

Graig Fan Ddu: crag of the black top

Neuadd: hall or mansion

Pen y Fan: *pen* can be variously translated as top, head, summit, end or edge; *fan* means peak or beacon

Pentwyn: top of the mound

Rhiw yr Ysgafarnog: hillside of hares

Taf Fawr: big Taff

Taf Fechan: little Taff

Torpantau: *tor* – a break, *pant* – hollow

Twyn Mwyalchod: blackbird hill

Y Gyrn: the cairn

Usk and Tawe

lift your eyes where the roads dip

USK	
SOURCE	Waun Lwyd, Fan Foel, Carmarthenshire
G.R.	SN 818 238
LENGTH	85 miles (137 kilometres)
TRIBUTARIES	Ebbw, Clydach, Honndu, Senni
MOUTH	Uskmouth, Newport

Usk carves an 85-mile (137km) sickle-shaped slash across south Wales as it makes its way from source, below Fan Brycheiniog at the north-eastern end of Y Mynydd Du, the Black Mountain, to mouth at Newport. It is called Wysg in Welsh, a name that may mean 'bountiful with fish', a truth to this day. The river first flows north to pass through Usk Reservoir before bending east and then south, dividing the Brecon Beacons from the Black Mountains, and visiting Brecon, Abergavenny, Usk and Caerleon, Isca to the Romans.

From the car park at Pont'ar Wysg, where the

Fan Dancers appear

road dips down to cross it, you can follow the river directly to its source. A meandering, strong-flowing stream with a channel braided in parts and cutting through banks of moraine, the Usk teases the walker with its constant changes of direction but a fair path soon develops above the west bank. Part hoof mark, part boot print and part tyre track, this descends to a little ford over the Nant y Lloi and soon the valley deepens and views north to the Usk Reservoir open out. After a particularly impressive set of meanders, the valley turns east-south-east and the stream narrows. Just as I was thinking that the path had given up, I came across a sort of ovine Clapham Junction, where many sheep tracks descend from the surrounding moors to cross the stream. Swinging round now to the south-south-west, the Usk becomes a narrow channel like a chattering gutter coursing through the reeds.

The head of the Usk lies in a rushy bowl below the final sharp climb up the prow of Fan Foel. It is a source seeker's delight, a series of lusty little springs, most just below the line of a prominent sheep track but with the main source set back further up the hillside. To make certainty even surer, it is marked by a stake, admittedly much smaller than the one at the Severn's source, but proof nonetheless that this is the true fountainhead. Near by someone has constructed a little belvedere from pebbly limestone and a couple of slabs where you can sit and gaze back down the valley over Waun Lwyd, to the reservoir, one of Swansea's watering holes, and its surrounding forest. This is ground known by Bronze Age farmers and Roman legionaries, both of whom have left their mark.

There is a 48 mile (77km) long Usk Valley Walk which, starting in Caerleon and finishing in Brecon, passes through some delightful and inspiring countryside. Like several other such routes, though, it fails fully to follow the river, although it would be possible to use footpaths and minor roads from its end to Pont'ar Wysg and this route to the source.

From the source, the easiest thing is simply to allow the river to guide your footsteps back down to the bridge, but there are better things to do around here – and more sources to see.

Fan Foel, the northern top of Fan Brycheiniog, summit of the Black Mountain, just peeps up over the moorland horizon and, like the county boundary which, give or take a few abandoned meanders, has followed the river from the reservoir, I decided to head straight for it. With Carmarthenshire to the west and Powys (formerly Brecknockshire) to the east, it is a steep pull up on to Fan Foel. A red kite was circling above as I reached the top.

Twenty years ago a fine, tall walkers' or shepherd's cairn, looking from a distance like a visitor surveying the scene, stood on the top. Ten years ago this had become a truncated, rather untidy affair. During the summer of 2004 the summit area was excavated to study the early Bronze Age round barrow which lay beneath. A rectangular central burial cist, about 6 feet long and 3 wide,

Above Pont 'ar Wysg

Llyn y Fan Fawr

was discovered holding a pile of cremated bones, some flint tools and crushed pottery. The remains of three people, an adult, a young child of no more than twelve years and an infant, were discovered as well as the burnt bones of two pigs and possibly a dog. A secondary cremation outside the cist contained the remains of two more people, one adult and one juvenile. Pollen analysis revealed that a floral tribute of meadowsweet accompanied the central burial. Perhaps through the swirling mists of four millennia we can picture a sad procession of people making their way to this hilltop, carrying the cremated remains and grave goods that were to accompany the dead to the other side and watch in imagination as they reverently place the bones, knives and decorated cup, with its food for the last journey, into the cist together with the creamy-white flowery garland. The covering slabs are then

dragged into place and the first of the stones which would build up over the years to separate ever further the living from the dead are laid on top. In later years the people would gaze up from the valley and see memories silhouetted on the skyline.

Around the outside runs a stone kerb with a diameter of about 12 yards (11m). Following the excavation the site was protected by geo-textile and backfilled with earth. There are similar cairns on many of the summits in the area, monuments to a forgotten era.

The view from Fan Foel is outstanding with the reservoir and Mynydd Eppynt conspicuous, as are the main Brecon Beacon summits away to the east. A short distance to the south-south-east is the trig point marking the top of Fan Brycheiniog and a nearby shelter. On the slopes to the west are springs marking the sources of Afon Twrch,

Proof!

which flows about 9 miles (14km) to its confluence with the Tawe.

A steep descent down a path undergoing repair led me to moraine-dammed Llyn y Fan Fawr, 1,600 feet (488m) below Fan Brycheiniog's summit and nearly 2,000 feet (610m) above sea level. Unlike most lakes in the area it is still natural, not being used for water supply. It has sparse aquatic vegetation and is said to hold no fish. Viewed from the tops it reflects the passing moods of the sky like a visual barometer. A stream flowing from the south-east corner of the lake is not, as might be thought, the source of the Tawe but a tributary of the river, Nant y Llyn. Tawe itself trickles out of an extensive boggy depression 600 yards (550m) north-west of the north-west corner of Llyn y Fan Fawr, although a medieval name for the lake, Llwch Tawe, suggests it was considered the source in times past. It

is easier to follow the little stream by sound than by sight at first as it makes its way through the tussocks and reeds. Soon joined by other streams, the Tawe, a river wrecked by industry but now recovering, flows south for about 30 miles (48km) to the Bristol Channel at Swansea – Abertawe.

A fine path from the north end of Llyn y Fan Fawr runs along below the towering cliffs of Fan Brycheiniog and Fan Foel, passing above Gwal y Cadno, a sheepfold or possibly the remains of a dwelling, before climbing gently to regain the bluff of Fan Foel and the path that leads down to the forest. I strayed off the track on Rhyd-wen Fach and came across a sad little memorial to the eight-man crew of a Lancaster bomber which had crashed here in 1943. Later I met the farmer on his quad bike with his dogs. They were moving the sheep further up the moor, a never-ending task. Passing more sheepfolds and crossing a minor col separating the headwaters of Nant Tarw and Afon Hydfer, both tributaries of the Usk, I entered the quiet forest and made my way back to the car park.

That night, by the Usk a few miles downstream from its source, I listened to owls screeching and watched a planetarium of the brightest stars before being lulled to sleep by its murmuring waters.

Glossary

Afon Twrch: boar river
Fan Brycheiniog: Brecon peak
Fan Foel: bare peak
Gwal y Cadno: fox's bed
Llwch Tawe: Tawe lake
Llyn y Fan Fawr: big top lake
Mynydd Eppynt: Eppynt mountain
Nant Tarw: bull stream
Nant y Lloi: calf's stream
Nant y Llyn: lake stream
Pont 'ar Wysg: Usk bridge
Rhyd-wen Fach: little white ford
Waun Lwyd: grey moor

THE WELSH DESERT

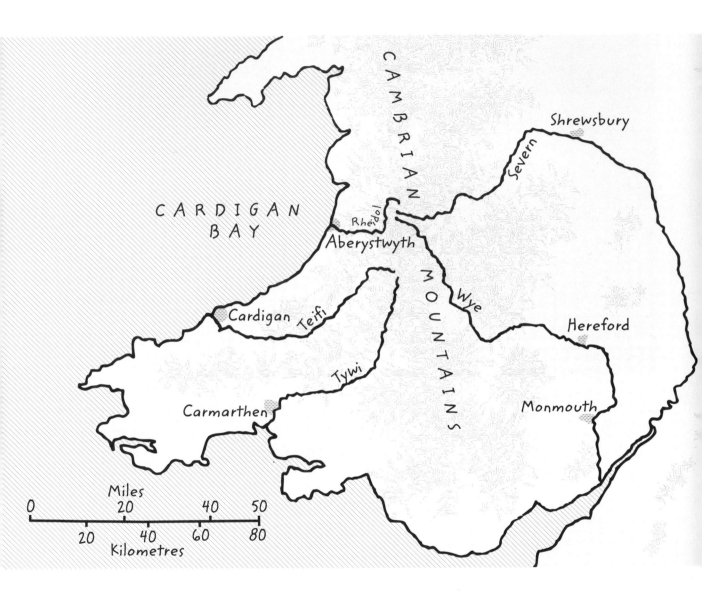

A large area of mid-Wales, with few roads and fewer towns, generally corresponding to Elenydd, the region at the heart of the Cambrian Mountains, has been described as the Welsh Desert for over a century and a half. An English visitor, John Henry Cliffe, writing in 1860, noted 'it has indeed with perfect truth been called the "great desert of Wales"'. As you will all too soon discover, this description is palpably not applied through the area's lack of rainfall – indeed it is home to many reservoirs and lakes – but rather a lack of people and this was certainly borne out on my visits, when I counted the folks I met during all the walks on the fingers of one hand. It is a glorious place of long views and distant glimpses, a tranquil and largely unspoilt landscape rich in echoes of the past and presently populated with a burgeoning number of soaring red kites.

Severn

a silence in the hills

SEVERN	
SOURCE	Blaenhafren, Pumlumon, Powys
G.R.	SN 821 898
LENGTH	220 miles (354 kilometres)
TRIBUTARIES	Vyrnwy, Tern, Stour, Teme, Avon, Wye, Avon
MOUTH	Severn Estuary

In Welsh Hafren and in English the Severn, the 220 mile (354km) long principal stream of Britain rises, together with the Wye and the Rheidol, on the slopes of Pumlumon, in a remote and desolate upland area of mid-Wales. One story tells of the three sister rivers deciding to visit the sea. Severn rose early, making her way through Wales before paying visits to friends in Shrewsbury and Gloucester. Wye started out a little later, taking a straighter path through Radnorshire and Hereford before joining her sister near Chepstow to go to the sea together. Rheidol slept in and was obliged to take the quickest route possible to get to the sea at Aberystwyth. Several other streams have their sources on these rolling uplands and not all of them find their way into the main three. On the northern slopes rises Dulas, which joins Dyfi near Machynlleth.

The Severn's source has seen many visitors over the years, perhaps the most famous being George Borrow, who came here in 1854 during his tramp around Wild Wales, as he called the book he wrote about it. It is most easily visited nowadays by following the Severn Way to its beginning. This 210-mile (338km) odyssey advertises itself as 'the longest river walk in Britain'. Well, it would be, wouldn't it? Borrow's guide was certain of the source: 'Now, master, I have conducted you to the source of the Severn. I have considered the matter deeply and have come to the conclusion that here,

and only here, is the true source. Therefore stoop down and drink, in full confidence that you are taking possession of the Holy Severn.' Reading on in Borrow's book, you may well have some doubts as to the guide's accuracy, for he goes on to discuss the source of the Wye and seems to place the two a bit too close together: 'A quarter of an hour will take us to it, your honour.' The distance, even as the red kite flies, is over 2 miles (3.2km)! The present-day visitor has no excuse for not locating the Severn's source, for it is marked by a large wooden stake, inscribed in Welsh and English, at 2,034 feet (620m) and has a made path leading to it, paved rather like stretches of the Pennine Way in the Peak District and across the Cheviots. On my first visit the stake was a much more modest affair and there was no made path, just a plod through the peat. There is certainly a great deal of the latter about. George Borrow commented that 'turf heaps, both big and small, are in abundance in the vicinity', and these are still higher than a man in places, the remnants of a thick blanket of peat which formerly covered the whole area. In such a maze of peat channels, there is some residual doubt about the primacy of the wooden post, for a small lake on the watershed beyond a fence may also lay claim to be the source, depending on which way the wind is blowing.

Covering about 25 square miles (65 sq. km), Hafren Forest was begun in 1937 when the Forestry Commission, having purchased twelve upland sheep farms, began planting conifers. One of the farms, Rhyd-y-benwch, is now a car park and picnic area with toilets and information boards. Still an active forest with areas being felled and replanted, Hafren has also been developed as an important local tourist attraction and wildlife habitat. A series of walks start from Rhyd-y-benwch and there are bridleways for horse and mountain bike riding.

The Severn Way follows the river from the car park to the source and is clearly marked all the way. A well-engineered path, part boardwalk, part

Lonely Hengwm

gravel and with the upper stages paved, means that the route is easy to follow. At the forest boundary the final part of the Source of the Severn Trail, a stone path through the wet moorland which is part of the Pumlumon SSSI, leads past the source stake to the watershed beyond. A slate boundary stone stands on a broad, rounded hilltop to mark the official beginning of the Severn Way, beside another, lesser monolith and a cairn of quartz boulders.

A return route from the forest fence follows a different route back to Rhyd-y-benwch, passing a waterfall, Bronze Age opencut copper workings and the remains of Nany yr Eira lead mine. The route descends alongside Afon Hore and returns to the car park.

Another fine approach to the source, and one guaranteed to be even quieter than the Severn Way, comes up from the west and follows the lonely valley

Source marker post, 1991 . . .

. . . and twenty years later

of Afon Hengwm for a couple of miles past the road end at Maesnant. The track soon deteriorates and a boggy plod follows until a clump of trees indicates the ruin of an old farmhouse. At the confluence of Hengwm and Gwerin, where a waterfall sparkles as it leaps down the rocks, you can tackle the slopes of Llechwedd y buarth, adding interest by following a curving, rocky rib, Craig yr Eglwys. The clump of trees spied earlier towers over the crumbling walls of a ruined farmhouse, one of two near the meeting of the streams. It is difficult for the modern visitor to comprehend life in such a situation without road transport, electricity and instant communications, the only noises the burbling of the stream, the rustling of the trees and the bleating of sheep. It was a life of self-sufficiency that changed little from generation to generation through succeeding centuries; a life encompassed by the neighbourhood when the word still had some meaning; a life lived by most of our ancestors but now irretrievable. A large cairn stands above the top of Craig yr Eglwys, looking down Hengwm; a shepherd's cairn visible from miles around. The rusting Kit-Kat tin which was lurking in the cairn in 1991 holding a visitors' book – noting that fifty-four people had come to this remote spot during the previous twelve months – was not apparent fifteen years later. It is about a mile (1.6km) walk across Bryn Cras and over the watershed to the source.

Glossary

Bryn Cras: dry hill!

Craig yr Eglwys: church crag

Gwerin: marsh

Hafren: Severn

Hengwym: old valley

Llechwedd y buarth: hillside of the farm yard/enclosure

Maesnant: meadow valley

Nant yr Eira: snow valley

Pumlumon: hill of five summits

Rhyd-y-benwch: upper ford

Wye
or why not?

	WYE
SOURCE	Blaen Avon Gwy, Pumlumon, Powys
G.R.	SN 802 871
LENGTH	133 miles (215 kilometres)
TRIBUTARIES	Ithon, Irfon, Lugg, Monnow
MOUTH	Beachley Point, Severn Estuary

The fifth-longest river in Britain at about 133 miles (215km), Afon Gwy has been anglicized as the River Wye. Unlike its close neighbour the Severn, the Wye's long-distance path, the Wye Valley Walk, does not visit the source. After 136 miles (219km) of 'a perfect mix of hill and river walking' this might seem something of an oversight, although the visitor to the lower slopes of Pumlumon is promised that 'a track to the left on the second bend leads to a viewing point that offers superb views towards the actual source of the Wye'. Any number of advertising slogans spring to mind: the Wye Valley Walk – like the meal without the pudding, the Manchester United match without the extra time, the honeymoon without . . . You get my drift and can no doubt think of several more. The Official Route Guide very kindly offers a photo of a walker with a pair of binoculars scanning the hillside 'towards the source' before directing you to join the Severn Way. I contacted the Wye Valley Walk website to see if there was any particular reason for the omission and received the following reply.

Hi Phil,
I am afraid there are no plans that I am aware of to take the Wye Valley Walk to the source. It has been discussed but due to the problems in accessing the site of the source and incorporate it within the guidebook it

was felt that we could just advise people who wished to pursue this the basic directions either in starting and finishing the walk. We do realise that people do like to walk from the source to the sea but we actually don't include either end in our walk. I will certainly mention this at our next WVW Partnership meeting as we are rewriting the guide shortly.
Regards Nikki Moore, Wye Valley AONB Information Officer

The Wye is not the only river to have a path that doesn't visit its source. The Teesdale Way, for instance, starts at Dufton on the western side of the Pennine watershed and only meets the river at Cauldron Snout, 10 miles (16km) from Tees Head, while the Ouse Valley Way begins outside a pub a couple of miles downstream from the source. None of this precludes the resolute source seeker from having a go, however, so why not?

Starting from Rhyd-y-benwch car park and picnic area in the heart of the Hafren Forest, the Wye Valley Walk climbs through the forest to emerge on the hillside before descending to join the river a mile or so from its source. Indecisive walkers who cannot make up their minds as to which long-distance path to follow have a half mile (800m) to decide, for the Severn Way and Wye Valley Walk share the same route from Rhyd-y-benwch to the confluence of Severn and its tributary Afon Hore. And what a half mile it is! The first part consists of a pink boardwalk with benches in little lay-bys every 50 yards (45m) or so and picnic tables overlooking the river. A good, hard-surfaced path then follows to the confluence. Here the adventurous will risk wet feet by crossing the Severn to gain the Wye-bound path on the far side, while the fainter hearted will use the bridge a couple of hundred yards upstream and double back to the confluence. The well-signed (everything is well signed in Hafren Forest) Wye Valley Walk heads upstream alongside the Hore,

passing one of the flumes that measure flow rates on the streams.

Wishing to look at the remains of the Nant–yr-Eira mine, I left the WVW and the forest to emerge on the slopes of Hore Fach. Radiocarbon dating proves that the mine was first worked, for copper and lead, during the Bronze Age but the late nineteenth century saw most work being undertaken after Captain Reynolds of Llanidloes rediscovered the mine. The ancient workings were 6–9 feet (1.8m–2.7m) wide, over 200 yards (183m) long and of depth unknown. A 38-foot (11m) diameter waterwheel and crusher were installed in the late 1850s and 33 tons of lead ore were recovered as well as several ancient tools. Further concerns worked the mine before the end of the nineteenth century and a total of 161 tons of lead ore were extracted. Still to be seen on the site are the remains of the wheel pits, crusher house and tramway, tumbled miners' barracks, tips and opencuts.

A sheep track took me above the forest to rejoin the WVW on a broad forestry track, which led to another mine site, Nant Iago. Here the way proper heads off downhill to join the Wye valley itself while a 'Permissive Path' – lovely phrase that – leads to the 'Viewpoint of Source of Wye'. This path contours round, high above the valley, giving views downwards an assemblage of large sheds and dirt roads which, from a distance, look rather like some of the ski developments in the Massif Central. Every few minutes a great cloud of dust erupts along the road as a vehicle travels along it at speed. This is the Sweet Lamb Rally Complex where 20 miles (32km) of tarmac and gravel roads are used for testing rally cars and off-road vehicles, staging rallying events and providing corporate hospitality. The name derives from an advertising hoarding, which has stood by the entrance to the complex on the A44 road for years, paraphrasing Peacock and proclaiming 'Mountain Lambs are Sweeter'. Thus is the economy of the area bracketed. Copper to cars, mining to motorsport, but always, hereabouts, the sweet

Nearing the source

lamb somewhere in the picture. It got me thinking about other unusual economic activities to be found in remote areas. Not that many miles to the north and not too far from the source of Afon Dyfrdwy the OS map used to indicate 'Pig Bristle Drying Depot'. This was an old army depot later used by Harris brushes. Sixteen tons of fresh pig bristles were delivered three times a week to the depot, which was sited because of its remoteness. Just imagine the stink and flies! Latterly redundant, brushes now using artificial bristles or ones imported ready dried from China, the site is now used by the Bala and District Motor Club as the Ranges Motorsport Centre. Those cars get everywhere.

At the end of the permissive path I hurried past several targets planted in the ground and was delighted by the view of the upper Wye valley stretching out ahead. From here to the source is all access land now and a tempting sheep track contours across the valley side, crossing several of the Wye's tributaries as the valley narrows and steepens with height. A large pile of rocks, terraced on its upstream side, marks the site of the Nant Iago mine dam of 1860, now breached. A leat ran from here to supply water to turn a massive 60-foot (18m) pumping wheel down at the mine. Such remains of old mining enterprises can be found dotted about the highlands of Britain and it takes some imagination to picture them in working days. Nant Iago epitomizes such enterprises. It stands in a remote, inhospitable site where men battled the elements for decades in the hope of turning a profit – a hope that seldom materialized. At many of these mines, shareholders poured in more money than was ever extracted as ore. Just down the valley from the breached dam was the shaft of the East Plynlimmon Lead Mining Co., developed on the back of the success of nearby Plynlimmon Mine in the 1860s. Founded in 1868 with a nominal capital of £7,000, the company purchased the Blaengwe mining grant for £3,000 and set about searching for the vein. One trial, in neighbouring Nant Cyff, failed to find a mineral-bearing lode, while an adit driven west from the Wye for 600 feet found a great deal of pyrite. This encouraged the owners to sink a shaft 90 feet below the adit level to where there appeared to be more galena (lead ore). Unfortunately it was at this point, in April 1871, that the Nant Iago dam burst, sweeping away the East Plynlimmon wheel. Work stuttered on until the end of the year, by which time the company had run out of capital, and

the mine was put up for sale in April 1872. The paucity of remains indicates that there were no takers.

The last stretch of the Wye is delightful, a southeast-facing suntrap on a good day, with little waterfalls, slides and rapids. A red kite was circling above the head of the valley as I climbed steadily. Once a common sight in towns and cities throughout Britain, these scavengers had been persecuted almost to extinction by the early twentieth century and there was only a small population of around five pairs left in the Cambrian Mountains. More

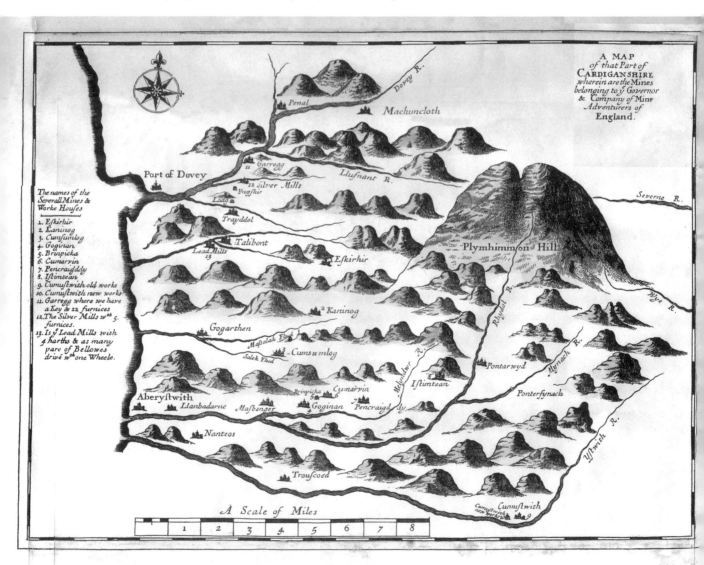

William Waller's map of the mining area, 1698

enlightened attitudes and the protection of nesting sites have led to a great improvement in the birds' fortunes and they are often to be seen around Pumlumon. There's even a Red Kite Café a few miles down the road towards Aberystwyth.

At the very top of the Wye valley three little dingles fan out and it is the northernmost which is the recognized source – Blaen Afon Gwy. There was still snow here in the middle of April and the drips from the highest bank coalesced to begin their 133-mile (215km) journey to join the Severn, whose own headwaters rise a mere 2½ miles (4km) away on the other side of Pen Pumlumon Arwystli.

At this point you can return to Rhyd-y-Benwlch, reversing the upward journey, or indeed continue down the long miles to the end of the Wye Valley Walk at Chepstow. I decided to visit a couple of hilltops before following the Severn back down. Just above the Wye's source a fence heads off south to meet another climbing north-west to a cairn on the very minor top sometimes called Pen Pumlumon Llygad-bychan. The lake after which the top is named, shown on large-scale maps to the east of the summit, lies virtually on the broad watershed, sometimes appears to dry up and has no apparent outlet stream, so its source claim seems pretty thin, unless there's a strong wind blowing, and even then it could feasibly feed the Wye to the south or Rheidol to the north. Following the fence west for half a mile (0.8km) will bring you to the highest summit between Cadair Idris and Pen y Fan, that of Pen Pumlumon Fawr. At 2,468 feet (752m) it is a hill we should appreciate but that intrepid nineteenth-century pedestrian George Borrow was not immediately impressed when he was taken there by his local guide. "'It does not look much of a hill' said I. "We are on very high ground, sir, or it would look much higher. I question, upon the whole, whether there is a higher hill in the world.'"

The summit gives long views in all directions but they are interesting rather than spectacular. All is remote, rolling moorland with only a few mountain

Source of the Wye, 1984

peaks to be identified. Chief among these are the tops of the Cadair Idris group and Arenig Fawr, while further away to the north are the Arans looking like the knuckles of a clenched fist. On a really clear day, Snowdon can be spied through the gap between Tarren y Gesail and Cadair Idris. The Black Mountains and Brecon Beacons show their profile away to the south. Nant y Moch reservoir and its dam stands out to the west. There is a fine sense of remoteness here and the area is certainly less populated than it was in the Bronze Age, when the summit cairns crowning many of the local tops were built. Apart from the trig point and the reservoir with its surrounding plantations, Borrow's description of the summit still stands today:

We reached the summit of the hill, where stood a large carn or heap of stones. I got upon the top and looked around me. A

Llyn Llygad Rheidol

mountainous wilderness extended on every side, a waste of russet-coloured hills, with here and there a black, craggy summit. No sign of life or cultivation were to be discovered, and the eye might search in vain for a grove or even a single tree. The scene would have been cheerless in the extreme had not a bright sun lighted up the landscape.

It is not too fanciful to imagine another famous visitor on these barren heights. Thomas Johnes developed his mansion of Hafod near Pontrhydygroes into a place of pilgrimage for the eighteenth-century romantics and Samuel Taylor Coleridge is believed to have based his epic poem 'Kubla Khan' on the place. It is not too fanciful to visualize the poet, filled with notions of the picturesque and whatever substances were available to expand his imagination, on the summit of Pumlumon Fawr, gazing around at the numerous, just out of reach, sinuous rills and pools and the distant Cardigan Bay and dreaming up some immortal lines from another of his works, 'water, water everywhere, Nor any drop to drink'.

Pumlumon's southern slopes fall away gently but its northern side, deeply gouged by a glacier, holds Llyn Llygad Rheidol, source of the 16 mile (26km) long river which joins the sea at Aberystwyth. In fact a couple of streams flow down into the lake, now a reservoir, from the crags of Graig Las and meltwater trickling from a patch of snow was the source when I was there last.

Back on the broad ridge, the watershed is tracked by several slate boundary markers inscribed 'W.W.W. 1865' and relating to Sir Watkin Williams

-Wynn (1820–85), who was the 6th Baronet in his line. He was MP for Denbighshire, most of which his family owned, between 1841 and his death, and a master of the hounds from the age of twenty-three. Hunting was one of his main pursuits as well as looking after the family interests, which included farming, mining and quarrying as well as canal and railway promotion on vast estates stretching from here to Ruabon, 50 miles (80km) to the north-east. A broad col, almost completely denuded of the peat that formerly covered it to a depth of several feet, is crossed before the path climbs to Pen Pumlumon Arwystli, easternmost of the Pumlumon summits, again crowned by a huge cairn. Its northern slopes fall away in a mile or so to the peaty desolation that spawns Severn and the 3-mile (4.8km) walk back down the Severn Way path to Rhyd-y-Benwch.

A 10-mile (16km) there-and-back walk along the Wye Valley Way from the main A44 at Pont Rhydgaled gives another fine approach to the source, passing through the Sweet Lamb complex and several mine sites before reaching the permissive path and the upper reaches of the valley.

Glossary

Afon Dyfrdwy: river Dee

Cadair Idris: Idris's chair

Hafod: summer pasture

Llyn Llygad-bychan: little source lake

Nant Iago: James's valley

Nant y Moch: pig valley

Nant-yr-Eira: valley of snow

Pen Pumlumon Arwystli: Arwystli is probably a personal name, so this was once likely to have been his bit of the five-summit hill

Pen Pumlumon Fawr: big hill of the five summits

Pen y Fan: top spot

Pontrhydygroes: bridge of the ford of the cross

Pumlumon: five summits

Rhyd-y-benwch: upper ford

Tarren y Gesail: hill overlooking a mountain recess

Teifi

from out the store-house of the sky

TEIFI	
SOURCE	Llyn Teifi, Ceredigion
G.R.	SN 780 674
LENGTH	76 miles (122 kilometres)
TRIBUTARIES	Grannell, Clettwr, Cych
MOUTH	Poppit Sands, Cardigan Bay

In this crowded land and this crowded age, a five-hour walk when you meet no one else is a treat. A five-hour walk when you see no one else is miraculous, but perhaps this was just a result of traversing the former lands of the abbey of Strata Florida. Such a walk I had when visiting the source of the Afon Teifi on a bright, clear and sunny June day. And when such a walk is made with the companionship of a famous earlier visitor, a man who left one of the first accurate descriptions of our landscape, the solitary walker has no need to feel alone. Our path will several times follow that of John Leland, Tudor traveller extraordinary, and we shall also walk with the shades of monks, pilgrims and drovers of former years.

The Teifi runs for about 76 miles (122km) from its recognized source in Llyn Teifi down the delectable upper valley past the remains of Strata Florida Abbey, through the great bog Cors Caron, near Tregaron, south-west through Lampeter and then west to Aberteifi and the sea. It is considered by many to be the most beautiful of all Welsh rivers; the derivation of its name seems lost to history.

The Teifi Pools Walk, shown on the Ordnance Survey map, can be used as a delightful introduction to the upper river and its source and can be augmented, if wished, by visiting several other worthwhile places off route. You can start the walk either at the abbey itself or near the head of the minor road following the tributary Afon Mwyro. It

Strata Florida

is about 11 miles (18km) for the former and 7 miles (11km) for the latter route.

The abbey is well worth a visit, although its very remoteness meant that on the day of my visit the staff appeared to have knocked off half an hour before closing time. Fortunately a gate at the side of the locked entrance building was still open, so I managed a look around. The abbey was originally founded in 1164 by Cistercian monks from Whitland Abbey on a different site by the Afon Fflur, a mile or so to the west of its present site, and the house was known as Mynachlog Ystrad Fflur. When, twenty years later and thanks to the grant of a huge tract of land stretching almost from Pumlumon to the sea from the great Prince Rhys ap Gruffudd, it moved to its new site, the name appeared in charters in its Latin form. Under such powerful patronage the abbey flourished and around 1238 the Welsh Prince Llewelyn ap Iorweth, Llewelyn the Great, held a council here, where he made the other Welsh lords swear allegiance to his son Dafydd. Throughout the thirteenth and fourteenth centuries, Strata

Florida's wealth, prestige and authority increased and hundreds of pilgrims were attracted. During the early fifteenth-century rebellion by Owain Glyndŵr, the abbey was occupied by English troops, and Henry IV and his son, later Henry V, were visitors. For years afterwards the abbey precincts remained a royal garrison and Strata Florida entered a long period of decline. When John Leland visited in the 1540s he found 'the Fratry and Infirmatori be now mere ruines' and on the eve of the dissolution it supported only half a dozen monks and an abbot. Subsequently many of the buildings were plundered for building stone and the abbey remains settled back into the landscape which they had so long dominated. The rediscovery of the site was largely due to the efforts of a man who might have destroyed the peace of the entire area, for in the 1860s civil engineer Stephen Williams was surveying the route of a proposed railway line from Rhayader to Aberystwyth when he came across the abbey ruins, half buried in vegetation. He returned later and excavated much of what is seen today.

To start from the abbey adds some miles of road walking but it is a quiet enough road. Further up the valley where the little Egnant stream is crossed by the road, there is a space for three or four vehicles to park and the path leaves the road a couple of hundred yards back in the direction of Strata Florida. It climbs through the bracken and flowery pastures before dropping to Troed-y-rhiw, a former farm and now a smart house with fine views back down the valley. John Leland, Henry VIII's Royal Antiquary and incidentally the only holder of that position, came this way in the 1530s during his journeys to visit the libraries of abbeys, cathedrals, priories and other places where ancient writings and records were kept. Although he later went insane and never published his findings, his records survived and give a valuable insight into the sixteenth century. A track leads you to Frongoch, an apparently deserted farmstead, and then swings away around the north of Craig y Fron-goch, from where there are retrospective views of the abbey. This ancient route, bounded by stones and marked by cairns in places, makes its way up Cwm Teifi, skirting boggy areas of cotton grass to reach the infant river by a prominent quartz-topped cairn and ash tree. A wheatear was chik-chacking on a fence post as I followed the stream past a series of little cascades before crossing it to reach a stile. If you haven't spotted it before, you will certainly notice the Llyn Teifi dam from here. Round one last little *twmp* and you reach the dam, with its pagoda-like valve house.

Llyn Teifi was dammed in 1958 and, together with the other Teifi Pools, provides the water supply for the towns and villages along the coastal belt as well as those in the valley. The lake, approximately 1,200 yards (1,097m) long from north-east to south-west and about 550 yards (503m) across from east to west, is a well-known fishing spot where trout are caught. Leland noted that 'Ther is in it veri good troutes and elys, and no other fisch.' Having climbed the concrete steps from the dam, you reach a track by a rusting corporation green gate and you can follow this up to the road. Walking along the track I could see red kites and buzzards circling overhead. Having recently seen the Battle of Britain Flight at an airshow, I was reminded of the Hurricane, and the broad rounded wings of the buzzard recalled the Spitfire. All that was missing was the Lancaster bomber, but the golden eagle hasn't been seen in Wales for over a century and a half.

The thin tarmac strip you reach through the Dwr Cymru gate at the end of the track is part of the ancient Monks' Way, rising from Ffair Rhôs 3 miles (4.8km) to the west, which once linked Strata Florida with its granges of Nannerth and Cwmdeuddwr on the river Wye and its sister abbey at Cwmhir, 25 miles (40km) away across the high green moors of Elenydd. The Teifi Pools were formed by glacial action and there is much evidence in the form of erratic boulders, the 'bare stonis' described by John Leland, and moraines in the vicinity. The Teifi Pools Walk follows the road around to the track to Llyn Egnant but an interesting variation

Strata Florida Abbey gateway

On Llan Ddu Fawr

is to head off north, along the ridge of Clawdd Du, and make for the trig point on Llan Ddu Fawr. As the ridge rises so the views back to Llyn Teifi and the rest of the pools broaden out. There are generally reckoned to be five Teifi Pools: Egnant, Hir, Bach, Y Gorlan and Teifi itself, all of whose waters find their way into the Afon Teifi. Although the lake is the recognized source, a stream that starts just north of the rocky top of Meincyn and has a fair flow while running beside the fence paralleling Clawdd Ddu could lay a claim. This certainly seems to be supported by John Leland's observation that 'Llin Tyve is fed fro hyer places with a small broket'. Nant Lluest, which flows from even further north, runs into Llyn Teifi's anonymous western neighbour and so may be discounted. On the way to the top of Llan Ddu Fawr (1,939 feet/591m) you pass a couple of concrete posts, presumably, like so many others round here, marking the boundary of the Elan and Claerwen water-gathering grounds. The trig point stands inside a circular shelter which could be the remains of a former cairn, and has quite wonderful views over the green Welsh Desert. Northwards Pumlumon is the main feature, with the wind farm at Cefn Croes which opened among much controversy in 2005 next in clockwise view. Across the peaty source of the Claerddu lie the two Fryddon lakes, followed by the upper end of the Claerwen Reservoir, and the pimple visible on Drygarn Fawr

is actually a 15 foot (4.5m) high and 25 foot (7.6m) diameter cairn. Away to the south the high tops of the Brecon Beacons and Carmarthen Fan come into view above glimpses of four of the Teifi Pools. Westwards the land falls away through a patchwork of fields and woods to the sparkling sea and away to the north-west rises Cadair Idris. And the trig point isn't even on the actual summit: this is 3 feet (0.9m) higher and 600 yards (548m) away to the north-east at Carnyrhryddod, and is graced by a quartz-capped cairn in a rash of stones which were once presumably a cairn of some significance, possibly to rams. When Leland came this way he noted that 'The hilles bytwyxt Llynne Tyue and Cragnaugllin were not in sight so stony as the hilles bytwyst Stratfler and Llin Tyue . . . I Standing on Creggenaugllin so in no place within sight no wood but al hilly pastures . . .' Carreg naw-llyn is half a mile (0.8km) east of the trig point on Llan Ddu Fawr and provides one of the best views in Ceredigion. Little has changed except for the appearance of the Claerwen Reservoir and the forestry. The walk from the road to the trig point and back will add 2 miles (3.2km) to the day.

A direct line back towards Llyn Egnant is straightforward on a clear day and you will cross a disused leat. This was constructed in the 1840s and carried water for over 10 miles (16km) from Llyn Fryddon to a series of lead mines between here and Pontrhydygroes. A track runs along the west side of Llyn Egnant to the dam at its south end. From here the Teifi Pools Walk descends Nant Egnant. Another diversion can be made at this point to follow the path eastwards for a mile or so to catch a view of the remote farm of Claerwen. This is one of the most open viewpoints in Wales and reminded me a little of the glimpse of Moor House which you used to get from the high fells in upper Teesdale in the northern Pennines. The curious will climb to the summit of the little hill on the south side of the path to see if the rain gauge shown on the map is still there. Looking southwards over Llyn Gynon, where there is the promise of another rain gauge, a ridge marks the watershed, for just beyond lies the source of the Tywi. Having gained the high ground, it makes sense to stay with it on the way back and I visited the bilberry-covered summit of the charmingly named Dibyn Du before dropping down into steep-sided Nant Egnant, whose descent follows a delightful path which gives intimate views into the gorge. Over the course of a couple of miles this changes from a grassy to a wooded valley and the path, rerouted near the end, joins the road near the parking place.

I had just come from a country music festival where the band had played John Denver's song 'Some Days are Diamonds (Some Days are Stone)', and this had definitely been one of the former, a jewel of a day with brilliant, sparkling views during a walk of many facets.

Glossary

Aberteifi: Cardigan

Bach: little

Carnyrhyddod: rams' cairn

Carreg naw-llyn: nine-lake rock

Clawdd du: black dyke

Dibyn Du: black edge

Dwr Cymru: Welsh water

Ffair Rhôs: fair moor

Frongoch: red round hill

Gorlan: sheepfold

Hir: long

Llan Ddu fawr: large black enclosure

Mynachlog Ystrad Fflur: abbey in the vale of flowers

Troed-y-rhiw: foot of the slope

Tywi

A step, methinks, will pass the stream

At nearly 70 miles (113km), the Afon Tywi is the longest wholly Welsh river. From its source on the southern slopes of Crug Gynon in the empty quarter of mid-Wales, it flows south through the Tywi Forest, marking the boundary of Powys and Ceredigion, to enter Llyn Brianne, a reservoir

TYWI	
SOURCE	Crug Gynon, Ceredigion
G.R.	SN 803 631
LENGTH	70 miles (113 kilometres)
TRIBUTARIES	Sawdde, Dulais, Cothi, Gwili
MOUTH	Carmarthen Bay

built in 1972. Running south-westwards through Carmarthenshire, the Twyi passes through Llandovery and Llandeilo before emptying into Carmarthen Bay, through an estuary shared with the Tâf and the Gwendraeth, east of the Pendine Sands. The river, anglicized as the Towy, is renowned for salmon and trout fishing, though acidification, caused by the planting of conifers, has been cited for the decline in fish numbers.

A couple of days after I said, 'It's about time I got rid of the bike, I hardly ever ride it, the tax and insurance blah blah . . .', the forecast was for clear, warm, dry weather over southern mid-Wales and so the bike came out of the garage, I fitted the top box and tank bag and off I rode. A lovely route, through Leominster, Kington, Llanfair-ym-Muallt, Cilmeri, Garth and Beulah, where I turned off on to the mountain road to Tregaron. This in itself is exciting, especially the Devil's Staircase, where the road zig-zags dramatically out of the Irfon valley before flinging itself down to the Tywi.

The map indicates that the route north from the tarmac just before the bridge at – I'll give a grid reference because, apart from the youth hostel at Dolgoch, there isn't really anything but trees, water, rocks and solitude in this wild and beautiful part of Elenydd – SN 803 571 is a 'Byway open to all traffic' in Powys and a 'route with public access' after it crosses the county boundary into Ceredigion. This means that you could drive or ride to within a mile or so of the source. Legally, that is. For reasons which will become clear, you probably won't. I like walking anyway and my bike is

'When they say ford round here . . .'

strictly on-road so, after riding a couple of hundred yards up the track, it was off with the leathers and on with the walking boots. The track was possibly a monastic route from Strata Florida Abbey and was certainly later a drovers' way. It was never surfaced like the Tregaron road and saw little traffic apart from locals and the odd, intrepid driver but more recently, with the growth of interest in off-road driving and riding, there are times when it becomes a busy thoroughfare with convoys of vehicles using it. This has had a detrimental effect on the surface and the chap who drove across in 1960 in his Ford Anglia certainly wouldn't traverse it now. One green lane enthusiast comments that this must be 'one of the finest in the country with its magnificent scenery and river crossings plus as an added bonus there are no ramblers because the river has no bridges'. Nice to see such an enlightened attitude among the off-road fraternity.

The farmer was bringing a trailer-load of livestock to Nant-ystalwyn as I passed above the farm, now only used for dipping and shearing. At one time a pair of otter's paws was nailed up on the barn door but the Tywi is now moribund here because of the surrounding plantations. The river may be dead but the forest was certainly active and at times the chainsaws sounded like a badly disturbed hornets' nest. At least the tree clearance revealed a glimpse of what a beautiful valley the upper Tywi must have been before the forest was planted. Farms were as far as three or four miles apart in this vast, sprawling upland and horse, cart or foot were the most usual ways of travelling. Despite the remoteness, or maybe because of it, there was a strong sense of community and people would visit each other's farms of an evening to play cards, darts or draughts, while farming tasks like shearing also gave opportunities to gather.

Much of the Tywi Forest was planted in the 1950s and '60s as part of the expansion of forestry in the uplands which followed the Second World War. In the early days a forest shepherd was employed whose job was to protect the newly planted trees from sheep, which would wander over the fences in the winter when mountain snowdrifts covered them.

The condition of the track begins to deteriorate north of Nant-ystalwyn, churned up by the off-road drivers and riders taking on the challenge, and some stretches are little better than linear lakes 50 yards long and a foot deep. Walkers who wish to stay dry-footed ought to cultivate 4x4-vehicle-driving friends or buy a pair of thigh waders. Even a prolonged drought would not do, as the route passes through several fords and, as one chap said in passing, 'When they say ford round here, they mean it.' The first couple, over tributaries, are tame enough but after the track has passed through a stretch of forestry it crosses the river itself. Here is a wooden cross with its sad memorial to an off-road expedition in appalling weather which had a tragic conclusion.

The problem with the fords is that they are deepened by the vehicles ploughing through them and the simple pedestrian is often better off wading across beside them where the water is a bit shallower. By the time I reached the confluence of the Tywi and the Nant Gwinau I had abandoned any attempt at keeping my feet dry and also abandoned the track to follow the Tywi along a bridleway north through the forest. Here stands the former farmhouse of Moel-prysgau, now a bothy. A night spent here will be as remote as any in Wales and England. The folk who lived here for generations had the chatter of the Tywi as a constant background to their lives; it would certainly have been more mellifluous than today's chainsaws.

I decided to climb the steep hillside behind the bothy, pausing only to eat some bilberries – one benefit of the lack of sheep – to reach a forestry road rather than follow the river itself. No sheep in the forest means no sheep tracks and the boggy, tussocky ground beside the stream is difficult walking

terrain. Most of the trees on the riverside had been cleared recently anyway, so I had good views into the declining upper Tywi valley. The struggle I had later to reach the forest edge after leaving the road certainly justified the earlier climb. The gathering ground of the Afon Tywi is a broad, boggy basin full of spongey tussocks and hidden hollows. Surrounded by tantalizingly dry-looking slopes, there are few defined watercourses whatever the map may say and what faint trickles exist are more audible than visible in the slough. The walker who had somehow managed to remain dry shod along the track would have to abandon hope here. Still, climbing the slopes of Crug Gynon, a 1,722-foot (525m) top, brings relief after the morass and an expansive view from the cairn on its summit. In a shallow depression to the north lies Llyn Gynon, while just over the next ridge, Dibyn Du, rises the Afon Teifi and I wondered if the buzzard mewing overhead was the same one that I'd seen a couple of years ago when I visited that source.

I didn't fancy recrossing the Tywi bog and anyway thought it would be churlish not to visit another of the river's high sources, that of the Nant Gorast. It rises in Llyn Gorast, the aptly named 'wasteland lake', and a stroll across the high ground soon brought it into sight. I decided that I'd had enough slough hopping for one day, so a view sufficed and I followed vague quad-bike tracks back to the Strata Florida green lane. Another series of linear lakes followed until I returned to the confluence by Moel-prysgau, which at least washed the mud from my boots before I followed the track back to Nant-ystalwyn and the waiting Yamaha.

Glossary

Beulah: home of the grape peelers
Cilmeri: brambly hollow
Dibyn Du: black slope
Garth: enclosure
Llanfair-ym-Muallt: Builth Wells
Moel-prysgau: hill of the brushwood
Nant Gorast: wasteland valley

QUIETEST UNDER THE SUN

Not among the best known of British rivers, the Teme and its main tributaries the Clun and the Onny rise in a magical few square miles around the haunted borderland of the Welsh Marches, an idiosyncratic country of ancient hills and rolling farmland, quiet roads and tranquil paths. Wandering around looking for sources is a perfect Bank Holiday activity in an area where the crowds can usually be counted on the fingers of no more than two hands and there are long views into the purple distance.

Teme, Onny and Clun

Far in a western brookland

The second largest tributary of the Severn, the Teme, or the Afon Tefeidiad, flows for about 75 miles (121km) from its source 4 miles (6.4km) inside Wales, through Ludlow and Tenbury Wells to the Severn south of Worcester. It rises in the Kerry Hills, at a spring in Bryn Coch quarry in the col between Kerry Hill itself and Cilfaesty Hill. The whole of the river was designated a Site of Special Scientific Interest by English Nature in 1996. The Teme flows through a landscape immortalized by A. E. Housman in his long, pessimistic work *A Shropshire Lad*. Though he had written most of the poem before he visited the county, he still captured the essence of this borderland which, even over a century later, seems to have changed less than most parts of Britain.

In valleys of springs and rivers,
By Onny and Teme and Clun,
The country for easy livers,
The quietest under the sun.

The Onny and Clun, tributaries of the Teme, we will return to later; first, an account of a hot, sunny afternoon stroll around, but not actually really visiting, the sources of three rivers. It was too hot,

TEME	
SOURCE	Iyrchyn, Powys
G.R.	SO 122 848
LENGTH	75 miles (121 kilometres)
TRIBUTARIES	Clun, Onny, Corve, Rea
MOUTH	confluence with Severn, Worcester

CLUN	
SOURCE	Anchor, Shropshire
G.R.	SO 175 848
LENGTH	24 miles (38 kilometres)
TRIBUTARIES	Unk, Kemp, Redlake
MOUTH	confluence with Teme at Leintwardine

ONNY	
SOURCE	West Onny : White Grit, Shropshire
	East Onny : Stiperstones, Shropshire
G.R.	(West) SO 302 977
	(East) SO 373 993
LENGTH	(West) 8½ miles (14 kilometres)
	(East) 10 miles (16 kilometres)
	R. Onny (from Eaton Bridge)
	c.12½ miles (20 kilometres)
TRIBUTARIES	(West) none named on map
	(East) Darnford Brook
	Onny : Quinny Brook
MOUTH	confluence of West & East Onny nr. Eaton Bridge
	confluence with Teme at Bromfield

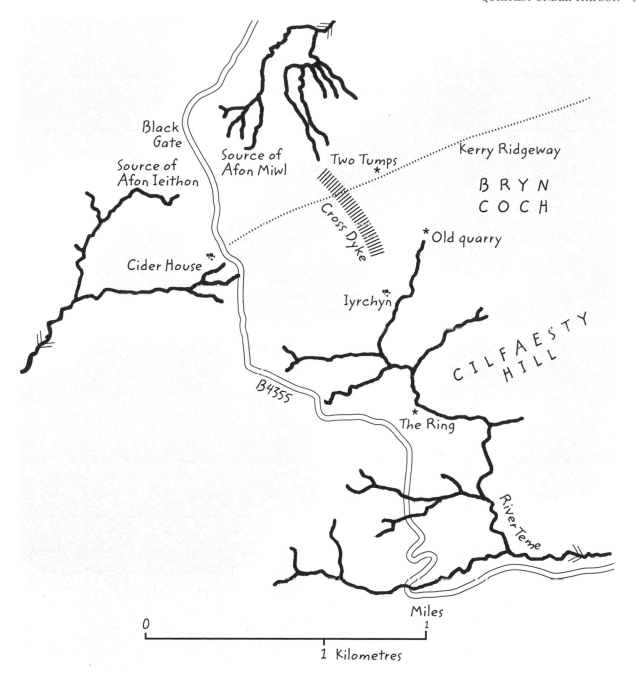

really, for serious walking, but I got my feet on the ground and set off. Staying at Cefn Lea Park, a conference centre with campsite off the A483 a mile or so south of Dolfor, I looked on the map and decided to walk up a sharp little hill, Glog, to get up to the top and find my bearings. I ignored signs at Cefn Lea giving directions to 'Top of Mountain', as their mountain isn't the one with the trig point to which I was heading. From the pillar there were fine views all around the dial and a chance to cool down in the slightest of breezes. Bridleways heading east, south and then east again led to Black Gate on the B4355. A few hundred yards along the road, just north of Cider House Farm, is a car park and picnic area at the start of the Kerry Ridgeway. From Black Gate a footpath crosses fields, passing above the source of the Afon Miwl, River Mule. This 9 mile (14km) long stream flows north then east, passing the village of Kerry before turning north again to Abermule and a confluence with the Severn. In early July, I had to make do with a barely damp patch in a sandy hollow as a source. The path climbs steadily to join the Kerry Ridgeway on the summit of the ridge.

This truly ancient track – in places Dark Ages and Iron Age earthworks cut through it – is a long lonely road as it strides across the crest of Kerry Hill, never dipping below 1,000 feet (305m). The Ridgeway stretches its hidden quality for about 15 miles (24km) between the Cider House and Bishop's Castle and makes a fine day's walk in itself as it crosses high heather moors and passes through shady woodlands; but today I followed only a short stretch of the route. By the tumuli at Two Tumps, at 1,660 feet (506m) the highest point along Kerry Ridgeway, the view is extensive and, even better, explained by the toposcope. The two Bronze Age burial mounds, now weathered to grassy mounds, would have been much more prominent when first constructed and visible from miles around. It is said that for a few weeks before and after the summer solstice, the sun is seen to rise between them when viewed from the Fowler's Armchair Stone at Banc Du 5 miles (8km) to the south-west. A fine place for the long-distance visionary dreamer. The Ridgeway, walked and ridden by people and animals for millennia, was last used regularly by cattle and sheep drovers in the mid-nineteenth century before the railways came to mid-Wales and took the trade away. It now once more makes its contribution to the economic life of the area, attracting walkers, riders and cyclists from far and wide.

A bridleway runs around the head of the Teme valley, above the disused Iyrchyn or Bryn Coch Quarry where the Teme flows from a small spring at around 1,500 feet (457m) above sea level and makes its way down a fairly broad basin to collect several more headstreams before passing through a small, rocky, steep-sided gorge. It sounded as though a

pack of hounds was baying down in the quarry, so I walked above the source and made my way up on to Cilfaesty Hill, its heather- and bilberry-covered summit decorated by a couple of branches and giving views over the rolling border country and miles of big sky southwards to the sharply etched peaks of the Brecon Beacons.

I dropped down to the Ring, an active land slip in the col between Cilfaesty Hill and Banc Gorddwn. Here gravel and silt deposits find their way into the misty water of the channel, which continues to be fairly restricted as it becomes Cwm Gwyn leading down to Crug-y-byddar and the river's first meeting with England. Having spent a few minutes sitting by the riverside, I followed the infant Teme upstream; a glimpse of the farm of Iyrchyn and its quarry had to suffice until I return at the end of the season and do it again.

A late afternoon lazy old sun was beating down, so I had a hot time of it walking back up to the road and it was predictable but still a shame that Cider

Teme trickles

House Farm no longer lives up to its name. An area of woodland to the west, a couple of hundred yards north of the farm, marks the source of the Afon Eithion, a major tributary of the Wye, which drains the western parts of Radnorshire before its confluence just below Newbridge-on-Wye.

From Black Gate I followed field paths past more earthworks and tumuli before following fences and, staying close to the wire, descended to the campsite, for a cold shower and an hour or so of sipping my ice-cold beer.

On a later visit it was the ground that was ice cold as I made my way along Kerry Ridgeway to find the source. It was a crisp blue-skied morning, so I extended my walk along the ancient way for a while before returning to cross into access land by the corner of a plantation where the bridleway crosses Kerry Hill between Ceulanau and Medwaledd. Trickles in the grass coalescing into a dammed stream indicated the birthplace of the Nant Mehel, a tributary of the Mule, but I soon crossed the minor watershed to find a rushy wet patch just above the bridleway gate which I deemed to be the head of Teme. As I followed the fence down to where a gap gives access to the top of Bryn Coch Quarry, the trickle was now a rivulet that tumbled over an icy little cliff and made its way down through the quarry to the basin below. The dogs were still baying at Iyrchyn farm.

The River Onny, a major tributary of the Teme, has two branches, East and West, which rise about 5 miles (8km) apart on either side of the Stiperstones, a jagged ridge as rich in myth as it once was in metal, south of Shrewsbury. During a brief thaw in what was an early and cold winter, I went to see if I could find the sources of the West Onny. The map shows that there are several, scattered about in an area promisingly bracketed by The Marsh and Black Marsh.

Starting at a sharp bend on the road on the watershed between the Onny and the Camlad and in a little salient of Wales which thrusts its way like

Cold source

a positive thumb into Shropshire, I quickly found myself back in England and with English Heritage at Mitchell's Fold. This Bronze Age stone circle once consisted of thirty stones, dragged from tors on nearly Stapeley Hill, of which about half remain. I didn't count them, supposing it to be unlucky or the precursor to madness, but contented myself with the view. To the north-west the aerials by Beacon Ring on Long Mountain above Welshpool just showed above the valley mist, while the Stiperstones to the east and Corndon Hill southwards raised themselves above valleys of springs and rivers. A New Age-type van was in the car park, its inhabitant stamping about and warming himself after an uncomfortable night halfway through the coldest December for a century. The circle has attracted many local legends, one modestly claiming that this was where Arthur withdrew Excalibur from one of the stones to seal his claim on the British throne.

Just north of the circle and above a cottage, a patch of juncus indicates one of the West Onny's sources. Turning eastwards and passing below the rocky summit of Stapeley Hill, I soon came upon another where a boggy little stream crosses the path. From here I made my way down a shelving path to Lower Stapeley. The owner had lived there for twenty-three years, he told me, and the previous week had been the hardest he could remember. The track had been so icy as to be impassable and it was the only time he had felt trapped in his own house.

Perhaps the harsh winter helped the folks in Nasz Dom just down the lane feel at home. A trickle from a spring by the house and a strong flow from another below Giant's Cave made their contribution to the branch of the West Onny flowing down the valley from its source in an area of rushes in the middle of Black Marsh. I made my way down to the main road, crossing the busy stream running out of Black Marsh and then quickly re-crossing it as I headed across the fields towards The Marsh, passing the gaunt remains of an engine house on the way. This area, around White Grit, formed the southern part of the western outcrop of the Shropshire lead-mining region, an area reputedly mined from Roman times until the end of the nineteenth century. Although the mine tips have been cleared and shafts filled, the landscape still holds clusters of cottages with their surrounding fields, the fossilized remains of lead miners' smallholdings.

At a right-angled bend on the road, you cross yet another West Onny feeder, possibly the favourite as it is followed by the Anglo-Welsh border here. There is also a tin tabernacle, a black-painted corrugated iron church which, at the time of my visit, sadly had an empty 'Next Service' board.

Popping down the lane just past the church took me to where a further West Onny headstream

Tin tabernacle

crossed under the road, mostly in a large black plastic tube. I decided to stay in Wales and, returning to the road by the church, followed it uphill and westwards until a footpath doubled back alongside a holly hedge and stone fence across a field to the foot of Corndon Hill. The stream I had earlier seen in its plastic pipe was still flowing lustily, so I decided to track it to its source. This turned out to be a much encrusted iron pipe sticking vertically from the ground in a wooded, formerly fenced enclosure.

Being so close to the hill, I decided to climb it and the view, even on a fairly dull day, was expansive. The upper West Onny valley spread out like a patchwork blanket of irregular fields and scattered houses with the tree-lined stream channels seaming through it. The summit, sporting its cairn, trig point and bench, is rightly popular with walkers. I dropped back down to the watershed to seek out the source of the rill, which is followed by the border, thrust north and west here by the bulk of Corndon Hill, and found the tiny stream flowing from an area of gruffy ground, the site of the filled-in Weston Shaft of the former Cliffdale mine. Worked between 1869 and 1927, the mine produced a large amount of barite and like many another abandoned mining sites now houses an eclectic collection of sheds, caravans, trailers, junk-filled hollows and even a narrowboat. An inauspicious start to what becomes a delightful, rural river.

A glance through the window two days before the end of the year revealed green rather than the all-pervading white of the last month, albeit a green shrouded in grey fog. Still, the latest thaw at least meant that I should be able to find water at the sources of the East Onny, which flows for about 10 miles (16km) to its confluence with the western version at Eaton Bridge. On the way I got to wondering if I would even find the right valley, as the fog was very dense for miles around the Severn. Arriving at Bridges, a truthfully named hamlet hedged in by shrouded sharp little south Shropshire hills where the two upper branches of the river meet, I found the Horseshoe Inn depressingly 'Closed Until Further Notice', a situation all too common these days.[5]

The fog was thinner here and some of the minor tops were visible across the valley as I walked up the road, once the main coaching route between Bishops Castle and Shrewsbury, towards the sources of the eastern branch. The thaw meant that there was plenty of water in the stream and I could hear it chuntering in the valley just below. Apart from the occasional crow there was nothing to listen to except for the odd, passing car. The sound lessened after I passed Hillside Farm, below which is the confluence of the headstreams and, what with the fog descending again, there was little to hear or see for a mile or so of gently climbing road until I passed Stitt Cottage, where the Eurythmics' 'Sweet Dreams are Made of This' was blasting out of the garage. Having spent part of the previous week in the horrors of the pre-Christmas city, who was I to disagree, especially as, like everybody, I was looking for something, even if it was only the start of a river.

With nothing distant to see I focused on the immediate and wondered why one white-painted milestone – 'B. Castle 9 Shrewsbury 11' – was shown on the map while the next one I passed wasn't. Also why was there an Old School House halfway up the road when the school, now the youth hostel in Bridges, was nearly a mile away and why are pheasants so stupid as to stand in the middle of the road? Perhaps they couldn't see the trees for the fog or perhaps they just like to watch Range Rovers swerve.

A powerful little rivulet was flowing down the Dingle and another was emptying itself into a drain

Roadside pawn?

by Lower Stitt Farm. A little further up the road the hedge on a sharp bend showed evidence of a recent visit by a car, ice or pheasant induced I could not say, while at the next kink another little stream pouring off the steep hillside dived under the road from its source up in the fog. A final feeder was found running along a wooded ditch between the road hedge and field fence; then it was a matter of a few more yards to the watershed where, just before New Leasowes Farm, a very minor road runs off. Turning round I should have had a lovely view down this little upper valley.

Following the road until the tarmac finished below the invisible Leasowes Bank Farm, I took to a track through a gate, making good use of a tree stump as its post. Was the field planned to have its corner at just that spot or was the tree planted by some far-sighted farmer? The next mile was to prove that there are nearly as many ways of fastening a gate as there are gates. I disturbed a disused quarry full of sheep while following the track across close-cropped turf with just the vestiges of snow alongside and in ditches. Briefly crossing to the northern side of this minor watershed, I found a delightful source – a spring gurgling up from the earth at the foot of a gnarled old birch tree – which flowed away to swell Hatherley Brook and then Rea Brook before joining the Severn at Shrewsbury. The way crosses the watershed by the next gate and ditches, draining both sides of the track as it descends to the road, feed the East Onny. Here, by a disused quarry, this branch of the river gains strength as several headwaters coalesce. Just across the road, in a wood, I found a little pool and a memorial bench.

My route joined the Shropshire Way for a while, climbing past a very basic campsite to The Hollies.

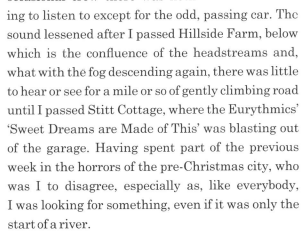

East Onny valley

The farm is well named, as its approach road is flanked by the evergreen, but it could also be The Leylandii from a screen planted further up. It was an archetypal hill farm in winter from the sheep in the surrounding pastures to the cattle in the steaming barns, the diminishing piles of hay and the tractor and muck spreader driving down the lane, the hens clucking around, odd piles of building materials here and there, rusting bits of agricultural machinery lying about and even an abandoned Fordson Major tractor. I followed lusty streamlets and the Shropshire Way to climb the bare pastures through the fog to the boundary wall. A short diversion southwards, across bog and boulders, brought me to another East Onny source by the corner of the intake next to a wood. Back to the gate and I crossed into the Stiperstones National Nature Reserve. Just inside is a board displaying byelaws. They are all very worthy but some are rather quaint – you can still pick berries but forget flying your kite and leave your iPod at home; it reminded me of the time we moored our boat at Maidenhead on the Thames and read the byelaws forbidding us from washing our clothes in the river or shaking out our rugs. The NNR General Prohibition xxxii might be of interest to the geocachers![6]

6   Intentionally leaving items in a place other than a receptacle provided by the Council for the deposit of litter or refuse.

The fog had never cleared, only occasionally lifting enough to give fleeting silhouettes and brief impressions of blue remembered hills, but it seemed even more solid as I walked the stony path along the crest. Fog lends beguilement to the view so that even the little scramble up and along the Devil's Chair was an adventure, given that the ground on either side of the rocky outcrop was invisible, and it was quite easy to believe the man in the party I passed in the mist who was calling the Stiperstones a mountain. I climbed to the trig point atop a tor but had to delve into memory and imagination for the view. At 1,760 feet (537m) this is the second highest top in Shropshire, after Brown Clee Hill, and usually affords prospects of nearby heights such as the Long Mynd and Corndon Hill as well as long vistas over the north Shropshire Plain to the hills of mid-Wales. This quartzite ridge stood proud of the surrounding ice during the last glaciation and was subject to a regime of constant freezing and thawing which shattered the rock and left the tors standing like the fins on a dinosaur's back.

I walked over rough ground to the wall around the now felled Gatten Plantation. Although this is still shown on the maps, the trees were cut down in the past few years as part of the Back to Purple project, which aims to return the land to its original heather-clad state. This has also involved planting thousands of heather seedlings to enhance natural regeneration. I followed the edge of the erstwhile wood down to an East Onny source pouring out of the ground below a clump of gorse and heather. It was not far to its first little waterfall but on reaching the road it disappeared down a drain and was not visible in the field across the road, although a ford and stream are both shown on the map. A visit after heavy rain would no doubt see it on the surface. I made my way along the road to the Stiperstones car park and wandered into the access land by the road to locate another headwater by a fence corner and gate close to the scant remains of a recently devoured sheep, one of several I saw that had succumbed to the snow; then I walked back to the road, crossing yet another little East Onny feeder. There are several cattle grids to negotiate before the road leads back to Bridges, but this at least means that you can walk on grass rather than tarmac. I had covered not much more than 8 miles (12.8km) in four hours, had seen little of anything off my route but had found several sources and had enjoyed my visit to the country for easy livers, a description given even more credence following the demise of the Horseshoe Inn.

The river Clun – Colunwy in the original Welsh – rises near the tiny village of Anchor to flow through its eponymous town as well as Clunton, Clunbury and Clungunford before joining the Teme at Leintwardine. Names are topsy-turvy in this cultural borderland and within half a mile of the source the two farms of Amblecote and Gwrid try to outstare each other across the infant Clun. Perhaps Æmell spent years trying to fathom his Welsh neighbours. Within half a dozen miles (9.6km), the Clun is crossed by one of the most magnificent stretches of Offa's Dyke and the echoes of a disturbed and disputed past seem out of place in such presently peaceful surroundings. Hereabouts Caractacus, Ancient British hero, fought the Roman invaders, in the eighth century King Offa of Mercia built his statement of power and possession across the landscape, while three hundred years later Edric the Wild, an English earl, harried the Normans. We walked Offa's Dyke Path one Easter when daffodils were bobbing and skittish lambs were just finding their feet and always recall these border hills with fondness.

Hopes of a lunchtime pint at Shropshire's second-highest pub led to another remorseful day as I parked on the Anchor Inn's ice-rink car park. A chalked sign said 'Open 7pm Every Day'. Surely, like the Yorkshire Calder's Portsmouth and Chatham, Anchor was christened by some returning sailor. Apart from the inn, a farm and a campsite – the Anchorage – there's not much to the place,

not even a chapel, although Wales is less than half a mile away from what's reckoned to be the most westerly English settlement on the Anglo-Welsh border. The source of the Clun is just south of the village at Foss y Rhess, variously translated as 'ditch' or 'swamp of the terrace or row'; there was certainly a vigorous stream pouring down the ditch alongside a field below Bettws Hill Wood and crossing under the road a couple of hundred yards south of the inn. The water seeps out of the ground in the gently sloping fields above the road.

This is grand walking country and a visit to the upper Clun valley can easily lead source seekers astray: less than a mile from the source are the earthworks of Castell Bryn Amlwg, one of the lesser-known border castles, while the Kerry Ridgeway stretches for miles just a couple of miles to the north.

Glossary

Banc Du: black bank
Bryn Coch: red hill
Castell Bryn Amlwg: castle on a prominent hill
Cefn: ridge
Ceulanau: riverbanks
Cilfaesty: corner house
Crug-y-byddar: deaf person's knoll
Cwm Gwyn: white valley
Nasz Dom: (Polish) our house

Clun rising

SNOWDONIA WANDERINGS

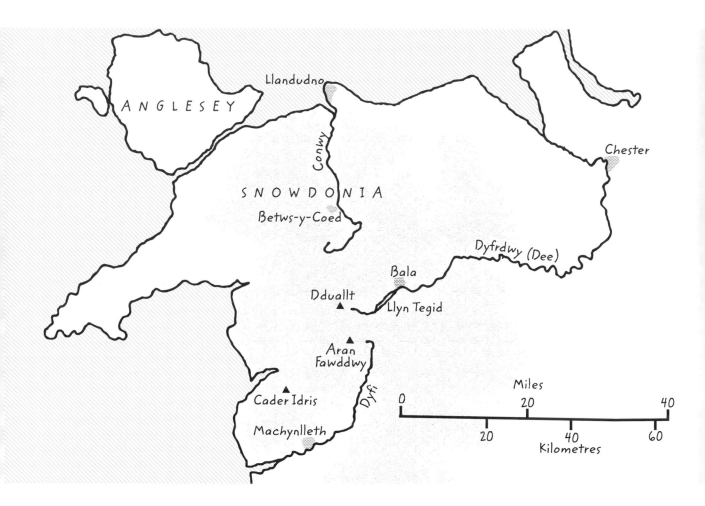

The north-western corner of Wales, Eryri, is one of the rainiest places in Britain and gives rise to many rivers. The sources of three of them are sought here. Two rise in lakes but they are very different in setting and aspect, while a visit to the third requires a traverse of one of the boggiest patches of land in the country. We occasionally follow in the footsteps of the restless Victorian traveller George Borrow on his tramps around Wild Wales.

Dyfrdwy
where Dee unmix'd doth flow

Deva Fluvius to the Romans who named their legionary fortress built on its banks after the river,

the Afon Dyfrdwy is better known as the anglicized river Dee. With a length of about 70 miles (113km), the Dee takes a circuitous route to its broad estuary between the Flintshire coast and the Wirral. The border between Wales and England twice

DYFRDWY	
SOURCE	Y Dduallt, Gwynedd
G.R.	SH 813 274
LENGTH	70 miles (113 kilometres)
TRIBUTARIES	Tryweryn, Clywedog, Ceiriog, Alyn
MOUTH	Dee Estuary

follows the river for a few miles and it enters England briefly, flowing through Chester, before returning to Wales to reach its mouth just beyond Connah's Quay.

Although some authorities give the source as Llyn Tegid, most agree that Afon Dyfrdwy rises some miles further south-west under the black crags of Dduallt. Although most of my source walks have been solitary, on this occasion, a foray into one of the loneliest parts of Wales, I had a companion. Geoff and I have walked together for many years, climbing most of the mountains of England and Wales. On our way to a mountaineering weekend in Snowdonia, I was certainly glad of his company during the crossing of Waun y Griafolen one late November day.

We started the walk by Dolhendre, a mile or so along a minor road that leaves the A494 Bala–Dolgellau route near a bridge over the Afon Lliw, one of Dyfrdwy's early tributaries. The confluence is 100 yards (91m) or so east of the bridge. Tarmac and then a track took us beneath the precipitous igneous crags topped by the remains of Castell Carndochan. A ruined medieval castle probably built on the remains of earlier fortifications, this still displays the remnants of a D-shaped southern tower and a round northern one with a rectangular central building between them. Dochan himself is said to have been a wise man who tutored the fifth-century king and saint Brychan Brycheiniog, founder of one of the three Welsh tribes. Fathering a reputed twenty-four sons would no doubt have helped his foundation. The castle itself may have been built by Llywelyn ap Iorwerth (Llywelyn the Great) during the late twelfth or early thirteenth century while he was consolidating his power base in Gwynedd.

The later constables and owners of the castle were presumably unaware that they were, literally, sitting on a gold mine, as there is no record of work on the site before the 1860s, by which time the castle was already a ruin. Gold fever had struck in the Dolgellau region in 1843 and it is perhaps a reflection of the remoteness of Carndochan

that it wasn't until twenty years later that a local shepherd boy spotted flecks of gold in rocks scattered around the hillside and even built into walls. The area was mined between 1864 and 1866, but the best ore was near the surface and yields soon declined. Later attempts proved no more successful and at one point it was reported that it 'cost one pound to produce 20/- worth of gold'. All meaningful operations had ceased by 1905.

Crossing a concrete slab over the Afon Fwy just upstream from a much more ancient clapper bridge, we headed into Coed Bryn Bras, climbing steeply past boulders thick with moss through the dark forest to emerge by a gate held together by that farmer's standby, binder twine. The adjacent stile fortunately meant that we didn't have to unravel it. The track climbed steadily above the forest, giving fine retrospective views northwards to Arenig Fawr, and it was obvious that the amount of water running down the path promised a good day for source finding, though possibly not for traversing Waun y Griafolen.

Crossing the Welsh watershed between Craig Llestri and Cerrig Chwibanog we were paddling in the headwaters of Afon Mawddach and gazing out over the hollow of Waun y Griafolen. It seems that the basin was initially scoured out of relatively soft mudstones by glaciers moving southwards from an Arenig ice field. As they melted the area was blanketed by boulder clay and a lake may have formed in the hollow. Around 9,000 years ago the climate had warmed enough for trees and moorland vegetation to return to this part of Wales and the glacial lake gave way to damp birch and alder woodland. With a return to colder and wetter conditions, the woodland died off and blanket bog developed. This continued for the following five millennia and a thick layer of peat gradually accumulated, with the lower peat layers becoming ever more compressed. Around 2,800 years ago a change to much wetter conditions resulted in erosion of the peat. Hags and groughs were formed and large river channels cut into the surface, draining to a large lake near the

'Lead the way, Geoff'

basin outlet north of Dduallt. Their remains are seen as meandering depressions in the surface of the blanket bog. More recently, with an improvement in conditions, a reduction in water flows allowed peat growth to resume. Heather began to colonize the drier old peat surfaces while the stream channels were filled with mosses, sedges and rushes, which developed into fresh peat deposits. This continues today and the site has been designated a Special Area of Conservation, reflecting the variety of wetland flora and fauna it supports.

Now bereft of the rowans which once grew here, this is one of the loneliest places in Wales. A 3-square-mile (7.7 sq. km) bowl of blanket bog, peat, tussock grass and knee-high heather, intersected by meandering channels and evil little vegetation-covered slits, it is a tough crossing in the best of weather. The path, clearly marked on the map, is a figment, its straight and narrow course heading towards the distant little rocky cone of Craig y Dinas merely mocking the faltering and floundering walker. Fears and doubts and discouraging apprehensions are apt to afflict the pilgrim negotiating this slough. Halfway over, we crossed a lichen-covered fence, the tops of its posts colonized by the bright red match-head-like British soldier fungus, and passed the skeleton of a dead tree, the only one we saw in the morass. Across the moor stands the elongated pyramid of Dduallt, the rocky summit of

which, we both decided, is a much better place to be than this. It took a long time, several changes of direction, a few leaps of faith, a couple of plunges and some choice language before we reached the base of the black crags.

Here we headed south, hugging the dry security of the foot of Dduallt's precipitous eastern face, passing patches of scree and car-sized boulders until, after noting a ruined round sheepfold, we found the source. A little rectangular structure, open to the sky, is built into the boulders right over the spring and from it the water gurgles away down a little rushy channel to start its journey to the sea. Surely this must be a shrine to the spirit of the divine water. There can be no other reason for its construction here and its moss- and lichen-covered stones speak of great antiquity.

We found a couple of flattish and dryish rocks to sit on – difficult by this great tumbled crag foot which the winter sun fails to catch – and ate our lunch, the silence broken only by the trickling of the water, the distant buzz of forestry chainsaws and the occasional roar of an invisible aircraft. Looking up the cliff I remembered the time I had scrambled down from the summit and first discovered this enchanted place. Dduallt is one of the less well-known Welsh mountains. Writing in the 1930s, Patrick Monkhouse stated, 'I have never heard of anyone ascending it,' and even in these days of peak-bagging the hill receives scant attention in the guidebooks.

We decided to follow a sheep track back along the foot of the scarp and climbed up on to the end of Dduallt's long north ridge. From here we looked across the bog to the twin tops of Moel Llyfnant and Arenig Fawr dominating the northern horizon and down on to where the Mawddach cascaded out of Waun y Griafolen to begin its 20-mile (32km) journey to Barmouth. Across the river a green track, part of the old coach road between Dolgellau and Bala, descended to a ford. Did it once cross Waun y Griafolen, on a causeway now buried in the peat, to join the track up from Llanuwchllyn? There was certainly no causeway as we splashed our way back across the moor. At one point Geoff said, 'Those two lakes we were looking for – I think we've just walked through one of them.' I've never looked forward to reaching a forest as much as I did that darkening late afternoon.

At last we regained the forest fence and walked down through the increasingly gloomy trees. We had walked about 8 miles (12.8km) and it had taken the best part of five and a half hours. It had been an experience, an adventure at times, but Geoff said when we reached the car, 'I liked it better when you dragged me up mountains.'

Glossary

Afon Fwy: winding river

Afon Lliw: bright river

Carndochan: Dochan's cairn

Cerrig Chwibanog: sharp-topped rocky place

Coed Bryn Bras: big hill wood

Craig Llestri: three crags

Craig y Dinas: rock of the fort

Dduallt: black height

Dolhendre: old house in the meadow

Dyfrdwy: divine water

Llanuwchllyn: church beyond the lake

Llyn Tegid: Bala Lake

Llywelyn ap Iorwerth: Llywelyn, son of the handsome lord

Moel Llyfnant: bare hill of the smooth stream

Waun y Griafolen: rowan tree moor

Dyfi
king of rivers

Rising in Creiglyn Dyfi beneath the beetling crest of the Aran mountains, the Afon Dyfi flows east for a couple of miles before being deflected south-westwards towards Dinas Mawddwy and its arcing journey to the sea. Reckoned by many to mark the frontier between North and South Wales, the river, anglicized as the Dovey, runs for about 30 miles

DYFI	
SOURCE	Creiglyn Dyfi, Gwynedd
G.R.	SH 867 225
LENGTH	30 miles (48 kilometres)
TRIBUTARIES	Cleifion, Twymyn, Dulas
MOUTH	Aberdyfi, Cardigan Bay

(48km) to its estuary by Aberdyfi on Cardigan Bay. The only town of any size it flows through is Machynlleth.

Creiglyn Dyfi lies in a glacial *cwm*, a cup-shaped hollow scooped out by the freezing and shattering of rock that accompanied the birth of a glacier which trundled down the hanging valley now occupied by Dyfi's headwater, Llaethnant. The Arans are real mountains, their bold, rocky crest standing out prominently when viewed across Llyn Tegid. The high ridge peaks on Aran Fawddwy, at 2,974 feet (906m) the highest Welsh ground outside the heartlands of Eryri.

Bwlch y Groes, with a summit at 1,788 feet (545m), was once reckoned to be the highest surfaced public road in Wales, but according to the Ordnance Survey it is now overtopped by Gospel Pass (1,801 feet/549m), birthplace of the Afon Honddu and the wonderfully named Digedi Brook, in the Black Mountains. The *bwlch* stands at the head of minor roads joining Dinas Mawddwy, Llanuwchllyn and Llyn Efyrnwy and is the key to visiting Creiglyn Dyfi and the high land around it. The cross at the road junction, replaced in 1989, commemorates the importance of the pass on a pilgrim route from north Wales to St David's in the south-west. I once drove up the icy road from Lake Vyrnwy late in December and met a motorist who was retreating. He didn't 'like the look of things further up', had turned around and missed out on a wonderful day. There is plenty of parking space at the top of the pass, though the easiest access to

Creiglyn Dyfi, at a hairpin bend in the road by the track to Blaen Pennant, is a mile or so down the hill. And what a mile! This southern approach to Bwlch y Groes has a total of eleven black arrowheads on the OS map with a steepest gradient of 1 in 4. It was notorious during the 1970s and '80s as the toughest climb on the Milk Race round-Britain cycle tour. During the glory days of the British motor industry, the route, also known as the Hellfire Pass, which wouldn't have pleased the earlier pilgrims, was used for testing Austin and Standard Triumph prototype cars. The road descends beside the Afon Rhiwlech, another of Dyfi's high headstreams, as it leaps down a very deep glen from its source besides the road by Bwlch y Groes.

A good track leaves the road on an acute bend and climbs above the buildings of Blaen Pennant to cross the tumbling waters of Nant Llewelyn-goch. Here you can abandon the track and follow a fence across Rhiw March, taking care not to trip over Blaen Pennant's water pipe, down to the river. There follows a splendid and adventurous half mile (0.8km) as Llaethnant tumbles, spouting and frisking, over a series of waterfalls, slides and rapids, all the while cutting a narrow gorge through the rock as it tries to get down to the level of the main valley. They say that this upper section of the Afon Dyfi has been known as Llaethnant since a local saint, Tydecho, changed the stream to milk during a famine. The sixth-century saint was also said to

Llaethnant

have stuck his king, Maelgwyn, to a rock for upsetting him. Anyone viewing the river here as it curdles over the crags will have little doubt that it needed no saintly input for the locals to call the stream milky; in the Lake District it would be Sour Milk Gill. George Borrow walked this way in 1854 and spoke to two inhabitants of Ty Mawr who told him that the waterfall he could see tumbling down the crag at the far end of the gloomy vale was 'the fountain of the Royal Dyfi'. From his description, the big house was Blaen Pennant.

The scramble beside the waterfalls opens out and the stream is more placid for a while before it is seen at the bottom of a deep, narrow gorge where you rejoin the main track. Once over the lip of the Llaethnant hanging valley and, just as suddenly as it started, the excitement is over. In front stretches a broad upland valley framed by the craggy slopes of Ogof Ddu and Llechwedd Du. The rounded bulk of Foel Hafod-fynydd rises further along the valley, with the Aran cliffs forming the backdrop. Here Llaethnant meanders as if hesitant before taking the plunge.

It must be admitted that the next 1½ miles (2.4km) to Creiglyn Dyfi itself is not a particularly pleasant walk when the ground is wet; the scenery is fine but the plod, through rush and tussock grass, can be trying, even when one remembers that these particular beds were once prized for the making of rush candles and that people travelled from far away to gather them. It's a pity they didn't trample out more of a path. The rush lights were made by stripping the green skin from the reeds and dipping the pith into hot fat. They could then be hung in holders and lit to give off light like a candle. The valley broadens out, numerous small Dyfi feeders can be seen descending from the dramatic precipices of the main escarpment and the upper couple of hundred yards of Llaethnant, in a grassy-sided little gorge, again remind you that this is the milk stream. Infant Dyfi has cut its way through banks of moraine to escape from the 15-acre (6ha) lake

Dyfi falls

which lies at a height of just over 1,900 feet (579m).

The ridge towering above the lake has seen its share of aircraft crashes and there were half a dozen during the Second World War. On 9 February 1944, a Mosquito crashed while carrying out a cross-country exercise. The wreckage and bodies of the two aircrew were not located until two days later. A year and a day after the Mosquito crash, a Bristol Beaufighter hit the mountain just below the summit on a day when snow showers and icing were being reported by other planes in the area. Again the two crew members were killed. Some pieces of wreckage can still be located but the sites have been badly looted over the years. Three or four headwaters join the lake beneath the crags and searching for water in them is a pleasant, though sometimes fruitless, way of spending a summer afternoon.

From Creiglyn Dyfi you can reverse the route, or cross a 2,000-foot (610m) hill, Foel Hafod-fynydd, before regaining the track back to Blaen-pennant.

This is such a grand landscape that a longer walk, taking in a circuit of the summits surrounding Creiglyn Dyfi, is included here. The starting point is, once again, the top of Bwlch y Groes. At one time this area was difficult of access with only a single 'permitted path' along the main Aran summit ridge to supplement the few rights of way. Now it's all access land apart from the valleys, so you can follow the fence along the broad ridge leading south-west from the car park with a clear conscience. The last

time I walked along this stretch, four orange excavators were at work, crawling over the hillside and doing the opposite of what their name suggests. As part of the LIFE Active Bogs in Wales project, they were blocking drainage ditches in order to raise the water table. This will improve the habitat for blanket bog plants, enhance water quality and, by preventing peat erosion, keep the carbon trapped in it.

This first part of the route well illustrates the difference between hills and mountains. Though the height of a mountain is often expressed as a figure, 2,000ft (610m) in England and Wales and 3,000ft (915m) in Scotland, there is more to it than mere maths. The first top along the watershed separating the head streams of the south-west-bound Afon Dyfi from the north-east-flowing Afon Twrch is Llechwedd Du, which reaches 2,010ft (613m). The way to it can be rather wet and interrupted by peat groughs but involves less than 300 feet (92m) of ascent in 1½ miles (2.4km). When I first came along here the summit was marked by a single white stone but now it possesses a cairn of sorts. Swinging round to the north, the fence meets another on the rounded top of Esgeiriau Gwynion, also capped with a white cairn, and here the scenic contrast becomes apparent. Looking to the east all is rolling and hilly but a view to the west shows up the Arans as proper, steep and craggy mountains. On one winter visit all the valleys were filled with the white cloud of an inversion and it took little imagination to visualize the Aran crags as they must have appeared around 12,000 years ago towards the end of the glacial era, rising above the ice. The reason for the difference is, as usual, the geology. Eastwards the landscape has been carved out of rocks of the Silurian era, millions of years younger but also softer than the gnarled, ancient igneous rocks to north and west.

The fence turns again, following the watershed down to Bwlch Sirddyn before climbing quite steeply on to Foel Hafod-fynydd. This is one of the finest viewpoints for the Arans, the whole ridge being spread out in one long sweep of crag and precipitous mountainside, the only obvious weakness being the grassy slopes of Erw y Ddafad-ddu. The summit also gives views down to Creiglyn Dyfi, which is easily visited from here.

At the foot of the broad ridge climbing above the lake to Erw y Ddafad-ddu stands a massive boulder. It can hardly be missed and is worth finding on a damp day, for it has a ledge on one side which makes a fine shelter for one. It has rested in this spot since the melting ice left it 1,800 or so lifetimes ago, and the block acts as a good perspective cultivator – something to contemplate while trudging up to the summit. Ambling up here on another cold, crisp day I clearly heard voices and turned around surprised, as they sounded just behind me, though I had not noticed anyone following me on the walk from Bwlch y Groes. There was no one in sight and it took me a while before I realized that, because of the stillness of the day and the clarity of the air, the voices belonged to a couple of walkers high up on the summit of Aran Fawddwy, half a mile (0.8km) away. Eventually the gradient moderates and you reach the top of Erw y Ddafad-ddu. There are several level acres but rarely black sheep at the summit, which has an untidy pile of stones with a rudimentary shelter as a cairn. If you turn south across broken ground, a rocky little wander through the boulders leads to the trig point on Aran Fawddwy.

The pre-eminent, though hardly best-known, mountain of sub-Snowdonian Wales, Fawddwy is 40 feet (12m) higher than Cadair Idris and almost 70 feet (21m) higher than Pen y Fan. A local story tells of the men of Dinas Mawddwy building the cairn on top of their mountain because they had heard that Cadair Idris was higher by 6 feet (1.8m) – a tale reminiscent of the 1990s film *The Englishman Who Went Up a Hill But Came Down a Mountain*, one of the few feature films to showcase cartography. The cairn in reality is another Bronze Age relic. Measuring about 45 feet (13.7m) across and rising to about 12 feet (3.6m) high, it has the trig point perching on top. The column has been rebuilt. It is now an elegant tapering affair built of blocks of the local rock but a photo in Poucher's *The Welsh Peaks*[7] shows it as a concrete pillar with a crack right across its base.

Wandering south from Fawddwy and keeping close to the edge of the crags, just below the very chine or ridge of the Arans, you pass several little pools and seepages, which give birth to tricklets forming the headwaters of streams joining Llaethnant below Creiglyn Dyfi. They also give a fine view straight down the broad U-shaped *cwm* in which the Llaethnant, far too small to have eroded the valley, is obviously a misfit. At Drws Bach is a cairn with a memorial, erected by the RAF in 1961, to Senior Aircraftman Mike Aspain of the RAF Mountain Rescue, who was killed by lightning here while escorting Duke of Edinburgh's Award Scheme candidates. The ridge, giving excellent views to Creiglyn Dyfi and along the Aran crags, continues round to Drysgol, whence a steep descent can be made to Llaethnant and the track to Blaen Pennant. A fine walk. Now there's just the little

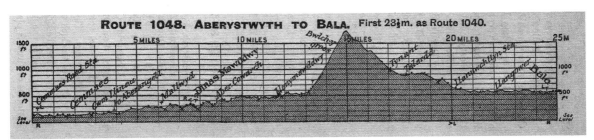

Bwlch y Groes, from *The 'Contour' Road Book*

7 W. A. Poucher, Constable, 1962.

Creiglyn Dyfi and Aran Fawddwy

matter of climbing that mile and a half of road with its eleven arrowheads. Maybe you'll be lucky, as we were once, and cadge a lift off a touring Canadian!

Glossary

Afon Rhiwlech: rocky hillside river

Afon Twrch: boar river

Aran Fawddwy: high place of Mawddwy (one of the cantrefs or hundreds of Merionethshire)

Blaen Pennant: top of the head stream

Bwlch y Groes: pass of the cross

Creiglyn: rock lake

Dinas Mawddwy: Mawddwy fort

Drws Bach: little door/opening

Dyfi: from *du* – dark/black

Erw y Ddafad-ddu: acre of the black sheep

Eryri: the highest land around Snowdon

Esgeiriau Gwynion: white ridges

Foel Hafod-fynydd: hill by the moorland summer dwelling

Llaethnant: milk brook

Llanuwchllyn: parish over the lake

Llechwedd Du: black hillside

Llyn Efyrnwy: Lake Vyrnwy

Llyn Tegid: Bala Lake

Nant Llewelyn-goch: red Llewelyn's brook

Ogof Ddu: black cave

Rhiw March: hillside of the horse

Conwy

one of the famous rivers of the world

The Afon Conwy, or river Conway in English, runs for about 27 miles (43km) through north-west Wales from its source in Llyn Conwy, on the northern Migneint moors, to its mouth at Conwy Sands. William Wordsworth wrote about the 'Alpine steeps of the Conway' and there are spectacular waterfalls a couple of miles south of Betws-y-Coed.

CONWY	
SOURCE	Llyn Conwy, Conwy
G.R.	SH 780 461
LENGTH	27 miles (43 kilometres)
TRIBUTARIES	Machno, Lledr, Llugwy, Crafnant
MOUTH	Conwy Bay

Historically the river formed the boundary between Denbighshire and Caernarvonshire.

Migneint is a large area of high, soggy moorland to the east of Ffestiniog. George Borrow came this way in 1854 during his pedestrian tour of Wild Wales and noted that

> the moor extended for miles and miles. It was bounded on the east and south by immense hills and moels ... Nothing could be conceived more cheerless than the scenery around. The ground on each side of the road was mossy and rushy – no houses – instead of them were peat stacks, here and there, standing in their blackness. Nothing living to be seen except a few miserable sheep picking the wretched herbage, or lying panting on the shady side of the peat clumps.

Borrow's 'dusty, hilly road' is still fairly empty most of the time and the Migneint maintains a deserved reputation for remoteness. Pont ar Gonwy, where the road climbing the upper reaches of the Vale of Conwy from Ysbyty Ifan crosses the infant river, makes a good starting point for a visit to Llyn Conwy and the easiest way is simply to walk up the grassy track heading north from Llyn Cottage. The lake and the estate around it were formerly owned and managed for sport by Lord Penrhyn and the Cottage was often used by the Penrhyns and their guests for night fishing. The lake reached its apex

as a sporting venue during the last couple of decades of the nineteenth century under the stewardship of Andrew Foster, who moved from Scotland to become Lord Penrhyn's Head Keeper of this area. He would surely have felt at home on these wide, wild moors. In June 1880 111 trout were caught in Llyn Conwy in two days.

A longer walk, of just under 5 miles (8km), giving a fuller view of the area, uses a couple of footpaths marked on the OS map. From Pont ar Gonwy, a semblance of a path runs just north of west to pass a couple of humps, the second graced with the name Bryn yr Hyrddod and a sheepfold (ramfold?). As you head down to Afon Ddu where, with luck, you will find a stake, the heather growing in abundance reflects the area's grouse shooting history and the path, such as it is, tends to avoid it and so sticks to the sphagnum. This stake points the way, via a wet, green corridor through the heather, to the next one which, on investigation, turns out in reality to be part of the remains of an old grouse butt with a little tree growing from it. The British soldier lichen looking like red-tipped matches sprouting from the top of the rotting wooden posts draws the attention but it is the British airman in the jet screaming overhead which is more likely to hold it. With luck you will be able to take a bearing on an occasional vehicle using the road the path is heading for, but I wouldn't bank on it. When eventually you reach the road, which drops down Cwm Hafodredwydd to the blind valley of Cwm Penmachno, Llyn Cottage is visible, so the conscientious walker could take a back bearing, just to check.

The way now leads downhill, past a milestone that informs the traveller, among other things, that Ffestiniog is 6 miles away and that Hugh Dwyryd Thomas was here on 2 May 1961. The number of empty Kronenbourg cans down the bank suggests this is not a road to drive along late on a Saturday night. But where are the can throwers heading to, or from? After a cattle grid and Pont Elen, the path turns up the hillside by a wall. It is probably just as easy to stay by the wall and fence, as the fisherman's path marked on the map is a little vague and soon meets a short stretch of wall by a stream. Continuing alongside the fence you cross a stile and a relatively easy way through the heather should open up around the southern end of a small rise (486m on the map) where, at last, Llyn Conwy comes into view. Lying in an elevated basin, at a height of 1,488 feet (454m), the lake is surrounded by little hills such as Pen y Bedw, Bryniau Duon and Bryn Owen. Outcrops of rock, some with quartz veins, make for pleasanter walking than the heather and, after crossing a wall, you reach an old boathouse on the north shore. This was struck by lightning and partially destroyed in July 1881 but was then repaired. Now it stands forlorn and roofless, with a little pile of litter in the corner.

Across the lake from the boathouse, three mid-Wales mountains, Arenig Fach, Arenig Fawr and Moel Llyfnant, stand on the southern horizon. Now managed by Dwr Cymru, the lake, which reaches a maximum depth of 16 feet (4.8m), is owned by the National Trust and is still fished, although acid rain has damaged the water quality. Liming has been tried but it is rather an imprecise exercise, which has effects on other parts of the ecology. Continuing along the shore, you pass a rectangular stone structure capped with quartz and with a pipe emerging from it. Four pairs of Canada geese were posturing and arguing loudly near by. With the whole 100 acres (40ha) of the lake to play with, why do they have to crowd together and fight? Perhaps,

like many humans, they are just naturally cantankerous. It is possible to stay by the rocky shore down most of the eastern side to a little slate-pebbly beach where you cross a stream descending from Pen y Bedw by a footbridge. The scrupulous may wish to follow it, as it appears to be the highest feeder. A quartz-topped cairn on a little island is a gull magnet and is overlooked by a little cliff which gives views of Snowdon over the lake.

An old door provides a useful little bridge and the path becomes more obvious as it approaches the southern end of the lake. Several buildings stand around the outflow, which you reach by the track from Llyn Cottage. A pleasant walk back to the road on a summer's day, the track was the scene of a tragedy at the turn of the twentieth century when Anna Jane of Swch, Penmachno, housekeeper at Llyn Cottage was caught in a blizzard while walking to her work. Although advised against making the journey in such conditions, the conscientious Anna set off and was never seen alive again. Her body was found within sight of the cottage.

Llyn Conwy is a pleasant place to while away a couple of hours in an area where, apart from the planes, all is peace and tranquillity.

Glossary

Afon Ddu: black river

Betws-y-Coed: chapel in the woods

Bryn Owen: Owen's hill

Bryn yr Hyrddod: hill of the rams

Bryniau Duon: dark hills

Cwm Hafodredwydd: valley with two summer dwellings

Cwm Penmachno: valley at the head of the Machno

Dwr Cymru: Welsh water

Ffestiniog: Ffestin's land

Kronenbourg: German-sounding French beer brewed in England

Migneint: swamp, bog

Pen y Bedw: birch top

Pont ar Gonwy: Conway bridge

Ysbyty Ifan: Ivan's hospital/lodging house

Above Pont ar Gonwy

A GREAT DIVIDE

The southern Pennines have acted as a physical and cultural barrier for centuries for the inhabitants to the east and west. The Snake Road is usually one of the first to fall victim to winter snow and it is appropriate to think about communications in a region where concerns about crossing the watershed have resulted in a richness of routes that have left their imprint on the landscape from Roman roads, packhorse tracks, turnpikes, canal and railway tunnels to the motorways and microwave masts of today.

Trent
a day's march

To the canal boater the Trent is ingrained on the consciousness; the Trent and Mersey, the Tidal Trent and Trent Falls are all there in the back of your mind. Memories of crossing the murky river in Stoke-on-Trent, of sharing its gentle, post-Stoke valley for mile after mile of quiet Staffordshire countryside near Stone and Salt, Hoo Mill and

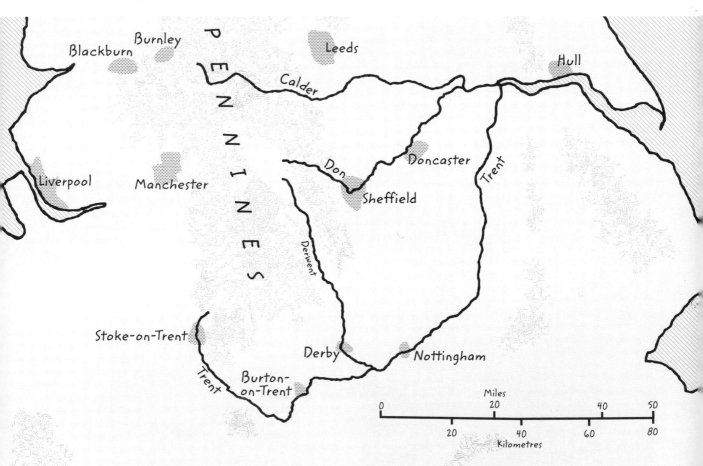

TRENT	
SOURCE	Wellfield, Biddulph Moor, Staffordshire
G.R.	SJ 913 583
LENGTH	185 miles (297 kilometres)
TRIBUTARIES	Churnet, Derwent, Dove, Tame, Idle
MOUTH	Trent Falls, Humber Estuary

Haywood, of towering power stations, of joining the river itself at Derwent Mouth, of Newark Castle and mighty Cromwell Lock, of gravel barges and serious boating. So it behoves the boater to go and see where the river that inspired Wedgwood and Brindley begins.

The source of the 185 mile (297km) long Trent is Trent Head Well on Biddulph Moor. So say all the authorities. Hmmm. We shall see.

A good approach to the head of the Trent starts from Greenway Bank, a couple of miles south of the source as the tricklet flows. Situated only 5 miles (8km) from the heart of the Potteries, the nineteenth-century landscaped estate of Greenway Bank, owned at one time by James Brindley's brother-in-law, Hugh Henshall, surveyor, engineer, canal proprietor and pottery manager, was bought by Staffordshire County Council in 1973. The house itself was in such a bad way that it had to be demolished but the 114 acres (46ha) of grounds, together with some of the outbuildings, are maintained as a country

Warden's Tower

park. A path, at times flagged, stepped and sleepered, makes its way down through quiet mature woodland to the Serpentine Pool, constructed in the 1780s as a water supply for the Caldon Canal. A dam separates the pool from the lower Knypersley Pool, designed by Thomas Telford as a reservoir for the Caldon and Trent and Mersey Canals and opened in 1827. It holds 930,000 cubic metres of water and is fished by the Cheshire and North Staffordshire Anglers Association for roach, perch with bream and specimen carp and pike. A stone on the dam is inscribed 'HHW', no doubt referring to Hugh Henshall Williamson, the first Hugh's nephew and mid-nineteenth-century owner of the nearby Chatterley Whitfield coal mine, who lived at Greenway Bank. He served as High Sheriff of Staffordshire in 1834. A leat feeding the Serpentine runs beside the track, which then makes its way round the north side of Knypersley Pool towards Warden's Tower, built in 1828 and once home to the gamekeeper. Occupied until the 1950s, it is currently empty but the Landmark Trust is said to be looking to lease it from the council. Near by is Gawton's Well, where a hermit was cured of leprosy by drinking the water and people came to use the medicinal waters of the spring. It is reckoned to be one of the most spiritual places in Staffordshire.

With so much of interest in the vicinity, it would be easy to abandon the quest for Trent's wellspring to another day but, as a true source seeker, I continued through the woodland, conscious of high ground to the left, and joined a public footpath just beyond the former estate boundary wall. The Trent is in the second little valley to the right, flowing through Crowborough Wood. The path swings to meet a track which gives views westwards to Mow Cop and which leads to the aptly named Rock End. Taking Crowborough Road I descended into the infant Trent valley and found two bridges, the first only really a culvert over a tributary. The little river announces its presence, gurgling alongside, before you cross the first road bridge over the river. Just upstream of the bridge is the confluence of two of the main feeders. Climbing out of the valley there are holly hedges and an interesting cottage before a crossroads where a left turn leads on to Barrage Road to go past Barridge Farm. The road gives good views across undulating, rocky-crested ridges to Mow Cop. Anyone interested in finding the first bridge across the Trent may like to follow an intriguing path just past Barridge Farm and, satisfied that they have seen the highest bridge, return to the road along the path to Bradds Farm.

Soon Trent Head Farm announces that the source must be near and a path turns off the road to pass an overgrown cottage before descending to Trent Head Well. Given that water was cascading down the concrete steps leading down to the well the last time I was there, it is pretty difficult to make a case for the well's pre-eminence. The well itself, standing at over 900 feet (275m) above sea level, is quite a substantial structure with a 3-inch (7.6cm) pipe protruding through a stone wall beneath a

Trent Head Well

headstone dated 1935. It's just that in coming down from the road you have walked beside a lively, gurgling stream with much more water in it than the trickle emanating from the pipe. Perhaps in time of drought the pipe continues to trickle when all else around has dried up. The streamlet from Trent Head Well follows a holly hedge to a boggy confluence with the stronger stream.

A glance at the map shows Wellfield Farm half a mile (0.8km) to the north-east with a tell-tale blue W, at a height of about 1,030 feet (314m) and much closer to the watershed, and even a thin blue line appearing and disappearing in the fields between. The pedantic pedestrian feels the need to investigate or at least circumambulate these highest gathering grounds of the Trent. So you can follow the tarmac up Leek Lane and on to Top Road, where a bench gives views of Leek and the high Staffordshire moorlands around the Roaches and Axe Edge. Jodrell Bank's great dish peeps over the housetops of Biddulph Moor and, looking north-west from this exposed crest, it is easy to see what the weather forecasters mean when they talk about the wind blowing showers through the Cheshire Gap.

There *is* a well in the field just north of Wellfield Farm and here, surely, is the true source of the Trent. The water oozing out here may sink back into the ground but it goes on to flow down that same stream, coursing not a hundred yards from Trent Head Well. Cogitating on all this I walked on to Rudyard Road and then Farmside Lane to pick up the footpath that leads back across the fields to Barrage Road.

Any number of ways back to Greenway Bank and Knypersley Reservoir can be devised but the Staffordshire Moorlands Walk keeps to the high ground and provides a variety of contrasting views in this interesting corner of Staffordshire. It was along here that I had one of those strange conversations that spark off memory. After I had overhauled a pair of hikers near a dog-barking, junk-cumbered, mud-splattered apology for a farm, one of them

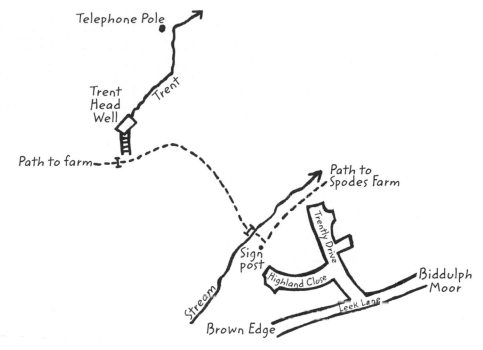

Author's 1984 sketch map

called, 'We thought you were the farmer come to call off his dogs.' I turned and said, 'Do I look like a farmer?' It reminded me of a time when, searching for a trig point just above the Trent valley north of Rugeley, I had trudged across some fields on what I'd thought was the right of way. Later I was heading back to my boat, moored on the canal, in which I'd been engaged with some engine 'ole tasks before setting off on a whim for my walk. As I reached the outskirts of Rugeley I became aware of a Range Rover following me slowly, so I stopped, thinking the driver might require directions – whenever I'm in a strange place, people stop me and ask the way to locations I've never heard of – but it was not the case. He informed me, somewhat sharply I thought, that there had been a number of burglaries in the houses by the fields where I'd been spotted walking. 'Do I look like a burglar?' I demanded, shocked by his insinuation and then looked down at my boating clothes!

The watercourse which flows south from Knypersley Reservoir is called the Head of Trent

and is thought by some to be the source, but anyone who has spent an hour or so exploring the little streams, rivulets, wells, hedges, fields and valleys around Biddulph Moor may well beg to differ.

Don
shimmer through this valley

DON	
SOURCE	Withens Edge, South Yorkshire
G.R.	SE 119 027
LENGTH	69 miles (112 kilometres)
TRIBUTARIES	Loxley, Sheaf, Rother, Dearne,
MOUTH	confluence with Ouse at Goole

This Don is a true Yorkshire mon. Born on the Bronte-esque Withens Edge, it flows through solid white-rose Sheffield, Rotherham and Doncaster. Originally a tributary of the Trent, it was rerouted by Cornelius Vermuyden to meet the Ouse at Goole, thus reinforcing its county credentials. There are plenty more Dons, including one in Scotland, one in Lancashire, another which joins the Tyne at Jarrow, a couple in Australia, one in Canada (incidentally, named after this one) and, of course, a famous example in Russia. The 1,220 mile (1,950km) long Russian version, outside the scope of this book, is longer than the top seven British rivers added together. Flowing across the south of the county, the Yorkshire Don was very industrialized and severely polluted along its lower course, although it has improved markedly in recent years as industry has waned. In some ways the Don is a mirror image of the Etherow flowing down t'other side of t'ills to meet Mersey in Stockport. Their topmost sources ooze from the same peaty ridge, their middle valleys are reservoir girt and their lower reaches densely urbanized.

An upper Don valley watershed walk, starting at Dunford Bridge, took me to numerous headwaters through a variety of types of terrain.[8] Parking is easy, beside Winscar Reservoir, by a picnic site on the Trans Pennine Trail (TPT) or in the village. The Windle Edge road aims arrow straight up the hillside, taking the TPT to its summit at 1,423 feet (434m), but I left the road to the left, opposite one of the Woodhead Tunnel air shafts, and descended along a bridleway, here part of the Barnsley Boundary Walk, to cross the stream, a Don tributary, flowing into Upper Windleden Reservoir. Climbing beside Woodland Clough (much clough, no woodland) you reach the main A628 Sheffield–Manchester road at Fiddlers Green, an obvious resting place. If the road should seem too busy then a short climb to the top of South Nab will provide a good view over the upper Don. On a dry day[9] you can lie at your leisure in the tussocky grass or, failing that, there's a flat slab to sit on next to the trig point. This concrete monolith, known to

cartographic aficionados as a Hotine Pillar and one of three we visit during the course of the walk, has a tale to tell.

Captain (later Brigadier) Martin Hotine was head of the Ordnance Survey's Trigonometrical and Levelling Division during the retriangulation of Great Britain, a grand new mapping of the land, initiated in 1935. Having been commissioned in the Royal Engineers during the First World War, he served in India and Iraq and later in Africa, where he made great strides in the accuracy of survey methods. This was a good grounding for his work when he was transferred to the Ordnance Survey in 1933. Hotine believed that all surveys should be made from a fixed platform rather than a possibly unstable tripod and so he designed and introduced the famous trapezial triangulation pillar. Made so that the theodolite sat squarely upon a bronze alloy plate set into the flat top of the pillar, each one, with its unique number cast into a flush bracket affixed to the side, had to be sited on open ground so that it was 'intervisible' with its neighbours. There were 6,173 of these columns, mostly handcast with great precision in concrete, although a

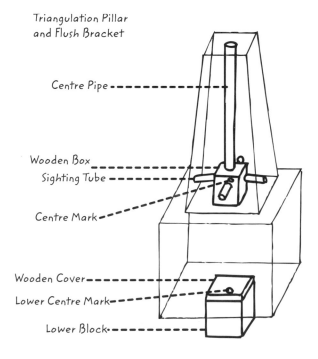

Triangulation Pillar and Flush Bracket

Centre Pipe

Wooden Box
Sighting Tube

Centre Mark

Wooden Cover

Lower Centre Mark

Lower Block

---

8   (Stifled laughter.)

9   (More stifled laughter.)

On Withens Edge

few are made from local stone, and standing 4 feet (1.2m) high and 2 feet (0.6m) square at the base, scattered the length and breadth of Great Britain. They took some building; the one on Cadair Idris in Wales took twelve days and needed packhorses to carry up over 2 tons of sand, cement and chippings. Some have disappeared over the years as a result of farmers ploughing them out or the encroachment of buildings. Even in the uplands trig points have succumbed, to lightning strikes and vandalism. There isn't a hill walker who hasn't been grateful (though that is nowhere near a strong enough expression of the emotion felt when reaching a cloud-shrouded, wind-battered trig point and realizing that this actually *is* the summit) to Hotine and his pillars. Those that remain, still over 6,000, are a fitting and lasting memorial to the man and his wonderful survey. On a clear day[10] it is theoretically possible to see ten more pillars from the one on South Nab, including the two yet to be visited.

Crossing the road at the top of the Woodland Clough path leads to another wide, grassy track on the far side. This is part of the original way over Woodhead before the current road, a turnpike authorized in 1731, was built. Here I was following the footsteps and hoofprints of jaggers, shepherds and packhorses laden with salt. The track passes

a memorial, a milestone inscribed with the ancient numerals XX and the remnants of the ancient Lady Cross, a possibly thirteenth-century monastic boundary mark, before swinging round to the north-west to rejoin the TPT, which heads north to recross the main road and rejoin the Windle Edge road. Here Uppermost Clough leads down to Upper Windleden Reservoir and sounds well named to be a contender for top source except that it is the valley of a tributary which meets Don at Dunford Bridge. A couple of hundred yards along the minor road, a track leads off to the left and curves around Carr Top and Wike Edge to arrive at a brick building on the line of the Woodhead railway tunnel. Another structure, to the south-west, is one of the 3 mile (4.8km) long tunnel's air shaft tops. I picked up a head stream of the Etherow and tracked it through a series of peat groughs in Upper Head Moss and Wike Head to the county boundary fence a hundred yards or so south-west of where it changes direction acutely. At this fence corner I was back on the watershed and rain falling on the northern side of the fence ends up in the Don. I followed the fence, just to the north of west, to the trig point on Dead Edge End which carries flush bracket no. S1779.

As you continue along the ridge the Holme Moss radio transmitting station mast, rising 750 feet (228m) above the moor a couple of miles to the west, dominates the scene. The fence follows the watershed, with the Don to the right and the Etherow to the left, over Withens Edge. Etherow-bound Withens Brook and its tributaries have cut deeper valleys than the Don head streams but the actual line of the watershed, as is usually the case on these Pennine moors, is debatable. Someone once wrote that to follow a watershed it is simply necessary not to cross running water. They should try it along here on a wet day!

Before the fence swings away to the north-west is a depression, laced with peat groughs, where the uppermost waters of the Don and Withens Brook seep out of the ground. Those that flow to the east coalesce into Great Grains, which itself becomes the Don below Grains Edge. Grains means branches and is highly descriptive of this dendritic moorland. I had to follow snow-packed Great Grains for a hundred yards or so before I found running – well, dripping – water. The weak winter sun, warming up the black peat, was just enough to melt the icicles hanging down over the grough.

The next section of the walk, following the watershed around to the green whaleback of Snailsden, can be pretty grim in poor weather but with the ground frozen solid, it was a pleasure. I watched a winter-coated hare skipping away across the snow and grouse skimming above the moor. Groughs and drainage ditches, which would seriously disrupt progress on most days, were filled with hard-packed snow and I had a deal of fun zig-zagging across the plateau. I even kicked steps up the higher slopes to Snailsden's flat summit. The third trig point of the day gave contrasting views. Southwards the many streams of the upper Don valley flow down solemn moorland to Winscar reservoir, while to the west the plateau rolls away to Holme Moss and Black Hill. Another mast, Emley Moor, is visible to the north-east and two wind farms and two power stations as well as the urban sprawl of Huddersfield can be seen. From the summit paths and tracks lead down, past grouse butts and through an old quarry, to the southern side of Harden reservoir and eventually,

after crossing the dam, the road to Dunford Bridge. A short walk along the road, past a boundary stone marked 'Holmfirth and Thurlstone', led me to the track down to Winscar Reservoir, the most extensive of five reservoirs around the upper Don valley. Winscar is one of Yorkshire Water's largest reservoirs. Opened in the late 1970s, it has suffered from leakage and a geocomposite liner has been installed across the upstream face to solve the problem. This gives the dam its blue-green appearance. At the end of my walk around the Don watershed, I took off clean boots.[11]

As an alternative, you can approach the source of the Don at the head of Great Grains from the car park near the Holme Moss mast. A there-and-back walk of just under 4 miles (6.5km) along the fence over Bleakmires Moss takes you over a triple watershed at Bailie Causeway Moss. To the south are Etherow's gathering grounds, eastwards water drains to the Don and streams flowing north form the Holme, which joins the Colne, itself a tributary of the Calder.

Derwent
out past the mill

This is the Derbyshire Derwent, of that there is no doubt. Rising in the bleak peat of the Black Peak, it is impounded in Derbyshire's Lake District, gave the impetus to one of the world's great early industrial centres, the Derwent Valley Mills, now a World Heritage Site, flows through the county town and joins the Trent having run its entire 60-mile (96.5km) course through the county. There *is* doubt about the derivation of the name. 'Bright water' or 'river lined with oaks' – take your pick. A visit to the source along the upper valley will lend credence to either derivation.

Fairholmes Visitor Centre stands in the middle of the Derbyshire 'Lake District', actually a

11   No need to stifle it any longer!

DERWENT	
SOURCE	Swain's Greave, Derbyshire
G.R.	SK 127 971
LENGTH	60 miles (96.5 kilometres)
TRIBUTARIES	Ashop, Noe, Wye, Amber, Ecclesbourne
MOUTH	Derwent Mouth, confluence with Trent

Derwent Dam

collection of reservoirs in the upper Derwent valley supplying water to Derby, Leicester, Nottingham and Sheffield. There are several free car parks on the approach road while the Fairholmes one is pay and display. Alternatively it is possible to continue up the valley to limited parking at King's Tree where the tarmac ends. This is not available on summer weekends or Bank Holidays, when the road beyond the visitor centre is closed and a shuttle bus service is run. On a lovely day in May I decided to go the whole hog and walk from the centre to the source and return over Bleaklow Stones and back along The Ridge, a walk of about 16 miles (26km).

Derwent Dam hangs over Fairholmes and the path, climbing from the road, shows you the massive scale of operations, with Tolkein and Hendrix both springing to mind. The west tower houses a small museum, open when the road is closed, dedicated to the Dambusters, the RAF's 617 Squadron, who used the Derwent Reservoir to practise their low-level bombing techniques before the raid on the Möhne, Eder and Sorpe Dams which supplied the German industrial Ruhr with water and electricity. An incredible combination of bravery and technical wizardry, the Dambusters Raid was a huge boost to morale in Britain, proving that, in 1943, the RAF could strike back effectively at the enemy. Its legacy has ranged from books to films, music to lager adverts, and with a remake of the

film projected for the next year or two it is still there in the national consciousness.

Derwent is the middle of three reservoirs with the later Ladybower lying downstream and Howden above. Work started on the solid masonry neo-gothic dam in 1902 with the huge blocks being transported along a railway from quarries at Grindleford before being erected by men with steam cranes and block and tackle. The thousand or so navvies who worked on the project lived, with their families, in Tin Town, a specially built, self-contained model village to the west of the river. Derwent started to be filled in November 1914 and was full fourteen months later. A surplus of water gives a spectacular waterfall as it pours over the dam between the towers.

The walk along a track on the east side is gentle, giving pleasant views across the reservoir. An electrician passed me in his van and I wondered at the limited prospects for wiring work in these parts until I met him, parked and unloading his fishing gear – 'Trout are rising, mate' – just below the next mighty dam, Howden. At the beginning of the twentieth century the upper Derwent valley was almost perfect for building the two reservoirs. The valley is deep cut, steep sided and narrow, making construction of the dams simpler while allowing huge amounts of water to be contained; well-placed rock outcrops could act as secure foundations, the high altitude meant high rainfall, gravity could supply the water to where it was required and few people lived in the area, so disruption was minimal. This was not the case when the later Ladybower Reservoir was built between 1935 and 1943, drowning the villages of Derwent and Ashopton.

The landscape changes as the valley constricts and the upper reaches of Howden Reservoir are squeezed into a Y shape, echoing the courses of the drowned Derwent and Westend Rivers. The Cow Heys shown on the map on either side of Howden were not formerly separated by a hundred yards of water and the scant walls remaining here once enclosed cattle, not trees. A sausage of fur, a little stoat, dashed across the track in front of me while a cuckoo called in the woods, no doubt busy prospecting some eviction job. Approaching the head of Howden Reservoir, having already walked for an hour, it is possible to look across at the cars parked at the end of the road and feel a sense of moral superiority over the walkers who have merely set off from there. It may be a feeling of physical inferiority by the end of the day.

Beyond the reservoir, at Slippery Stones, a seventeenth-century packhorse bridge, in excellent condition, crosses the Derwent. Threatened with drowning when Ladybower was being built, the scheduled ancient monument was dismantled and reconstructed here in 1959. The name comes from the large stepping stones that were formerly the only way to cross the river. It is a popular stopping place for walkers and cyclists, for the round of the reservoirs is a popular route, and the latter are nannied – 'Caution. Steep Descent. Rough Ground' – and this on the track! You cross Bull Clough at the Fred Heardman Memorial footbridge. Fred was a former landlord of the Old Nags Head in Edale at the start of the Pennine Way. Known as Bill the Bogtrotter, he set up the first Edale Mountain Rescue Team in the early 1950s and was an inveterate walker who had been the first to cross the 56 miles (90km) of Kinder and Bleaklow and back in

under ten hours while negotiating the bogs and avoiding gamekeepers.

The valley continues to narrow and turns to climb gradually to the west by Oaken Bank, a semi-natural pocket of ancient woodland which has aspen and hawthorn as well as oak and birch. The valley seems to be richer in wildlife than many in the Pennines, possibly as a result of sheep being excluded. I put up my first grouse of the day at the end of the woodland and followed the track to its finish at Lands Clough, where a corrugated-iron shelter stands, presumably connected to the grouse butts on the hillside above. The moor rising on the far side of the valley reminds us of the earlier name of this stretch of the Derwent, Ronksley River. A path, in turn stone-flagged, a narrow trod through heather, a sandy-bottomed groove in the peat and a broad sphagnum squelch, continues to follow the Derwent, now a smaller stream in a wider valley. Its bright water skips and slides over little falls and rapids, and views open up of Barrow Stones and Shepherds Meeting Stones on either side of the valley. Someone was sitting on the top of the latter and waved, although if it was a shepherd vainly waiting for his fellows I couldn't tell. A sudden narrowing of the valley into as classic a V-shape as you're likely to see and a sharp turn to the southwest mark the beginning of a steeper climb, which ends in the upland bowl of Swains Greave.

With the cloud down and the rain pelting, this is an inhospitable spot, where myriad headstreams come together to form the Derwent. On a warm, dry day, with the larks singing, it's pleasant enough and on this warm, dry day I found the source in an area of sphagnum moss below the final climb on to the high ground stretching from Barrow Stones to Bleaklow. A filigree of dry gullies and groughs stretches away which, in a wet spell, can be transformed into torrents and soggy channels draining off the moors.

Crossing the fence built around the upper slopes of Bleaklow as part of the Moors for the Future

Partnership project I climbed up the dry channel that, on a wet day, would be the furthest headwater. Part of the way up I found a little spring whose water soon sank back into the peat and higher still disturbed a grouse nest. Mother shot off into the air while her half dozen or so chicks exploded from the nest, scattering in all directions. They are wonderfully camouflaged and if they weren't moving it would be all but impossible to see them against the heather. Above Swains Greave is the Bleaklow plateau. When you remember that 'low' is derived from an old English word for 'a hill', Bleaklow becomes one of the most descriptive of place names. It is a strange place, a sprawling, sodden, peat-hag-ridden plateau with gritstone outcrops round the edges; a degenerate, leached-out landscape. The top of Bleaklow has been likened to a desert and the scenery certainly gives the impression of emptiness, while some of the hags have the shape, if not

the colour, of dunes. Mind, when the rain is sheeting down as it often does, the desert imagery is hard to take.

The Moors for the Future Partnership is aiming to halt the deterioration of these uplands and restore the vegetation in order to prevent further large-scale erosion of the peat. The fence is to keep out sheep while the new heather is established and the area certainly seems to be more vegetated than it was a few years ago before the project started. There are still deep groughs where the peat has been eroded away to a bed of sand underneath. These meander around in all directions but rarely the one in which you wish to go. Some of the groughs have had piles of logs dumped into them, part of the gully-blocking programme which aims to prevent further erosion in the channels, trap peat particles and raise the water table. I popped out of a grough and Bleaklow Stones, one of the hill's summits

Upper Derwent valley

though it hardly deserves the name on this vast plateau, appeared half a mile (0.8km) away along the broad ridge. Sporadically marked by stakes, this is the watershed of England, a fact that will elicit a hollow laugh from anyone who has experienced it on a wet day. As a watershed, Bleaklow has a lot to learn.

The Stones are fascinating. A collection of sandblasted aeolian statues, the Anvil is the most easily recognized while some of the others look like Henry Moore cast-offs. The walk back to Fairholmes took me over Westend Head, source of one of Derwent's early tributaries, and along The Ridge, where I was surrounded by clouds of aphids. It's a long trek, most of the western stretch of the Derwent Skyline Walk, taking in Alport Moor, Westend Moor with its lonely trig point and Rowlee Pasture. The highlight is the sight of Alport Castles, reckoned to be the result of the largest landslip in Britain, with its spectacular Tower and the strangely semi-detached Little Moor.

When I reached the top of the forest below Lockerbrook Heights, a concession footpath took me down through the woods and back to the visitor centre. One of these days I shall find out the difference between a permissive path and a concession footpath. Perhaps the former is for young, thrusting types while the latter is aimed at the elderly, clutching their bus passes. I know which I felt more like after my six and a half hours out on the moors.

A shorter source walk of about 8 miles (12.8km) can be started, access permitting, from King's Tree at the end of the Derwent valley road. From the barrier the track leads down to stepping stones across Linch Clough and goes through the trees to cross the packhorse bridge at Slippery Stones to climb and join the track on the east side of Derwent by the Fred Heardman footbridge. From here the route is the one described above up to Swains Greave and the source. From the watershed you can follow the ridge across to Grinah Stones and Barrow Stones, the walk between the two outcrops giving fine views over the valley to Derwent Edge and the chance of passing a small sign, in a cairn on the side

Bleaklow Stones

of a grough, proclaiming this spot to be the source of the Derwent. A lack of any water in the vicinity seemed to gainsay the bold statement, but at least someone's taken the trouble. Returning to the large outcrop south of Barrow Stones, the next target is the cairn shelter on Round Hill. Heading down towards Lower Small Clough, you will meet a track that was excavated to transport the grouse shooters to the stone-walled, corrugated-iron-roofed huts located at the head of the valley. These are generally open, contain a visitors' book and are a boon in poor weather. Continuing in virtually the same direction you will meet the head of Linch Clough – 'ridge valley' rather than the place where irate grouse shooters, or football supporters, sort out walkers, or Derby County managers – and you can follow this down to a grassy path which leads through the trees back to the stepping stones and King's Tree.

You can make an approach to Swains Greave from the north, from the car park by the western end of Woodhead railway tunnel. The first part of the route follows the Trans Pennine Trail to cross the A628 to a stile. Walking up the hill you reach a broad track, now part of the TPT but formerly an important packhorse route between Cheshire and Yorkshire. The track contours below Longside Edge to cross the A628 again and descend to Lady Shaw Bridge at Saltersbrook, the seventeenth-century bridge overshadowed by its later counterpart. Further up the track divides, with the TPT heading off on the left. Continuing straight on and crossing a stile to a wall end, you can avoid a wet section of the track by taking a path to the right which rejoins it further along. Arriving at the remains of the medieval boundary marker of Lady Cross you abandon the track for a path, generally clear but sometimes boggy, that leads over Round Hill and up to the watershed by a small cairn. To the north rise headstreams of the Don and the Etherow while southwards everything is draining down to Derwent. Heading right along the path as it traverses peat groughs and hags, you reach Swains Head. Here a

fence and stile help with location. There are good views of the upper Derwent valley and across the fretted basin of Swains Greave to Barrow Stones. The committed source seeker may wish to drop down into the hollow to find the first trickle of the Derwent but those content to view from afar will continue along the watershed until, after a third of a mile (0.5km), the path swings away to the south. From here a walk of about 300 yards (275m) west across the moor leads to a path heading north into Far Black Clough. With its crags and waterfalls, this is a fine little Pennine valley. Further down the path becomes a track serving grouse butts and, having crossed the stream at a ford, follows the Etherow back to the car park.

Of course, to pay proper homage to the Derwent it is necessary to walk the full 40 challenging miles (64km) of the Derwent Watershed, the classic High Peak challenge, taking in Mam Tor, Lose Hill, Win Hill, Margery Hill, Howden Edge, Bleaklow Stones and Head, Kinder Scout and Brown Knoll; the secret is to not lose Hope early on.

Calder
Castleford lasses must needs be fair

	CALDER	
SOURCE	Heald Moor, Lancashire	
G.R.	SD 880 268	
LENGTH	45 miles (72 kilometres)	
TRIBUTARIES	Hebden Water, Ryburn, Colne, Smithy Brook	
MOUTH	confluence with Aire, Castleford	

The Yorkshire Calder is one of half a dozen rivers with the name, derived from the Old Celtic for 'violent stream', in Britain. The two or three small streams which are the headwaters of this Calder actually rise just across the county boundary, in

Lancashire, while another river of the same name has its source less than a mile away and heads off down the other side of the watershed to join the Ribble. The Yorkshire version flows generally eastwards for about 45 miles (72km), through Hebden Bridge, Halifax and Wakefield, to its confluence with the Aire near Castleford. The upper reaches of the Calder valley are narrow and deep, for five or six miles rarely attaining a width of more than a couple of hundred yards, and hemmed in by steep slopes. At Hebden Bridge the Hebden joins the Calder and the valley gradually widens out until, beyond Halifax, it meanders across a broad, level plain.

I drove along the upper length of the Calder Valley above Todmorden, a place that my father always said would scare the pants off any German alighting from a train and reading the station sign. Passing through the little linear settlements of Vale, Cornholme and Portsmouth with their

In Ratten Clough

towering mills, railway viaducts and hemmed-in terraces, it is difficult to picture the valley in its natural wildness, for the entire area is imbued with the remains of industry. However, wild it once was, and never more so than during the last Ice Age, when escaping glacial melt water flooded over the watershed, exploiting the fault lines that seam the Cliviger Gorge, to gouge out the valley we see cluttered now.

One of the Pennines' lesser-known gems, Cliviger is well worth exploring and a walk around the area, criss-crossing the watershed, has the added bonus of visiting three river sources. A parking place at the foot of Ratten Clough, oxbowed by road straightening, is a good place to start. It promises information as well as parking but, apart from an overgrown sign – indicating that this was a millennium project – standing forlornly in the bracken, there was none. A field gate gives access to the clough and it is possible to climb steeply and tentatively beside the Calder, and sometimes in it, past a series of waterfalls and slides, to a gritstone-walled amphitheatre, where a final fall tumbling over a rocky bastion bars passage to the sprawling moorland above. Well, it barred my passage and I had to skirt under the crag across bilberry-clothed terraces to climb steeply up a grassy nose to a broken wall leading back to the stream tumbling down rocky little falls across the moor. During the scramble up Ratten Clough the geologist will enjoy examining the Holcombe Brook Grit, the Lower and Upper Haslingden Flagstones and the Rough Rock Millstone Grit, while the ordinary mortal will be pleased to have survived.

You can follow the young Calder from here, along its upper valley hanging high over Cliviger to the source, but there are easier ways than the ascent of Ratten Clough. Just along the grass verge south of the car park, the road crosses the Calder at the bottom of the clough and a path heads off through Chatham Hill plantation to reach the open moor above a farm. From here the townships of the

Yorkshire Calder's source

Calder valley can be seen stretching away south-eastwards from Portsmouth. You may wonder why such maritime-sounding place names exist in an area so far from the sea but the explanation lies in a local lad who joined the navy. When he came home from the sea he named the local pub Portsmouth, the dairy Whitehaven and the joiner's house Chatham.

Above Green's Farm I followed the Burnley Way along a track for a short distance before it veers off to the right to climb on to Heald Moor. The track continues alongside Green's Clough, one of Calder's headwaters, and soon passes Hill Top Colliery, a drift mine, gently humming away to itself but at the time of writing due to close in less than a year. Several abandoned lorry trailers add little to the scenic beauty and a line of electricity pylons marches across the col between Heald Moor and Carr and Crags Moor where the various sources of the Green's Clough stream are to be found. One spring emerges from beneath a pile of gritstone boulders beside the track.

A stretch of tarmac leads to the unprepossessing environs of Heald Top Farm, which was having a hay delivery as I passed through. Numerous paths and tracks converge here confusingly and the

farm is just on the crease of the map so, not for the first time, I mouthed my thanks to Mr Bender. He was an employee of the Ordnance Survey who, in the 1930s, invented the concertina-style 'Bender Fold' which allows any part of the sheet to be looked at without opening it out completely. Mind, that was not the only reason I had to be grateful to the Survey as I was sporting a pair of their socks, emblazoned with the distinctive blue and pink OS symbol, given away free with the purchase of a map at my local outdoors store. Heading north-west through two gates, I followed a green road, formerly a section of Limers Gate, an ancient highway between Rochdale and Clitheroe. There are several so named in the area, reminding us that lime was essential for improving the poor soils of the Pennine moors and that gate is a northern word for 'a path or track'.

I had crossed the watershed before Heald Top Farm and was now in the Irwell's gathering grounds. I was to cross it twice again before I got to the Deerplay Inn, clearly visible a couple of miles away, behind which Irwell rises. A track climbing on to Heald Moor led past tumbled drystone walls and sheepfolds, where I marvelled once more at the skill and tenacity of the wallers who had threaded these moors with miles of their craft, to an old quarry currently embellished with oil drums and scrap metal. A slight descent across one of the most tussocky moors I can remember brought me to the source of the Yorkshire Calder, the North Sea-bound water trickling away from a rushy depression in a gentle col. The shaley ground beside the stream had been churned up in places by mountain bikes and traversing some sections was like walking across a colliery yard.

A gentle climb over soft moss and then more tussocks and rushes took me over the watershed again, crossing the Burnley Way to a descent alongside a field wall to a footpath and a crossing of the culverted and gated Irwell. The river was once given the sobriquet 'the hardest worked stream in the world', and even these upper reaches betray their industrial past, as the bed is stained red with ochre from the Deerplay Colliery which worked the Union Seam under these bleak moors. It was so high up that in winter the miners sometimes had to dig their way into the mine through the snow and the management ran the ventilation fan in reverse to force out the warmer air to defrost the motors for the coal conveyor in the surface drift. Deerplay was the highest mine in Lancashire, started in the mid nineteenth century and closing in 1968 when nearly 94,000 tons of coal were raised. It was a sad day locally when the pit closed and the miners had a farewell drink in the Deerplay Arms standing at the colliery entrance. This was more than I did and it was a sad day for me, as the pub doesn't seem to open at lunchtime these days. A curving tarmac road behind a locked gate and a few piles of bricks are all that remain of the colliery now, apart from the polluted water, which is treated before it is discharged into the Irwell.

Further along the A671 Bacup–Burnley road, beside more old quarries, stands the war memorial erected in memory of the men from Weir village who died during the First World War. At the time the village was the site of the Irwell Springs Dyeworks and the land for the memorial was given by its owner. A west-facing stone bench behind the Scots granite cross proved to be a sun trap even in the middle of October. Looking east-south-east from the grassy quarry tips above the war memorial, the upper Irwell valley runs away towards Bacup. There are many springs on the south-western slopes of Heald Moor, Thieveley Pike and Deerplay Moor which contribute to the river but one spring is given singular predominance by its naming as Irwell Spring. This lies, not surprisingly, behind Irwell House, and is one of a couple of springs rising in a boggy field. The highest one now appears to flow from the corner of a building but the ground around here has been much disturbed

and the water runs away down an artificial ditch. This rather sums up the Irwell, as it spends a great deal of its early course trammelled and channelled when not actually culverted over. The river eventually runs for about 39 miles (63km) from source to its confluence with the Mersey east of Irlam in Manchester.

Climbing up for the fourth time today to the watershed by the trig point on top of Thieveley Pike, I mused on the reality of this Pennine divide. Not far away north or south any number of routeways speak of our ancestors' struggles to cross these moors: packhorse trails, the seemingly endless lock flights carrying the Rochdale Canal over its summit at Summit, canal and railway tunnels hacked and blasted through the rocks at Standedge and the giant cuttings and embankments on the M62 motorway all speak of the tremendous effort involved in getting from one side of t'ills to t' other.

Thieveley Pike, an ancient beacon site at 1,473 feet (449m) and the highest point on the Burnley Way, gives long views north across the urban sprawl of Burnley and Colne to distant Malham Cove and Fountains Fell. When you look east across Cliviger the two dozen turbines of the Coal Clough Wind Farm are prominent. One of the oldest onshore wind farms in England, Coal Clough generates enough power for 5,500 homes. Except it wasn't, not today anyway. The anticyclonic conditions that gave me October sunshine meant that there was no flap of wind to turn them.

I still had one more river to find and one more watershed to cross, and so made my way northwards along the Burnley Way to descend quite steeply over Deerplay Moor and then Dean Scout to a gate at a path junction with a multiplicity of signs. Near by is a picnic site at the ruins of Thieveley Farm, a popular spot for outings since Victorian times. A prominent rock pillar protruding on the south-eastern flank of Dean Scout is known as Beacon Rock. The crags of Thieveley Scout stretch

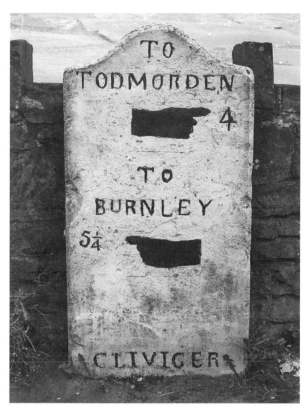

This way, that way

Thieveley welcome

away south towards Todmorden and I turned right to follow a path parallel to them, helpfully labelled 'TO CALDER HEAD'. I could soon hear the unmistakable sound of running water below me to the right and there, in the middle of a boggy basin, partly planted

with trees, is the source of the Lancashire Calder. At first the stream heads off south-eastwards, as if intent on joining its Yorkshire namesake.

This area is now part of the Forest of Burnley, a project started in 1997 to create 1,000 acres (405ha) of new native woodland as well as improving existing woods to double the town's woodland cover. Around Thieveley Scout over 90,000 trees have been planted and the exclusion of sheep has allowed some natural regeneration to occur. Many of the forest projects are along or near to the Burnley Way, a 40-mile (64km) route taking in lengths of the Lancashire Calder riverside and canal towpaths as well as the wilder land of the south Pennine moors. It is a walk that neatly contrasts the past and present, visiting Burnley's historic Weavers' Triangle and disused quarries as well as passing the Coal Clough wind farm and the regenerated countryside. For the visitor with two or three days to spare who wishes to gain an insight into the geography and history of the Lancashire Pennines, the Burnley Way gives an elucidatory introduction as well as a memorable walk. And that's from a lifelong Blackburn Rovers supporter!

The Lancashire Calder flows towards its Yorkshire sister for less than half a mile before being deflected through 180 degrees to begin its 15-mile (24km) journey north-westwards to the Ribble. The path follows it for a while before crossing the little stream at the top of a steep, wooded clough down which tumbles the Calder to Cliviger. This stretch shows the continuing forces of erosion where new gullies caused by heavy rain seam down from the crags above. The path soon loops round to bury beneath the railway before joining the A646 Burnley–Todmorden road via a dinky little gate. A walk along the road, over the barely perceptible Calder divide at a fine milestone, soon led back to the car park. I reckoned I'd crossed a watershed five times today and, thanks to my OS socks, I hadn't got lost once.

URBAN INTERLUDES

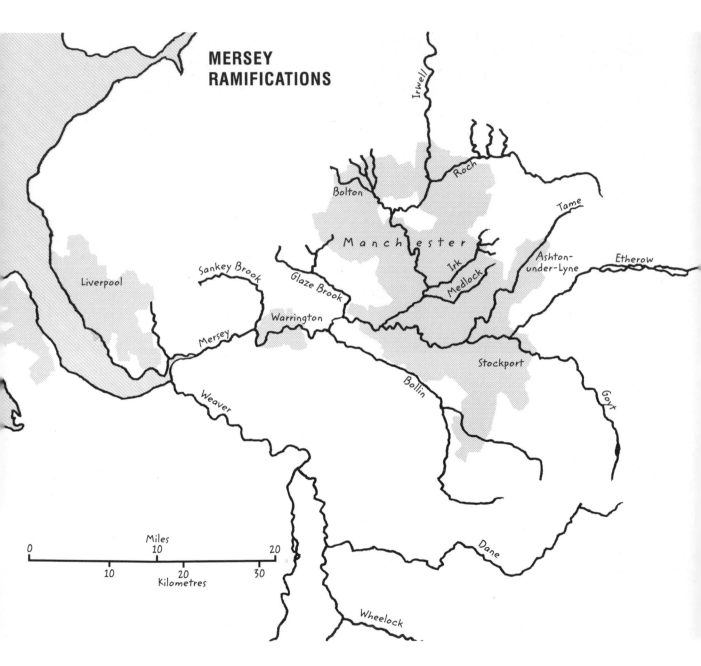

A couple of trips down some of the more recondite alleys of source hunting. The Ordnance Survey map and compass can be replaced by an A–Z while a bus pass will be handier in some places than walking boots. In more extreme cases dowsing rods might be called for. As a relief from the solidly urban, in this chapter Mersey's headstreams are tracked back to their sources far away from all the soot and noise of the city, high up on the Pennine watershed.

Tame

damp tips . . . of weak headwaters

TAME	
SOURCE	Oldbury Arm - Blackheath, West Midlands
	Wolverhampton Arm - Wednesfield, West Midlands
G.R.	SO 978 872
	SJ 954 009
LENGTH	25 miles (40 kilometres)
TRIBUTARIES	Rea, Blythe, Cole, Bourne
MOUTH	confluence with Trent, Alrewas

Wood Green, Friar Park, Stowheath, Priestfield, Blackheath and the Rowley Hills, bucolic-sounding names which echo a time when this midland Tame flowed free, when this dark river was dark in name only. In 1817, the Staffordshire historian William Pitt described the valley as 'rich, fertile and pleasant, and the surrounding countryside picturesque'.

The Tame is my nearest real river but it is one of those streams that you can cross thousands of times without knowing it. It has two main sources which feed headwater tributaries known as the Oldbury and Wolverhampton Arms. These join at Bescot under the long legs of the stilted M6. This is a secret spot known by millions as 'that place in Brum, you know, where the RAC Centre is', from where the river flows eastwards to the north of Birmingham city centre. The river Rea joins the Tame in Nechells, just east of Spaghetti Junction, the Gravelly Hill M6 motorway interchange. Flowing out of the conurbation the river then turns north after its confluence with the rivers Blythe, Cole and Bourne and passes through a series of purification lakes at Lea Marston. After this, the Tame continues to flow northwards, through Tamworth, eventually joining the Trent by the National Memorial

Arboretum, just east of Alrewas. The Tame is the Trent's largest tributary and the major river system in the West Midlands conurbation. Its catchment covers an area of over 900 square miles (2,331 sq. km) with a main river length of about 25 miles (40km). Flowing through an area with a population of 10 million and with an industrial history stretching back four centuries, it is hardly surprising that the river is officially described as being 'heavily modified', meaning that it bears scant resemblance to its natural form in terms of its channel characteristics and course, with large sections being culverted or canalized.

The wide upper Tame valley through which the river once flowed gently was for centuries a heath, hardly disturbed by man. This monotonous landscape broken only by low hills of glacial drift, the sites of Darlaston, Wednesbury and Bilston, became one of the most concentrated industrial regions in the world between the mid-eighteenth and the mid-twentieth centuries. The river helped the industrialization by supplying water and powering early mills but was later exploited and forgotten, the banks, and the river itself in many places, built over and the water polluted with industrial waste and sewage. In 1921 the Ministry of Agriculture and Fisheries had established a Standing Committee on River Pollution (SCORP), tasked with investigating polluted rivers. The Committee's report in 1930 described the Oldbury Arm at Bescot as 'dirty, yellow, opalescent and . . . turbid'. Three years later the Wolverhampton Arm at Bescot was 'exceedingly foul and turbid with all the appearance of stale, crude sewage. Masses of black sludge were floating on the surface of the water. Gas was bubbling freely all over the bed of the river. Masses of grey fungus were waving in the water.' By the end of the Second World War the Tame was so filthy it supported no life.

Rather like the coal miners who once hewed a living in the upper reaches of the Tame's catchment area where an almost horizontal 30-foot (9m)

thick seam was found close to the surface, the river spends a lot of its time underground, culverted and hidden from sight, so that its present course is sometimes different from its natural route and often difficult to follow. According to the SMURF[12] Project website, the source of the Oldbury Arm is adjacent to the M5 motorway, just to the south of Titford Pools. These were originally created as a reservoir for the Birmingham Canal and date from 1773–4 when a dam was raised to enclose a 9-acre (3.6ha) site. The pools were supplied with water from the Rowley Hills, where several springs and runnels could lay claim to be the Tame's source. If they could be found! A short stretch of infant Tame can be seen, behind steel fencing and running through a concrete channel, behind a children's playground at the north end of York Road. Emerging from beneath no. 75, it quickly scurries away beneath the motorway. Visiting fairly early on a Sunday morning turned out to be a boon, for at the end of York Road, where it joins Penncricket Lane, is a mini-roundabout, in the middle of which is a manhole cover, beneath which can be heard running water. Come here at any other time, except in the middle of the night when your motives might be suspected, and you wouldn't hear the water for the traffic. A series of manhole plates with names reminiscent of tanks or quidditch brooms – Ductile, Stanton PLC, M IV, Chieftan 600 – leads the explorer up to the crossroads and into Mincing Lane, where the subterranean sound seems to disappear.

Urban source seeking is a somewhat esoteric pastime and a fluorescent Severn–Trent jacket and a set of divining rods would be a useful bit of kit. Comparisons of old maps with present-day ones point to a couple of headsprings rising in Blackheath. The Blackheath of today would be barely recognizable even to someone who knew the place forty years back and finding locations marked on maps of over a century ago is not easy. However,

Visible Tame!

there is certainly a bit of a dip in Cardale Street where several manhole covers are found and just off Birmingham Road is the suggestive-sounding Spring Avenue, which stands close to the site of a range of buildings, indicated on the 1902 Ordnance map, by which another stream rose.

The Wolverhampton Arm itself has two branches which rise in the Neachells and Stow Lawn areas, about 1½ miles (2.4km) apart. Watery Lane is as fine a clue on the map as any and this, leading from Neachells Lane in an indistinct area between Wednesfield and Willenhall, is a good starting point for an exploration of the upper reaches of the north branch, hereabouts known as Waddens Brook. Walking along Watery Lane past burgeoning industrial parks, Taylormade Forging and Bespoke Bolting seem to speak of Savile Row as much as

12 Sustainable Management of Urban Rivers and Floodplains.

this part of industrial greater Wolverhampton. As you head north, towards the source, across a typical twenty-first century Black Country landscape of wasteland, warehouses, fly-tipping and tethered horses and with birdsong twittering incongruously above, the stream meanders through naturally regenerated woodland and past boggy little pools. In contrast to the lower stretches of the river, here the water is crystal clear and populated with water skaters. Turn-of-the-twentieth-century maps show Waddens Brook flowing through the disused Merrill's Hole Colliery and you will see, in the damp swags and eroded remnants of pit heaps, echoes of the vanished landscape. Ahead is the embankment of the former Midland Railway's Walsall-to-Wolverhampton line with the brook emerging from a brick culvert at its foot.

On the far side of the railway embankment, several pipes feed a murky pool almost beneath a factory wall and this seems to be Wadden Brook's first sight of daylight. Early maps show the brook extending further north and rising in the vicinity of Moat House but there is little evidence any more above ground. A public open space now stands south of the Lichfield Road across the road from the site of the former Moat House Farm and I found a pair of Silent Knight manhole covers where the path leads on to the open space. There is a strong flow under the western one and this appeared to be as close as I was likely to get to this northern source of the Tame.

The southern section of the Wolverhampton Arm of the upper Tame rises on the border of Stow Heath and Priestfield, an area arguably more interesting in the past than today, when it is covered by acres of housing. The river is certainly easier to follow on old maps than present-day ground. The Moseley Road Open Space car park makes a good base for exploration here. When I left it in bright sunshine, a flock of Canada geese occupied what they had left of the grass by the pool but when I returned twenty minutes later, in rain, they had been replaced by a multitude of pigeons. In the meantime I had followed a line of inspection covers across the open space behind the blocks of flats on Park View Road to a boggy area beside an air-quality monitoring station, which would appear to be the present start of this headwater. Turn-of-the-twentieth-century maps indicate that the source is further west and I suspect that there is a spring somewhere beneath the Stowheath Day Centre, and the slight dip in Stow Heath Lane by the currently derelict Hare and Hounds is where tiny Tame crossed the road to run down the north side of the pub's grounds.

Partially shadowed by the M6, the confluence of the headwaters lies in a complex area with a complex history at Bescot, south of Walsall, almost within tow-rope distance of the landmark RAC Operations Control Centre and kicking distance of Walsall FC's Banks's stadium. And, 'spake it loud an' spake it proud', very definitely not in Birmingham. This Black Country confluence can be approached from the south by way of St Paul's Road, Wood Green, which starts confidently between two schools but soon degenerates into post-industrial squalor, passing through a fly-tipped, graffiti-smirched wasteland. The road turns into a path, hemmed in by fences, and the Oldbury Arm appears on the right, a shallow weir directing most of the flow to a complexity of concrete channels which disappear beneath the railway line. Here, in times of heavy flow at least, is the confluence, for the channel that parallels the railway is the Wolverhampton Arm and a spillway connects the two. The river was re-aligned when the M6 and M5 were constructed in the 1970s. It is difficult to conceive, in this desolate spot, that here stood a thriving industrial concern which lasted for four centuries and almost impossible to imagine the water meadows that existed along this broad, flat valley before that. The grazing cattle of Bescot, having once been supplanted by tilt hammers and iron forges, are now echoed by the Holstein-Friesian-patterned Robert Wiseman Dairy lorries passing on the M6, an event which, during a Walsall FC home game, occasions loud mooing from the home fans.

It surprises the modern-day visitor that so many water-driven mills once existed along these upper reaches of the Tame. Nearly fifty stood on the various branches of the river in Staffordshire alone, some of them on streams that seem too small to turn a wheel and some on stretches where the water is now underground. Our ancestors were very skilled in the control and use of the resources they possessed and some of the water mills worked for centuries, grinding corn, dressing leather, sawing wood, crushing seed and pumping water as well as being used for the iron-working processes which proliferated later.

The industrial history of this site at the confluence of the Tame's headwaters is a microcosm of the economic narrative of the Black Country and, in some ways, of Britain. It is believed that there was a water-powered forge on the Bescot site from about

1590. Standing by the confluence, the mill had the benefit of supply from two dammed sources and had floodgates to control the flow. The mill, known as Wednesbury Forge, eventually came under the control of the local iron-making Foley family and in the years 1667–72 it was producing between 67½ and 141 tons of iron annually.

Wednesbury Forge continued to be used for iron working and at various times during the eighteenth century it was rolling iron, making saws and grinding gun barrels. It saw its tragedies as in 1758 when a boy, William Toms, fell into one of the forge pools and was drowned and nine years later when Joseph Stevens was killed by a grinding stone breaking while he was working on it. In 1817, Edward Elwell took over Wednesbury Forge and started to develop it into a large concern, building a tall chimney that was a local landmark for decades and constructing a new pool fed by Tame water.

The railways had a large effect on the local

Underneath the arches, Tame confluence, Bescot

landscape, starting with the Grand Junction Railway, opened in 1837 and following the easy gradients along the Tame Valley. Running from Birmingham to join the Liverpool and Manchester line near Warrington, it was part of the first trunk railway and was one of the major limbs of what later became the London & North Western company. The Wolverhampton Arm of the river was diverted to run alongside the railway, passing under it through the triple brick arches visible today. In 1850 the South Staffordshire Railway was built at right angles across the Grand Junction and passed over Elwell's Pool on a wooden viaduct. Nine years later a goods train came off the rails and fell into the pool.

During the American Civil War in the 1860s, Elwell's sold large quantities of edge tools to the States and developed important export markets around the world. The company's catalogue listed over 1,200 kinds and sizes of hand tools, such as forks, hoes, pick axes, spades, axes and shovels. The Elwell family, who built nearby St Paul's Church and a school for the workers' children, maintained control until 1902 when Alfred, a grandson of the founder, died. The concern became a private limited company, combining with the Chillington Tool Company of Wolverhampton around 1930 to become Edge Tool Industries. Latterly it was part of the Spear and Jackson group but the Wednesbury Forge site was closed in 2005 and the site cleared.

Excavation work by Ironbridge Archaeology Projects has revealed a wealth of evidence about the long history of the site. The area, fast reverting to scrub, is currently known as Opus 9 and is described as the Black Country's largest industrial development scheme. It will no doubt spring back into life when the recession ends.

Having crossed the main railway line, the footpath from St Paul's Road descends, only to climb once more, above the overhead power transmission cables on the line to Walsall, and this time it runs alongside the motorway for a few yards, giving a rare close-up view of the traffic speeding or crawling along this the busiest length of motorway in Europe. The bridge also gives a bird's-eye view over the river and railway line. On one visit, little groups of Eddie spotters were ensconced on the walkway, binoculars at the ready, looking out for Stobart lorries. They certainly had time to note down the lorry names as, on this Friday afternoon, the water in the river below was flowing faster than the vehicles above. I wondered if these elderly men had been here half a century and more ago, looking the other way for Coronations and Britannias.

A little further on and you reach the confluence. In fact there are two. When the M6 was built across the Tame's flood plain and along much of its urban section through the Black Country, it was constructed on stilts. Here, on the section known as the Bescot Viaduct, a quartet of them stands on a serpentine concrete island, with the waters of the Wolverhampton Arm flowing along both sides to join the Oldbury Arm and make the river proper. Here, beneath the roadway, the concrete columns sprout like some dystopian temple, decorated by the daubings of the votaries, 'Licka, Jake and Dane, the WS10 boyz'. But even in this labyrinth nature fights on: pigeons roost in the shadows while a couple of apple trees bear fruit and the brambles spread their branches through the litter.

The sources of the Tame have none of the grandeur of some of the others described here, they and their surroundings posses nothing of beauty about them, but they are witnesses to an intriguing past and they have survived centuries of abuse. Who is to say that in another half millennium the Tame will not once more flow through a heath, hardly disturbed by man?

Stour
how calm and clear it flows

Of the several rivers with the name Stour in England, this is without doubt the most crossed but

STOUR	
SOURCE	St. Kenelm's Well, Worcestershire
G.R.	SO 944 807
LENGTH	30 miles (50 kilometres)
TRIBUTARIES	Smestow Brook
MOUTH	confluence with Severn, Stourport-on-Severn

least acknowledged. Just over 8 of its 30 or so miles (50km) lie within the West Midlands conurbation and the river has suffered for its location at the heart of the industrial revolution. At one time there were forty-two forges, furnaces and mills using water power on the 5 miles (8km) between Halesowen and Stourbridge. Half a dozen major roads and nearly twenty lesser ones now cross the Stour in its urban journey from Halesowen to Amblecote via Cradley, Quarry Bank, Lye, Stambermill and Stourbridge. Some stretches are culverted over and in many places the river is secretive and hard to follow. Freed from its workaday shackles the Stour then meanders gleefully for a couple of miles through meadows around Prestwood until at Stourton it is crossed by the Staffordshire and Worcestershire Canal (the second time it has flowed beneath an aqueduct, for the Stourbridge Canal crosses just as it leaves the conurbation) and is joined by its major tributary, the Smestow Brook. Here the river turns south and, hounded by the canal, flows through woods and meadows by Kinver and Wolverley to Kidderminster, where once more it is canal-crossed and culverted. Its final few miles take the Stour ruefully past sewage works and under electricity cables until it apologetically joins the Severn, its murky waters being prevented from joining directly by piling which deflects it 50 yards (46m) downstream of the natural confluence.

The Stour's end may be disappointing but its beginning is delightful. Around 800 feet (244m) on the eastern slopes of the Clent hills a number of springs vie to be the source. Legend grants the honour to St Kenelm's Well but another lower down at Spring Farm has a stronger flow, while local historians have identified a further well to the north of the deserted village of Kenelmstow. Given the springs rising in Uffmoor Wood and further headwaters starting by St Kenelm's Road there is ample scope for exploration.

A walk of less than 2 miles (3.2km) is enough to visit the main sites. From the car park on Uffmoor Lane a well-walked path heads north, running parallel to the lane and crossing several tricklets before emerging on the road opposite St Kenelm's Cottage, a building named with fine Victorian understatement. Crossing the road and the infant Stour, a narrow, well-walked, stream-side path runs off on the left, through wild garlic and dog's mercury, to climb gently through woods across a succession of small fields. There are many holly trees in the woods, bird boxes and human-scale baths, and the path crosses into Penorchard Meadows, a large area of semi-natural grassland looked after by the Worcestershire Wildlife Trust. The fields have never been ploughed, no artificial fertilizer has been used and grazing has been minimal for a long time. The meadows are therefore home to a number of rare plant species, including crested dog's-tail, common bird's-foot trefoil and the common spotted orchid. Damp areas host species like water mint, lesser spearwort, ragged-robin and jointed rush, and other plants of interest in the reserve include eyebright, yellow rattle, dyer's greenweed and yellow-wort.

St Kenelm's Church comes into view and with it the first of the Stour's sources. According to legend the spring rises over the spot where the boy king Kenelm was buried after being murdered and beheaded at the behest of his sister, Quenrida, in AD 821. Buried under a thorn tree, his body was later discovered by missionaries from Rome alerted by a scroll, dropped by a white dove, Kenelm's own soul, at the feet of the Pope. The scroll carried the message 'Low in a mead of kine under a thorn, of head bereaft, lieth poor Kenelm king-born' and the Papal emissaries were sent to investigate. Meeting an old woman tending a herd of cattle on the slopes of the Clent Hills, they noticed one cow standing on its own by a thorn tree. Although the cow neither ate nor drank, it never went hungry and they surmised that it must have been guarding the spot where the

St Kenelm's church

St Kenelm's well

king lay. As they dug to find the remains a spring started to flow: St Kenelm's Well. The well quickly gained a reputation for its healing powers, a shrine was founded and the village of Kenelmstow grew up around it. Pilgrims travelled from far away to visit the healing well – and the Red Cow, named in honour of the legendary beast. Strips of cloth, including a tie, hanging in a bush over the site of the well, showed that it was still visited. The nearby stone well head with its two low walls to channel water was built in 1985 by Lord Cobham of Hagley Hall. The area has been landscaped with flights of wooden steps, and the Kenelm legend was interpreted and celebrated in wooden and stone sculptures by Michael Fairfax and the people of Romsley and Hunnington in 1995. A dozen or so of the stones alongside the channel have been carved with scenes from the legend and several pairs of wooden columns stand around the site.

The church itself has a twelfth-century red sandstone nave that links directly into the chancel, a greenish sandstone fifteenth-century tower and a timber porch. Weathered gargoyles and carved initials decorate the outside of the building while the inside is cool and peaceful.

The walk continues northwestwards across a couple of horsey fields which give fine views to the north-east over the Black Country conurbation of Halesowen, Stourbridge and Dudley to the ridge, stretching from Sedgley Beacon, Dudley Castle Hill and Turners Hill with its masts across to the topknot of Frankley Beeches. This side of the ridge is the drainage basin of the Stour while the far side is the Tame catchment, and so it forms a section of the English watershed with the Stour draining into the Severn and the Tame into the Trent.

As you cross a sunken lane, humps and hollows indicate the site of the lost village of Kenelmstow. Growing with the popularity of the healing well, it probably declined with the ending of pilgrimages after the Reformation. A pool, surrounded by trees and bushes, in the corner of a field on the north edge of Kenelmstow, is reckoned by some to be the Stour's source and a neolithic place of worship. A path heads off downhill and crosses another at a hedgerow. A right turn here follows the path down through trees towards Bogs Wood. The path crosses a strong stream, originating at the aptly named Spring Farm and a good claimant to be the true source, before it joins the farm road to arrive back at St Kenelm's Cottage and Uffmoor Wood. Possibly named after Offa, King of Mercia and Kenelm's grandfather, the wood was used by local people for centuries and parts of it were coppiced. In the 1970s Uffmoor was owned by a brush-making firm who planted many non-native pines and larches. It was acquired by the Woodland Trust in 1980 and a long-term plan is in place to replant it with native species. Bluebells were just starting to flower at the end of March and buzzards were mewing overhead as we made our way back to the car park.

Mersey, including Tame, Etherow and Goyt

water is life and heaven's gift

MERSEY	
SOURCE	Stockport, Greater Manchester
G.R.	SJ 897 908
LENGTH	69 miles (111 kilometres)
TRIBUTARIES	Irwell, Bollin, Weaver, Gowy
MOUTH	Liverpool Bay

For the dedicated source seeker, Mersey is the bonus river, for no fewer than five locations with some kind of claim can be visited. The river is now generally accepted as starting at the confluence of the Tame and the Goyt in the middle of Stockport, once of Cheshire and now in Greater Manchester, but some earlier authorities mark the source as the junction of the Goyt and the Etherow, about 7 miles

(11km) further upstream as the river meanders. The main river itself, at about 69 miles (111km), has a distance virtually equal to the sum of its three major feeders. In length order they read Tame, Goyt and Etherow, although there is but little more than a couple of miles' difference between them all. The tributary trio all have moorland birthplaces but Mersey is essentially urban.

It was just above a ford near the confluence of the Tame and that Goyt that Stockport first grew as a Saxon village. By Tudor times it was a small town on the south bank of the Mersey, growing hemp and making rope. In 1732 a water-powered silk mill was built on a Mersey meander and this early introduction to textiles meant the town was well placed to join in neighbouring Manchester's nineteenth-century cotton bonanza. Stockport also grew as a centre for hat making and by the 1880s the town was exporting more than six million a year. It now has a hat museum that you'd be mad to miss.

According to the philosopher Friedrich Engels, the town, in 1844, was 'renowned as one of the duskiest, smokiest holes in the whole of the industrial area'. Post-industrial Stockport has cleaned up its act, mills have become bedroom furniture emporia, railways are now horse, cycle and pedestrian trails and the site of an eighteenth-century water-powered calico printworks is a butterfly conservation area in the Reddish Vale Country Park. The park, a 398-acre (161ha) area of open space along the lower Tame valley, makes a good starting place for a walk, confusingly downstream, to the rather odd, confluential source of the Mersey. The visitor centre, closed on Fridays so no prizes for guessing which day I was there, and car park are at the foot of a steep lane near the millponds of the former printworks. A railway viaduct dominates the scene but the area seems remarkably rural after the motorways and urban roads taken to reach it. The park is well pathed and well signed but I had to do a little trespassing to stay by the river, which passes through the middle of a golf

In Reddish Vale Country Park

club. As it had snowed the previous night, active golfers were at a premium and he ignored me. As you cross the river from what had been Cheshire to what was once Lancashire, a faint path appears through the woods and a pleasant stretch follows along the hogweedy and knotweedy bank and then over river bluffs and along a cobbled track. A footbridge crosses the river once more, downstream from a weir that used to feed the Portwood Cut, a leat supplying a number of mills.

A path across snowy dog-walking meadows led me to a car park and once again to the riverside. First mills and then tower blocks came into view before the road, Tiviot Way, crosses the Tame. The six-storey brick-built Meadow Mill, built in the 1880s for cotton and wool spinning, contained 120,000 spindles in 1914. It now serves a variety of uses, like many of the surviving textile giants. The path, now part of the Trans Pennine Trail, follows the Tame as it curves round behind the mill

complex, overlooked by the green pencil blocks of Hanover and Pendlebury Towers on Lancashire Hill. Soon walls and piling enclose the river and the remaining stonework of a demolished railway viaduct gives way to the concrete motorway bridge. A path, part of the Fred Perry Way designated in honour of one of Stockport's greatest sons, runs beneath the bridge to the confluence. Here beneath the M60 and overlooked by an old stone bridge over the Goyt, a sculptured steel fence informs that this watersmeet is indeed the source of the Mersey: 'HERE RIVERS GOYTS AND TAME BECOME MERSEY FLOWING CLEAR FROM STOCKPORT TO THE SEA.' The clarity of the water may sometimes be questioned but not that of the message, which was erected in 1995, a collaboration between local artists and schools. The immediate surroundings of the confluence are not inspiring but then Stockport's relationship with the river it conceives leaves a lot to be desired, as most of its first few hundred yards are culverted and covered

Confluence fence

by Merseyway, now Stockport's major shopping area, which was built in the mid-1960s on giant stilts above the river. In a no doubt millennium-inspired fit of optimism, there were plans in 2001 to install glass panels in the pavements within the shopping area in order to reveal the river and boost tourism. The scheme has not yet been developed and this first length has not seen the light of day since 1934, when the Merseyway road was originally built over the river.

From east of the Reddish Vale Country Park forward views open out towards the Pennine moors above Denshaw and Stalybridge, where the various branches of the Tame rise 15 or so miles (24km) to the north-east. There are two other rivers with the same Tame name in England. The west Midlands one is the major tributary of the Trent and the other rises in North Yorkshire, being a feeder of the Leven, which joins the Tees. Closely related top-onymically are Thames, Thame, Tamar and Taff, all versions of a Celtic word possibly meaning 'dark' or simply 'river'. Like its west Midlands namesake, this Tame has a dark history of pollution. It flows through towns like Uppermill, Ashton-under-Lyne, Dukinfield, Denton and Hyde and its indus-trialized valley bequeathed a litany of muck. The bleaches and dyes of the woollen, cotton, felt and hatting trades, effluent from the manufacture of papers, batteries and engineering products, chemicals from the Denton coal-gas plant, rain drain from pit heaps and roads as well as sewage efflu-ent all contributed to the river's insalubrity. By the time it met the Goyt in Stockport, up to two-thirds of the Tame had passed through a sewage works. During the past forty years, largely as a result of anti-pollution measures and the decline of manu-facturing, the water quality has improved and fish populations have revived.

The Tame's headwaters rise in a fretted filigree of peat groughs north-east of White Hill, a mile or so south of the M62 as it cleaves its way across the Pennines between Manchester and Leeds. This is a wild and bleak area where the place names – Windy Hill, Moss Moor, Blacker Edge – say it all. The source can be most easily visited by following the Pennine Way north-west from the A640 Rochdale–Huddersfield road. The path crosses the little rise of Rapes Hill, which gives a good view across to the gathering grounds above Linsgreave Head. It is then a matter of following the stream, from where it is crossed by its highest, single-flagstone bridge, to where it begins in the peaty waste. A there-and-back stroll of a couple of miles will give a taster of this high moorland but a longer walk around the

Castleshaw and Denshaw valleys gives a fuller introduction to the upper reaches of the Tame valley.

Castleshaw fort guarded the Roman road between Deva (Chester) and Eboracum (York), where it began its climb up to the Pennine crest at Standedge and lies in what must have been a remote and exposed location, with clear views up to the hills and down to the Tame valley. Although it was probably only in use for about forty years around the end of the first century AD, after which it was superseded by neighbouring forts at Slack and Manchester, its outline is still etched into the landscape and it surveys the fields and factories as it once looked out over the forest. From the car park below the fort a path leads past the Castleshaw Centre, an outdoors centre since it was opened in 1895 by the Oldham Poor Children's Holiday Association, across fields in which a class of excited children was studying mole-hills, to Hull Beck. The path beside the beck leads past Hull Mill Dam and climbs above Eagle Mill Dam. Pennine water works! Once it powered mill after mill down the valley; now it fills reservoir after reservoir to wash clothes, flush toilets and make ice cubes. Hull Mill started as a cotton mill in the 1780s and during its two centuries of working life was used for wool carding and spinning, brick manufacture, shawl making, bleaching, dyeing and making industrial garments and surgical lint. It was demolished and the site is now occupied by housing. Part of Eagle Mill is incorporated into the Eagle Court housing development. At Delph, an archetypically Pennine name like nearby Dobcross, Denshaw and Diggle, all parts of the township of Saddleworth, Hull Beck joins the Tame. Although on the western side of the Pennines, Saddleworth was part of Yorkshire from the Middle Ages. The 1972 Local Government Act placed it in Oldham, in Greater Manchester, but the locals are resolutely Yorkshire in outlook and many houses sport the white rose.

At the confluence of Hull Beck and the Tame, a wall plaque marks the height reached by a flood of July 1872. The path follows the riverside past trim allotments where one of the holders reckoned that finally, in the first week of March, 'Spring has sprung, it's just around the corner.' This indecision surely reflects that of the Saddleworth mindset – definitely not Lancashire but not quite Yorkshire. Just past a lovely stone bridge a bench was graffitied 'DELPH collecting and harbouring weirdo's and misfits since 1854'. Judging by the dog mess carefully wrapped in a black plastic bag and left on the seat, it still is. This is one of the banes of the twenty-first century. Are these people simply so stupid as to think wrapping the stuff up is all they need to do, or is it some kind of twisted protest? It is not a problem confined to Delph; I've also seen it during my source searching at Syresham by the Great Ouse, in Malham near the incomparable Cove and above the Storey Arms in the Brecon Beacons. I've spoken to dog owners who, to a man and woman, condemn the practice. Delph also seems to suffer from another contemporary affliction – misplaced apostrophes.

As you continue up the Tame valley you pass a series of mills and former mills between Linfitts and Denshaw, which neatly illustrate the recent history of the British textile industry. There were once around thirty mills tucked into the Castleshaw and Denshaw valleys of the upper Tame. Most have been demolished and it came as a surprise to find one still working and producing textiles. It was the smell that did it for me and transported me back half a century to my cotton town childhood. The sweet, oily scent that I recognized immediately, wafting through the open doors of Pingle Mill, would have been known by most of my ancestors for generations back. My father worked as a tackler, maintaining and repairing the looms in a cotton mill, and I once spent a memorable few weeks working as a loom sweeper in a mill that's now a housing development. If you've ever seen those famous pictures of children crawling about under machinery, at Swainson and Birley's mill at Preston in 1834, you'll get the idea. The hot, humid, fleck-laden atmosphere of the weaving shed in the dying years of the old Lancashire cotton industry was more akin to the nineteenth century than the swinging sixties but it was the noise, an everlasting cacophony of mechanical discord, that left the greatest impression and lasted the weekend through. They're still spinning woollen yarn at Pingle Mill and, like the rest of the remaining British textile industry, they survive through specialization and innovation. Still, the smell's the same.

Readycon Dean reservoir

Just up the valley I passed the scant remains of Linfitts Mill, a few huge blocks of gritstone lying scattered about, one like a giant's dining table, while beyond an embankment are the remains of the mill pond. The 1891 OS map of Linfitts Mill shows lines of tenters, a tenter being the framework from which dyed or washed cloth was hung out to dry evenly with tenterhooks. There's no need to pass the site in a state of anxious suspense, however, as the path continues placidly onwards, giving views of the steepening valley ahead. The hamlet of Slackcote, reached up a rhododendron-flanked lane, was once a centre of hand-loom weaving, as is evidenced in the cottages with their broad mullioned windows which allowed in the maximum amount of light.

A particularly well-signposted stretch of path leads across Tameside meadows towards Denshaw, where you are welcomed by pigs, geese, hens and, when I was there at least, a contented ram stretched out on a pile of sacks. The riverside path runs past a new housing development, Denshaw Vale, which incorporates a couple of buildings from the large print works formerly standing here. The Tame passes under the main road, which can be followed left to a five-way junction in the middle of Denshaw. Roads from Rochdale, Ripponden, Huddersfield, Oldham and Manchester converge at the early nineteenth-century Junction Inn, making this a busy little place. It is even busier on Whit Friday when over a hundred bands congregate to

take part in the annual Saddleworth and District Brass Band Contests, staged at a dozen different locations in the area. From late afternoon a succession of bands play two pieces, one marching and one static, while an adjudicator, hidden away from sight, judges their performance. Then it is back on the bus to head off for the next venue. A spectator at one of the busier spots might expect to listen to fifty bands before the winners are announced late at night or even early the next morning. Denshaw's contest is a relative latecomer, started as recently as 1993, while some of the other Saddleworth villages have been blowing their own trumpets since the nineteenth century.

There is a choice of ways from Denshaw to the Tame's source, all of which have an element of road walking. I decided to head straight up Ripponden Road, opened as a turnpike in 1798 and taking a more direct route across the moor than the older road that ran further to the east. It provided a pavement and then a verge as far as the Ram's Head Inn, at 1,212 feet (369m). From here you can pick up the Pennine Bridleway and follow it across the hillside to the lush green of the grassed earth dam, constructed in 1883, that contains Readycon Dean reservoir. Just after the bridleway turns away from the water a track leads off through a gate to the head of the reservoir and you can follow the infant Tame fairly steeply past a rocky outcrop, pools and miniature waterfalls to where it is crossed by the Pennine Way. Just above the well-paved path a stile gives access to the moor above Linsgreave Head and, in the midst of this Tame wilderness of peat, you can choose your source. The streams running just yards away down from the other side of Linsgreave Head will end up in the Ryburn, a tributary of the Yorkshire Calder. One visit here coincided with a thaw, so progress was halting across banks of snow which couldn't quite make up their mind as to whether they were still frozen enough to support my weight or thawed enough to let me crunch through to the peat beneath. A couple of tennis rackets would have been handy.

Peat covers large areas of the Pennines around here and a walk along the Pennine Way in its early years taught me probably more about the stuff than was really necessary. Peat is formed when soft vegetation such as mosses and grasses die but only partially rot. On high ground this is due to waterlogging and low temperatures. Peat has been forming for thousands of years and built up to a depth of several yards on moorlands over vast areas of the Pennines. During the past couple of centuries, pollution by industry, over-grazing by sheep and burning have all contributed to the degradation and erosion of the vegetation cover, leaving large areas of bare, soggy, boot-trapping, strength-sapping peat. Further south, on Bleaklow, Black Hill and Kinder Scout the peat has deteriorated badly and schemes are currently in place to attempt to re-vegetate it. This is far more than a cosmetic exercise as carbon dioxide, locked into the peat as the vegetation slowly decomposes, is released into the atmosphere when it degenerates. The peat also regulates water flow by storing and gradually releasing it.

I first came this way in 1975. Like most good ideas – [it felt like a] and [at the time] may be inserted where best fits – the Pennine Way walk notion started in the pub and neighbour Mike and I were soon committed to a summer jaunt from Derbyshire to Scotland. The 270 miles took us fourteen days and by the end of it Mike had just about

broken in his boots. I don't think he's walked anywhere since. Obviously the Pennine Way passes close to many river sources but I didn't pay particular attention at the time, except when they came over my boot tops.

From Linsgreave Head it is only a short walk to the trig point on White Hill, a place where Alfred Wainwright, author of the best-selling *A Pennine Way Companion*, commented 'You will question your own sanity.' Thirty miles into the PW from Edale, the worst of the peat is behind the Wayfarer and nowadays much of the path has been improved. Our notes written at the time on my copy of Wainwright range from 'horrible' and 'a mess' to 'you must be joking' and 'you must be bloody joking'. Following the Pennine Way generally southwards from White Hill, the path enters the National Trust's massive Marsden estate to cross the Tame at two stone slab bridges before climbing Rapes Hill and dropping down to the A640 road between Rochdale and Huddersfield. Here, at Haigh Gutter, the Way passes another of the Tame headwaters before crossing Oldgate Moss to Northern Rotcher, a millstone grit outcrop which gives good views down into the Castleshaw valley. For the poetically inclined a diversion south-east of less than a mile, along the scarp which guards the cold, grey hills of the Tame–Colne watershed, takes you past the aptly named, flat-topped Dinner Stone to a memorial to a much-loved local poet and writer.

White Hill

Ammon Wrigley put into verse and prose his deeply personal views of the local world he knew was disappearing around him. On a day when the winds of the Pennines fresh and free are beating up on to Standedge from Castleshaw, it is very moving to stand at the 'green church' where his ashes were scattered and view the landscape that inspired his work.

On this occasion, though, I turned right at the Northern Rotcher on to the Oldham Way. This is a 40-mile (64km) circular walk around the borough visiting Oldham's countryside and industrial heritage. The section I walked along was the wet bit over Hind Hill, marked by cairns and posts through the peat. Still, I was safe in the knowledge that all the numerous little streams I forded ended up in the Tame and eventually the Mersey. Heading south and joining Moor Lane, a walled track with OCWW boundary stones, I was back in the canine world. I found the ball that a man and his spaniel were seeking and had a conversation with a woman with wolfhounds who was searching for a stray Labrador. At the end of the wall is a mounting block, which informs passers-by that this is on the Edith Boon Way, part of the Pennine Bridleway, which has followed a lower route from Readycon. Dropping steeply down Low Gate Lane, you reach the dam of Castleshaw Upper reservoir, from where a clean Dirty Lane leads back to the car park. The Roman fort remains are in a field just east of the reservoirs and beneath their waters lie the remains of a couple more of the woollen mills that gave this unique landscape much of its character .

Although the source of the Mersey is now fairly firmly fixed by the decorated railings already visited, in the middle of Stockport, some older authorities give the higher confluence of the Goyt and the Etherow the honour. Indeed such an erudite informant as the *Encyclopaedia Britannica* in its 1911 edition stated, 'It is formed by the junction of the Goyt and the Etherow a short distance below Marple in Cheshire on the first-named stream.'

There even seems to have been confusion about the name of the river itself. When the canal-carrying Marple Aqueduct was built, at the very end of the eighteenth century, the river at Marple was known as the Mersey or sometimes the Etherow. In 1898, the Director General of the Ordnance Survey agreed that the river Mersey, upstream from its confluence with the river Tame at Stockport, should be renamed the river Goyt. The Goyt/ Etherow confluence is found within Brabyns Park, 90 acres (36ha) of park and woodland and formerly the grounds of a hall built in the 1740s. During the First World War Brabyns Hall served as a hospital and convalescence home for injured soldiers but the building was demolished in 1952, three years after the estate became a public park. This source/confluence can easily be visited during a stroll around the park, but a longer walk gives more of a sense of the history of the area.

Etherow Country Park, one of the first country parks to be developed in Britain, at Compstall, south-east of Stockport town centre, was established in 1968 around the leats and reservoirs of a former cotton mill. It has since expanded to cover an area of 240 acres (97ha) of the lower Etherow valley and is a mixture of water, woodland and wildlife haunts. It has a large car park, information centre and café and so makes an ideal starting point. Compstall Road, passing the last throw of the industry that gave the place its meaning, leads down to the bridge over the Etherow and past the George Inn to Rollins Lane, where the residents have a struggle to maintain the surface, especially in a hard winter. It gives us some idea of what it must have been like in pre-tarmac and pre-local authority days when the people of the parish were, no doubt unwillingly, expected to look after their local thoroughfares. The lane soon reaches the delightful Iron Bridge of 1813, spanning the Goyt just before the confluence. Built by Salford Iron Works as a carriage bridge for Nathaniel Wright of the Brabyns estate, it is an elegant structure which has been sympathetically restored as a sort of bridge within a bridge. A listed structure of national importance, it is the only known surviving cast-iron bridge of its age and style in the north-west of England. Intact and unaltered, it remained in daily use until 1990, when a survey determined that it was at risk. The following year a temporary Bailey Bridge was built over it and ten years later a campaign was started to restore the bridge. The project was able to move forward with the help of Lottery Heritage Grants and the bridge was re-opened in 2008. It is to be hoped that the adjacent gatehouse, currently boarded up, will also be restored.

The Goyt Way, which runs for 10 miles (16km) between Etherow Country Park and Whaley Bridge, here turns down a muddy track to the confluence with the Etherow. What a contrast there is between this placid, parkland scene and the sources of the two rivers high on the Pennine moors! The Way crosses the park and, deserting the river, ascends through woods to join the Peak Forest Canal at Marple locks. Here the route turns right, down the towpath, but few would spurn a walk up at least a part of the flight. Opened in 1804, the sixteen locks take the Peak Forest Canal up 209 feet (64m) from the level it has followed since its junction with the Huddersfield Narrow and Ashton Canals at Ashton-under-Lyne, 6½ miles (10.4km) to the north-west, to a junction with the Macclesfield Canal in Marple. The flight was not built until four years after the rest of the waterway, and a tramway was constructed to fill the mile-long gap until the locks were finished. The locks are a tribute to the engineers and masons who worked on them and number 8 in particular is as elegant in its form as any example of Georgian design. For the visitor it is visually pleasing and for the boater everything is just where it needs to be for efficient working. The observant and imaginative will see faces in the keystones of the lock bridges.

Iron bridge, Brabyns Park

Aqueduct and viaduct, Marple

When you return down the flight the canal and railway are seen to be running close together, with the rails burrowing under the water between locks 5 and 4. At the foot of the flight a bridge takes the trains over the boats, neatly demonstrating the change in canal level. Marple Aqueduct, designed by Benjamin Outram, carries the canal almost 100 feet (30.5m) above the Goyt. The Grand Aqueduct, as it became known is 309 feet (94m) long and contains 8,000 cubic yards (6,116 cu. m) of masonry. It is a fine, three-arched structure whose pierced shoulders and different colours of gritstone are best appreciated from below.

It took nearly seven years to construct, while the adjacent twelve-arched railway viaduct, benefiting from fifty years of development in building technique, was put up in just one, between April 1862 and April 1863. A graffitied signpost at the end of the aqueduct promised 'nudist camp' but a couple of days before the end of January, no nudists were about. Steps lead down to the river and a path burrows under aqueduct and viaduct before climbing up through fields to reach Water Meetings Lane. You can follow this down towards the river, passing first Upper and then Lower Watermeetings Farm, which give reassurance that the confluence is near. Crossing the fields, you pass a modern sign erected by a venerable organization. The Peak and Northern Footpaths Society was founded in

1894 as the more Victorian-sounding Peak District and Northern Counties Footpaths Preservation Society. It has roots going back as far as 1826, when the Manchester Association for the Preservation of Ancient Footpaths was set up to oppose a landowning magistrate who was attempting to deny public rights. The society has campaigned for the cause of maintaining rights of way, has erected over three hundred signs and continues to be involved in resolving access problems. As recently as 1967, the British Waterways board was still trying to prevent the scheduling of the Peak Forest Canal towpath as public, an action which the society resolutely, and succesfully, opposed. When you consider that five years earlier the board had seriously entertained the idea of demolishing the aqueduct after frost damage to the structure during the severe winter weather had caused part of the north face of the east arch to collapse, this is perhaps not so surprising.

The path beside the Etherow, now part of the Midshires Way as well as the Etherow–Goyt Valley Way, passes through Redbrow Wood and back to Compstall Bridge and the country park. Compstall developed mainly during the first half of the nineteenth century after the Andrew family from Rochdale established a water-powered calico mill on the other side of the bridge from the present mill complex. Beginning with dyeing and printing they quickly expanded into spinning and weaving, and a large range of mills and associated buildings grew up on either side of the new turnpike road. By 1849 Compstall comprised a printworks, cotton mills, a fine house (Green Hill, now Compstall Hall) and 200 mill workers' cottages. The village was as much George Andrew's own as Saltaire was Titus Salt's or Bournville George and Richard Cadbury's. The man himself is supposed to have quipped, 'The earth is the Lord's and the fulness thereof; but Compstall and all within is Juddy Andrew's.' He built St Paul's Church, maybe to thank the Lord for his good fortune, and the Athenaeum, a fine stone building provided for the education and recreation of the villagers and now maintaining its role as the Kiddi-Winks Children's Day Nursery. Although the mills closed and the Andrew family are long gone, echoes of their influence still remain. Streets of terraced cottages are named George, John and Thomas after family members and in 1970 the only pub in Compstall changed its name frrom the Commercial Hotel to the Andrew Arms.

Water power for the mills was provided by the Etherow and a large weir, extensive mill ponds, a mill race and two huge waterwheels were engineered. The key feature which singles out Compstall from scores of other little industrial settlements was the use of the mill race as a canal, the Compstall Navigation. This was designed to transport coal, bricks and tiles in iron tub boats from near the weir to the village. Watching the miniature rainbows refracting in the rising spray above the Pennine-peat-stained water roaring over the weir, the bystander is struck by an irresistible urge to go and see where it's all coming from.

Well, this one was and a couple of days later I was travelling up the Etherow valley, Longdendale, past the string of reservoirs which leave you in no doubt about the water-supply capabilities of the river and its tributaries. The five valley reservoirs (a sixth, Arnfield, hangs above the valley on a tributary) were built between 1848 and 1884 to provide the growing populations of Manchester and Salford with fresh water. Designed by John Frederick Bateman, they were constructed to supply water 'nearly as pure as if it comes from the heavens'. This was a definite bonus for folk who had relied on often foul wells and springs, witnessed by the fact that in 1832 a cholera epidemic in Manchester had killed 674 people. The highest three reservoirs (Woodhead, Torside and Rhodeswood) are for drinking water, and the lower two (Valehouse and Bottoms) are compensation reservoirs to maintain the flow of the river. Longdendale, with its

Etherow weir, Compstall

Compstall Navigation

reservoirs, main road carrying over 25,000 vehicles per day between Manchester and Sheffield, and giant pylons, has often been cited as a spoiled landscape but on a sunny day, with dinghies sporting on the water, it has its attractions and the upper reaches are powerful in a way that eighteenth-century visitors would no doubt have called sublime.

Salter's Brook is often given as the upper feeder of the Etherow and I took a moorland walk to a couple of locations which can claim to be the source. On a bend to the west of the summit of the A628, a minor road heads north, before veering north-east towards Dunford Bridge, and a vehicle can be parked by the roadside. A grassy track leads off through a gate and stile, curving around Carr Top and Wike Edge to reach a brick building. This one has a roof and I noticed unmistakable signs of ovine and human visitation, but another rectangular structure on the south-west side of the track has a different tale to tell. This is one of the air shafts of Woodhead Tunnel. Built to carry trains between Manchester and Sheffield, the first tunnel opened in 1845, with the second following eight years later. The main traffic was coal and by the mid-twentieth century the twin bores were being used by up to 250

trains a day. The narrow tunnels were nicknamed the hell-holes by the engine crews who had to work steam locomotives through them. In 1953 the tunnels were replaced by a completely new one, bored to carry a newly electrified route, trumpeted as 'Britain's First All-Electric Main Line', from the south Yorkshire pits to Lancashire. At first traffic was heavy but the unique 1500V direct current system was not followed when other parts of the BR system were electrified and the Woodhead route remained as a non-standard, rather antiquated, entity. Passenger services were cut from the beginning of 1970 to allow the route to focus on freight, still predominantly coal, but, with changing industrial patterns, even this declined and the line was closed in 1981. Since then the trackbed through the Etherow valley has become the Longdendale Trail, part of the Trans Pennine Trail, itself a section of the European Long Distance Footpath E8, which may eventually lead the walker from western Ireland to the Bosporus. The two old tunnels were used from the 1960s to carry electrical cables and the new tunnel is currently being converted for the same purpose. This will presumably end the hope of the tunnel ever being used again by trains, although they were saying that about Standedge canal tunnel[13] and boats at about the time the new Woodhead was opening!

From the brick building I followed a branch of Salter's Brook through Upper Head Moss and Wike Head, along peat groughs and across a fence, to its source just below Dead Edge End. A slightly lower headwater starts at Redhole Spring, source of Upper Head Dike, a third of a mile (0.5km) across the boggy hillside. Visiting on the last day of January in the coldest winter for thirty years has its advantages: the route between the two spots would be a quagmire most of the time but all I had to worry about was skidding on the ice. From here another of the Woodhead air shafts is visible to the

13   Ten moorland watershed miles to the north-west, Standedge, on the Huddersfield Narrow Canal, was legally abandoned in 1943; it re-opened in 2001.

south-east, this one circular, and from it a good track, used by the TPT, leads away south-westwards past old quarries to join the bridleway running across Longside Edge to cross the A628 before descending to the old bridge over Salter's Brook. From the Middle Ages salt was an important commodity carried by packhorses through Longdendale from Northwich and Middlewich in Cheshire to Wakefield and Sheffield. Lady Shaw Bridge, crossing Salter's Brook, which here marks the boundary between Derbyshire and Yorkshire, is first mentioned in 1695. It is believed that the bridge was originally wider and that it was rebuilt when the new turnpike was opened just up the hill in the late 1730s, the bridge being narrowed to prevent carts using it to avoid paying the tolls. The remains of Salter's Brook House, an inn from 1795, stand near by, as does an old milestone. Patronized by jaggers, travellers and shepherds, the inn received a boost from the coming of the railway and it survived until after the completion of the early Woodhead tunnels. When the navvies moved on, the inn closed, in

1852. To the south and east rise other headwaters, such as the Small Cloughs – Far, Middle and Near – and Long Grough, which flow down from Round Hill and Featherbed Moss to join Salter's Brook and form the Etherow proper. Up the track from Lady Shaw Bridge you reach a junction where the packhorse trails from Barnsley and Wakefield met, accounting for Saltersbrook's importance as a staging post on the route. Here I took the northern track which leads back to the road junction and the car.

Etherow was said to rise at the ancient boundary of Lancashire, Yorkshire and Cheshire, a length of the Goyt separated Cheshire from Derbyshire and part of the Tame formed the border between Lancashire and Cheshire. This makes it all the more apt that the name of the river which is formed from these three, Mersey, is derived from the Old English for 'boundary river'.

Mersey's third headwater, the Goyt, rises not far from the Cat and Fiddle Inn, on a grough-traceried hillside just on the Cheshire side of the county boundary with Derbyshire. The stream flows down

Upper Etherow valley

Upper Goyt valley

Goyt's Clough to feed the Errwood and Fernilee Reservoirs before running through Whaley Bridge to join the Etherow at Compstall. The Goyt must have a higher quotient of demolished mansions near its extremities than any other British river, for if the erstwhile Brabyns Hall, by its confluence with Etherow, marks its end, then Errwood Hall stood but a couple of miles from its source. The hall was built in the 1830s for Samuel Grimshawe, a rich Manchester man of business, and was occupied by three generations of the family. In 1930, following the death of the last direct descendant, the 2,000-acre (809ha) estate was bought by the Stockport Corporation as part of the plans for building Fernilee Reservoir. The hall was used as a youth hostel until, in 1934, it was demolished together with several farms and cottages at the hamlet of Goyt's Bridge. Fernilee Reservoir was completed in 1938 and Errwood followed in 1967.

A car park by Errwood Reservoir makes a good starting point for a walk to the source and around a part of the Goyt watershed. The road, which is subject to one-way traffic (uphill only) and closure at busy times, follows the river upstream through woods. A signposted riverside path allows diversions away from the tarmac and into the wooded valley, returning to it at Goytsclough Quarry, from where, legend has it, Thomas Pickford started a

business mending roads, carrying stone from the quarry in panniers on packhorses. The family later diversified into general transportation and the firm is now one of the largest removal and storage concerns in Europe. A bridge crosses the Goyt here but was not used by the Pickford packhorses, having been removed from its original location, Goyt's Bridge, now beneath the Errwood Reservoir, and rebuilt here in the 1960s. Further upstream, where the narrow valley is almost bare of trees, is the river's confluence with Berry Clough. It is difficult to appreciate now but this upper stretch of the Goyt valley was peppered with the pits and shafts of a coal mining industry that lasted from the start of the seventeenth to the beginning of the twentieth centuries. Criss-crossed by roads and trackways, this exposed stretch of moorland, between 1,300 and 1,800 feet (396m and 549m) above sea level, must have been one of the bleakest industrial sites in the country.

The valley narrows further through Goyt's Clough, and you pass a waterfall on the right and mine drainage sough on the left before, at Derbyshire Bridge, so called as it was on the boundary between that county and Cheshire, the road crosses to the east side of the river. Just beyond, at the car park and Ranger Centre, the road meets the old Buxton-to-Macclesfield turnpike, which parallels the Goyt, here less than a yard wide, for half a mile as it climbs towards the Cat and Fiddle Inn. Following the river, now a trickle, away from the tarmac, it climbs away to the south-west and disappears under the A537 in a concrete pipe. A couple of hundred yards above the main road, the flow became intermittent and I walked up a 6-foot-deep dry grough to emerge on the flat moorland of heather, cotton grass and cloudberry. Here, near the line of stakes running along the watershed, were two little peaty pots marking the Goyt's highest source. A tinker's spit and stride away is the head of Tinkerspit Gutter, one of the river Dane's headwaters. The Goyt flows north to join the Mersey in Stockport and the Dane runs south from here to join the Weaver near Northwich, before meeting up again with the water that started its journey a few yards away, in the Mersey near Runcorn. Walking down towards the Cat and Fiddle, past little green plastic trays of grouse grit, I crossed several more streams and ditches, all feeders of the Goyt. Larks rose, curlews were chasing off a buzzard and a grouse shot out from virtually under my foot.

The Cat and Fiddle is at or near the top of several lists. Despite 'a recent measurement commissioned by the landlord' that amazingly suggested it was higher than the Tan Hill Inn in Yorkshire, the Cat and Fiddle is the second-highest pub in Britain. Indeed, to be at the height claimed, 1,770 feet, the building would have to move up on to the moors half a mile or so north or south. The notorious road from Macclesfield to Buxton, which passes the pub and is a motorbike mecca, is currently rated as the most dangerous in Britain, having overtaken the A889 between Dalwhinnie and Laggan in Scotland. Carefully crossing the road, I made my way on to a stretch of the old turnpike which leaves the present road at a sharp bend. I passed an old milestone before turning right along a track above Stake Farm where a late cock (it was 10.53) was crowing. There is a plethora of signs along the track, including the rather prissy 'Walkers Only Thank You', and it would be logical to carry on down the direct route to Errwood, but a path glistening in the sunshine led off tangentially towards Shining Tor and how could I resist a walk along part of the Goyt watershed coupled with a visit to a trig point and the top of Cheshire. The highest point of Cheshire – a county not generally noted for elevation – used to be on Black Hill, a slough visited by Pennine Wayfarers, but since the boundary changes of 1974 it is the far more pleasant Shining Tor. A wall marches along the watershed and there are seats, signs and a flagged path. A gate that didnae quite shut gives

access to the pillar. The views are wide ranging and take in the distinctive summit of Shutlingsloe, hyperbolically, or some might say oxymoronically, referred to as the Cheshire Matterhorn, as well as the white dish of the Lovell Telescope at Jodrell Bank and the sugar-loaf-shaped folly White Nancy. Further away are the great sprawl of Manchester and the cooling towers of Fiddler's Ferry power station, ultimate destination of much of the water falling on these slopes, and which consumes about 43 million gallons of Mersey water a day.

The path along the watershed is paved and easy to follow through an area of peat stabilization. On the Shining Tor side of the col before the rise to Cats Tor, you can desert the path and follow a track down towards Errwood. It was a delightful descent through lovely woods, which gave glimpses of the reservoir. It was only when I reached the bottom that I noticed the sign informing visitors that in order to protect wildlife the track was shut. I spent a few minutes looking around the remains of Errwood Hall. It must have been an idyllic spot and was particularly beautiful with the rhododendron and azalea in gorgeous flower. Many of the trees planted by the family are at their zenith these days and the contrast between the subtle shades of green of the leaves and the bold colours of the blooms was spectacular. The Grimshawes had their own private burial ground atop a little knoll above the hall and a mausoleum stands nearby. Besides the family graves, there is one of John Butler, who was captain of the Grimshawes' yacht *Mariquita*, on which they cruised extensively in the Mediterranean, visiting Spain and Italy, and collecting plants to grow at Errwood.

Of the hall itself, little remains but the floors, some arched windows and the pillars of the main doorway. The Grimshawes are remembered locally for their hospitality and generosity; what they would make of the raves held in the valley these days is anybody's guess.

YORKSHIRE DALES AND MOORS

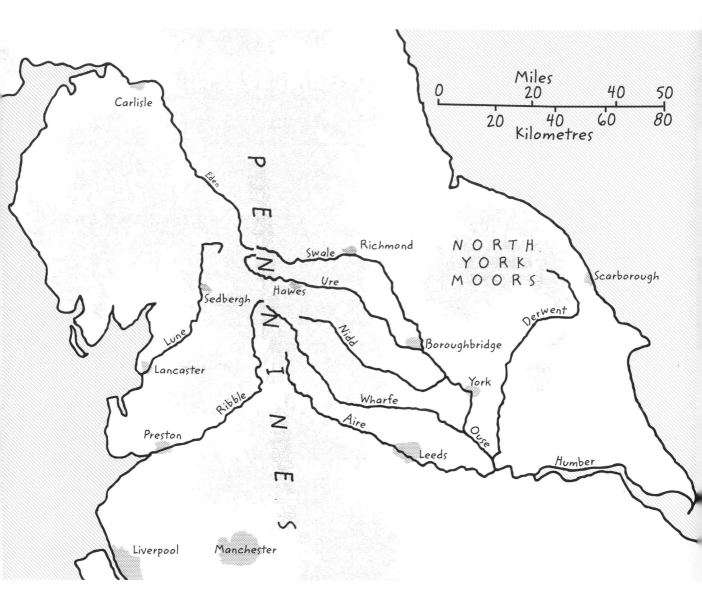

As I am a Lancastrian married to a Yorkshire lass, for me the Dales and Moors have always been a favourite walking area. Here are to be found a couple of staunchly Lancashire rivers that actually rise outside the county – in one case in Yorkshire! There are also tales of fluvial brigandage on the fells, fine jaunts among the singular geography of the delectable Dales and a visit to the heathery acres of the North Yorkshire Moors.

Swale

this dear spot

SUNWAC was one of my schooldays mnemonics: the order of Yorkshire rivers from north to south. Swale, Ure, Nidd, Wharfe, Aire and Calder are all tributaries of the Ouse, Yorkshire's main drain. The 73 mile (117km) long Swale is the most unruly of this sextet and some may put this

SWALE

SOURCE	confluence of Birkdale & Great Sleddale Becks, North Yorkshire
G.R.	NY 856 008
LENGTH	73 miles (117 kilometres)
TRIBUTARIES	Whitsundale Beck, Gunnerside Gill, Brough Beck, Wiske
MOUTH	confluence with the Ure by Myton-on-Swale

down to its being the most northerly. In its upper course it is fast flowing and rises rapidly in flood times. The headwaters emerge on the slopes of High Seat and Nine Standards Rigg close by the old border between Yorkshire and Westmorland (now Cumbria), which here does its best to follow the English watershed along the high ridge marking Mallerstang's eastern wall. The Swale itself is said by most authorities to begin at the confluence of Birkdale and Great Sleddale Becks, from where it descends quickly past Keld, taking the waterfalls of Wain Wath, Catrake and Kisdon at a leap before flowing for a further 20 miles (32km) to Richmond Bridge followed by a more placid old age and ultimate confluence with the Ure by Myton-on-Swale near Boroughbridge.

A walk of about 12½ miles (20km) around the head of Swaledale took me to several of the sources scattered around a large and remote area of moorland. People of the past are more apparent in the landscape than those of the present and I did not meet another living soul in the five hours I was out.

The B6270 road through upper Swaledale is mostly unfenced and there is a parking space just to the west of its junction with the very minor road to the delectable Ravenseat in Whitsundale. From here a farm road leads down towards the confluence of Birkdale and Great Sleddale Becks, the

official start of the river. Burnt Moor was living up to its name as I walked down the track towards the end of a very dry March; a pall of smoke rose from a fire set by the gamekeeper to encourage the growth of young heather for the grouse. The red grouse is endemic to the British Isles and mainly lives on heather moorland in northern England and Scotland. Shooting is big business around here and I was to see much more evidence of the sport during the rest of the day.

By Stone House, a substantial but apparently deserted farm near the confluence, stands the first bridge across the Swale. Built about 1840 using stone from nearby Hill Top quarry, a slender arch sweeps across the river carrying a lane to – well, nowhere really, just a barn and a couple of outbuildings. From Stone House the track heads across fields between a pair of well-built drystone walls built with three sets of throughstones. Lapwings circled overhead, their call echoing their common name, peewit, and local one, tewit.

Fording Birkdale Beck at the confluence, I followed Great Sleddale Beck past the remains of Lane, or Loanin, End lead mine. A shakehole or shaft top, filled with old beds and fridges, the engine shaft covered by a row of iron pipes and the shells of buildings are all that remain. Worked from the middle of the eighteenth century, the mines were further developed in the 1820s when a steam engine was put on the shaft in an attempt to drain the workings. Another nearby shaft used a wheel driven by water from Birkdale Tarn but in spite of these efforts the mines were drowned out. I followed a Land Rover track which criss-crossed the beck and noticed narrow plank bridges on many of the streams. They were not for humans but, with a wire netting tunnel holding a trap, were designed for stoats and weasels, which feed on the eggs and young grouse or even adult birds. Predator control is one of the main jobs of the gamekeeper, involving killing foxes, stoats, weasels, magpies, carrion crows and rats. Hundreds of stoats, for instance, can be caught each year in spring-operated fenn traps on a typical grouse moor. More controversial is the disturbance and illegal killing of raptors such as hen harriers, peregrine falcons and even, in Scotland, golden eagles, which prey on grouse and their chicks. The Royal Society for the Protection of Birds recorded that in 2008 only five successful hen harrier nests were recorded on driven grouse moors in England and Scotland, even though there was enough suitable habitat to support nearly five hundred pairs. Not surprisingly, the shooting lobby fails to recognize that any raptor persecution problem exists. A 'driven' moor is one where beaters flush the birds towards the guns, while 'walked-up' shooting is where the sportsmen walk across the moor and drive the birds themselves. Grit trays are also found on the managed moors. The grit helps grouse to digest the heather, which is their staple diet, while some of it is medicated to treat worms and other parasites.

When you reach the highest buildings in Great Sleddale, standing at about 1,300 feet (397m), the fellside above is striped with walls, the remains of the enclosures of Sleddale Pasture, a landscape of lost endeavour where grass was once grown for hay by the farmers of Angram half a dozen miles down the valley road. Here, Leaden Haw and Hush Gutter remind the passer-by once more of the importance of lead mining in these remote dales, while higher up a small, square, roofless, stone building stands across the beck from a low cliff with a horizontal mine tunnel, a level, at its foot behind a pile of excavated stone. I wondered if this was the copper mine said to have been leased to a man from Reeth who set two men to work it. They soon struck the vein and one miner stayed to work the ore while the other walked the 14 miles (22.5km) down the valley to tell the proprietor the good news. The two men returned in a horse and cart, the round trip taking several hours, and by the time they were back at the excavation the ore had all been worked out.

In places banks of stones tossed up between the

Great Sleddale Beck

stream and a dry channel speak of the force of the beck on less benign days than this and in places Great Sleddale Beck has carved through the limestone, scalloping the bedrock or tumbling noisily over little steps. At the confluence of Long and Short Gill, which looks obvious from a distance but less so with proximity, you follow Long Gill past the shaley bank of Scriddles. Seldom have spurs been so interlocked as in this highest section of the valley. Looking back the vast bulk of Great Shunner Fell fills the horizon while ahead the land rises fairly gently to crest Mallerstang Edge. Many of these Pennine hills, even some of the biggest ones, aren't as exciting as the rocky mountains of, say, the Lake District, which will soon become visible over the Eden valley, but you've got to take the smooth with the rough.

Eventually running water becomes harder to find and the head of Long Gill, which becomes Great Sleddale Beck which becomes the Swale, is just a seepage from a sphagnum-covered, rushy depression, one of a series scaling the upper eastern slopes of Hugh Seat, which become a little drier with height and depending on season and weather.

Watched by a couple of sheep that had escaped the latest round-up, I reached the bare, except for a fence corner, top of Hugh Seat. The fell stands in a pivotal position on the watershed, with streams draining from its slopes into the Swale, Eden and Ure. Following the ridge north along the Eden/Swale watershed, passing Eden Springs and the Long Gill Head, which is the head of the other Long Gill, the one that becomes *Little* Sleddale Beck which joins Birkdale Beck which becomes the Swale, I crossed my favouritely named 2,000-foot hill. Archy Styrigg is a wonderful name with a fine ring about it. Though not immediately springing to mind as a name for a hill, once encountered it is undoubtedly a memorable one. According to large-scale maps Archy Styrigg is the name of the fell while the summit is properly referred to as Gregory Chapel. Great names but surely more appropriate to a 1930s murder mystery than a hilltop – Gregory,

the dashing second son of some cinctured earl, and his sidekick, the ever-faithful, though rather naïve Archy. We can see the latter most at home with practicalities – engines, wiring diagrams and foot-slogging – while Gregory pursues the more cerebral problems of solving society murders . . . "'Good man, Archy!' exclaimed Gregory. 'Oh, I say, do you mean that Greg, old man? Thanks awfully.'" The ridge culminates on High Seat, which gives fine views over the Eden valley to Wild Boar Fell and the Howgill Fells with Lakeland beyond. Down in the valley stand the gaunt remains of Pendragon Castle, an atmospheric place above some fine meanders.

. . . moorland seemed to stretch interminably through the all-enveloping mist. It was so absolutely impenetrable that Gregory Chapel had lost all sense of being, let alone direction. That the famous, priceless Mallerstang gems, stolen only yesterday from Lord Edenside's seat of Pendragon Castle and buried somewhere, somewhere in this vast waste, would ever be found seemed most unlikely, nay impossible to contemplate. Was this to be the first failure, the end of a glittering career which had seen so many solutions to so many seemingly baffling crimes? Then through the mist Chapel saw something glittering. Could it be? Was it possible? 'Greg, old chap, they were buried in the cairn!' It was Archy Styrigg, saving the day once more!

'Good man, Archy!' exclaimed Gregory.

'Oh, I say, do you mean that Greg, old man? Thanks awfully.'

'I think it's best if I take those now, Archy, old bean . . .'

From High Seat the broad ridge continues

Near the source of the river

around the peaty head of Uldale Gill, another of Swale's major headwaters, to High Pike and fine views out over the head of Birkdale to Nine Standards Rigg with its summit cluster of cairns, said to have been built to scare off marauding Scots, and Birkdale Tarn, a blue mirror among the duns and drabs of the moors. I was once walking towards the top of High Pike when I noticed what, at first sight, looked to be an oddly shaped khaki-coloured boulder just off the path. I'm glad I didn't wander over to investigate because half a minute later, with a whistling and a hollering, it leapt into the air with several more on the lee side of the hill. That was no boulder: rather it was a beater waiting patiently for the signal to start the grouse drive. The year 2010 was a very good one for grouse shooting, with a number of moors noting record bags. The severe winter may even have helped the grouse, which after all is a subarctic bird, by killing off parasites. Old hands recalled that 1963, after another big freeze, had also been an exceptional season.

I made my way down to the head of Birkdale, remembering the time we'd come down here from Nine Standards in the mist to find a party of sportsmen shooting across the road, an activity we felt was highly questionable, especially on a Sunday afternoon. Still, some people live for the sport. Captain Horatio Ross, Admiral Lord Nelson's

godson, brought down 82 grouse in 82 shots on his 82nd birthday, while the 2nd Lord Ripon reputedly once shot 28 birds in a minute and over half a million head of game during his lifetime. He was on the moors 30 miles south-east of here one day in September 1923 and had just killed 51 grouse during a drive, when he dropped dead in the heather aged 71.

Belying its name, Birkdale is virtually devoid of trees and is now a lonely and all but uninhabited valley, which was probably at about its most crowded in 1819 when it had a population of forty-seven people. At its head, a gently sloping, boggy and peaty expanse known as Lamps Moss gives out its stored-up water equally generously eastwards to Uldale Beck or west to Kitchen Gill. Two old boundary stones stand at the top of the road, or rather the one announcing 'HAMLET OF BIRKDALE: COUNTY OF YORK' does; the other, informing the traveller of arrival in 'TOWNSHIP OF NATEBY', in Westmorland, is a hundred yards down on the Yorkshire side of the summit − evidence of some past border dispute. They used to reckon it was the best-maintained bit of road anywhere, as it was looked after by both sides. Current authorities, including the counties of North Yorkshire and Cumbria and the Yorkshire Dales National Park, agree with the Birkdale view of things and have positioned their signs on the watershed.

Half a mile (0.8km) down the road, at Beck Meetings, Uldale Beck meets Crooked Sike running down off Coldbergh Edge, part of the southern continuation of Nine Standards Rigg, and Birkdale Beck is born. Just beyond is forlorn Black Scar House, an old shepherd's hut and fold, looking out across a mosaic of managed moorland to Great Shunner Fell. Below here the valley constricts and Birkdale Beck is deeply entrenched as the road runs high above it, hugging the contour. Tracks run off to the shooting huts and grouse butts along Great Lodge Gill and Little Sleddale Beck. A driven moor may be worth around £3,500–4,000 per brace of bird to the owner while walked-up shooting could fetch about half that sum. The land may look poverty stricken but a quality grouse moor could set you back £5–10 million.

As I plodded down the road it struck me that, apart from during my first decade, I had hitched a lift in every succeeding one apart from this. In my teens and early twenties it was my main means of travel and several jaunts have since been helped along by application of the thumb. I once walked across the Lake District and ended up, soaked as usual, in the pale leather upholstery of a two-seater Saab. The driver and I had a lively conversation about walking and climbing but few words were spoken when I finally got out leaving a dark silhouette behind. I now decided that I would try to hitch a ride from the next car that passed me and carried on down the tarmac in a pitch of anticipation. The trouble was that not a single vehicle came down that road, with the exception of a solitary cyclist, and only three went up it in the next twenty minutes. I was in sight of the van overlooking the source of the Swale when a car at last appeared and I thought that it would be pushing my luck a bit far to try to stop somebody for the sake of a hundred yards. Next time![14]

Ure
a trickle in the grass

The Yorkshire Ure (there's another in western Scotland, a tributary of the Creran) is about 50 miles (80km) long from its source above the Mallerstang valley to its confluence with the Swale 3 miles (4.8km) beyond Boroughbridge. Although many authorities give this as the beginning of the Ouse, the river is still named Ure on the map for a further 5 miles (8km) until, at the confluence of mighty Ure with tiny triply tautological Ouse Gill Beck, the name changes. The beck itself rises in the garden of the former Great Ouseburn Workhouse and a column by the original source (the spring now appears 40 yards/36.5m away) carried the inscription 'OUSE RIVER HEAD OUSEGILL SPRING Ft. YORK 13miles BOROUGHBRIDGE 4miles'. The beck flows for about 4 miles (6.4km) before it joins the Ure and appropriates its waters. At one time there was a wooden signpost on the riverbank by the confluence which had 'Ure' on the arm pointing upstream and 'Ouse' on the downstream one.

Most rivers share a name with their valley. Not so the Ure, which flows down Wensleydale. The name Yoredale, now generally reserved for the rock strata characteristic of the Yorkshire Dales, was the ancient name for the Ure's dale until about the beginning of the eighteenth century, when it was usurped by the use of Wensleydale. Perhaps some far-sighted cheesemakers were thinking of future marketing prospects: 'Have some Uredale, Gromit' doesn't fall quite so trippingly from the tongue.

URE	
SOURCE	Ure Head, North Yorkshire
G.R.	SD 805 968
LENGTH	50 miles (80 kilometres)
TRIBUTARIES	Bain, Cover, Burn, Swale
MOUTH	confluence with Ouse, Cuddy Shaw Reach

Moorcock Inn at the head of Wensleydale, John Pratt

Wensley is a small village halfway down the valley, which was a market town until Tudor times when, in 1563, it was visited by a plague 'most hotte and fearfull', so that many people fled and few visited 'for a long season'. The place never recovered, its trade and market migrated to Leyburn, but the name stuck.

The Ure and the Eden are really twins divided at birth by a few hundred yards of peat and a few thousand years of geological time. Hell Gill, the Eden's main headwater, was formerly the Ure's source until glacial drift dumped at the end of the Ice Age diverted its course northwards. The present source is plain for all to see, for on the map is simply stated 'Ure Head'. It stands near the summit of Sails, which is both the most southerly and lowest of the Mallerstang Edge summits. Half a mile (0.8km) to the north, the top named Little Fell on the maps rises to a height of 2,188 feet (667m) and is thus the mathematical summit of the fell. The Ordnance Survey chose the slightly lower Sails for its unusual horizontal ring trig point and this spot is certainly superior as a viewpoint. Ure Head lies in between.

The source is in the shallow, boggy, intervening depression, a confusing area of peat groughs, confusing to the source seeker anyway, for not all the rain falling in this waste is destined for the North Sea. A drop or two finds its way westwards into the Irish Sea because tributaries of Hell Gill Beck also drain away from the dip between Sails and Little Fell. By far the majority of the water landing on Sails, however, finds its way into the Ure, either directly or through its tributary West Gill, which flows through secretive Cotterdale.

The ascent to the source is an easy matter, for it is simply a case of finding a suitable spot to leave the old High Way, which runs across the western and southern slopes of the hill at an altitude ranging from 1,300 feet (397m) by Hell Gill to 1,600 feet (488m) on Cotter End, and striking up the fellside. There is no difficulty, for the gritstone edge that is such a feature of the more northern parts of

Ure Head cairn

Mallerstang is absent here.

The Ure itself can be followed, for it has carved a little valley in which the water slides and tumbles over boulders and around angular blocks of stone. It is a chattering, lively mountain stream and a good companion on the ascent, which is otherwise a dull walk over grassy sheepwalks. At one point it runs through a deep-carved ravine and the last time I was here I disturbed a deer, grazing beside a ruined circular sheepfold, which ran off skittishly across the fellside.

The area marked 'Ure Head' on the map is a boggy depression with a considerable amount of tall rushy grass and large areas of swampy ground. Ideal for breeding rivers but not so good for the pedestrian. I almost came to grief a couple of times attempting to cross it and at one point wondered if I was ever going to leave it.

A substantial cairn standing a couple of hundred yards west of Sails' summit and overlooking Ure Head is about 5 feet square and 6 high (1.5 x 1.8m). It makes a good belvedere from which to study the swamp and the headwater channel of the Ure. It is also a good spot to take off the boots, wring out the socks and question the sanity. The cairn, moreover, gives exceptional views – is that really Lakeland's Mickledore appearing between Wild Boar Fell and the Howgills? Unlike several other large cairns further north along the Mallerstang ridge, this one does not mark the old county boundary, but standing so close to the source perhaps it was built to note the fact.

The observer may be lulled, by the openness or wild nature of the view, into believing it to be somehow natural, but, in truth, almost every aspect of our landscape has been shaped by human endeavour. This is a continuing process and changes are happening in the uplands that may have further effects on the scene. Some of this has come about through the Alice in Wonderland workings of the Common Agricultural Policy. In 1977 information from the Ministry of Agriculture, Fisheries and Food showed that 71 per cent of moorland in England and Wales was stocked at about one ewe per acre. By 1987 this had trebled in some areas, as farmers were encouraged by subsidies to increase stocking levels. At the same time moorlands and blanket bogs were 'improved' by drainage. Channels, called grips, were cut into the fellsides to drain the land and this has led to damage

Crossing the High Way

to the delicate balance of upland plant species, an acceleration in peat erosion and a greater risk of flooding downstream caused by increased run-off speeds. Increased grazing adversely affected sensitive habitats and along with afforestation and encroachment by bracken, 200,000 acres (8,937ha) of heather moorland were lost.

More recently, changes in the CAP have been reflected in the way farming is carried out in the uplands, with a change from the encouragement of high yields to more of a focus on environmental benefits. The Single Farm Payment scheme, introduced in 2005, cut the link between yield and subsidy payments and paid farmers by the area of land held. For many farmers, especially those with smaller acreages, the result has been a decline in income and the National Trust, a major uplands landowner, has expressed concern about a real threat of farmers no longer keeping sheep and cattle because they would not be able to make an economically viable living. Although the CAP reforms are designed to bring environmental improvements, this would hardly happen if farmers can no longer make a living by doing their core work using expertise built up over generations. A better balance needs to be struck between the needs of farmers and the environment.

The Ure, which bears its name straight from its source, spends a couple of miles travelling westwards and disappearing for a while as it crosses the limestone, before correcting itself at Ure Crook and turning to flow south-east towards the old white walls of the Moorcock Inn and the head of Wensleydale.

Nidd

nothing could be serener

The Nidd is given a distance of anywhere between 50 and 59 miles (80–95km) by different authorities, although, looking at the extravagant succession of meanders it negotiates between Knareborough

NIDD	
SOURCE	Nidd Head Spring,
	North Yorkshire
G.R.	SE 002 752
LENGTH	59 miles (95 kilometres)
TRIBUTARIES	How Stean Beck, Darley Beck,
	Crimple
MOUTH	confluence with Ouse,
	Nun Monkton

and Nun Monkton where it meets the Ouse, this is maybe not surprising. The river rises in the eastern Pennines, on the dip slopes of Great Whernside, and runs south-east and then east through Pateley Bridge and Knaresborough before flowing north, south, east, west and all points between before joining the Ouse about 6 miles (9.6km) north-west of York. Although it lies outside the Yorkshire Dales National Park, the upper valley is recognized as the Nidderdale Area of Outstanding Natural Beauty, which covers 233 square miles (603 sq. km) from the bare high fells to the more wooded and pastoral landscapes further downstream. The valley is narrower than most of the other Yorkshire Dales and the fact that it has no through road across the valley head adds to its sense of remoteness. The head of Nidderdale contains three reservoirs, two of which can be visited in the course of a 12-mile (19.3km) walk around a section of the upper watershed.

A road leaves the Nidderdale village of Lofthouse quite shyly, through a gate on the right after crossing over the river. This leads through the lovely upper valley to a car park by Scar House Reservoir dam. Scar House and Angram were built by the Bradford Corporation, with the smaller and higher Angram Reservoir opening in 1919 and Scar House following in 1936. The numerous concrete slabs at the side of the road approaching the car park are the bases of buildings which made up the village of

Scar. Built to house the workforce, it was a complete community in itself with 10 large hostels for workmen, 28 houses in five blocks and 34 semi-detached bungalows. Also provided were shops, a canteen, a 600-seat cinema, a school, a library, a hospital and a mission hall. Scar village had its own hairdresser, fire brigade and policeman, and for a time a post office with its own postmark. During the Depression years of the 1920s and '30s, conditions were so much better in Scar than in the nearest town of Pateley Bridge that the workers were warned that any misbehaviour by themselves or their family members would result in instant dismissal – there were plenty waiting who would take their job. Even so the Scar Village Notes newsletter of October 1927 reported local indignation at the wanton damage that had occurred on two occasions to railway carriages on special late trains. The Nidd Valley light railway had been built to deliver materials for the project from the railhead at Pateley Bridge to Angram and for a time passengers were carried as far as Lofthouse. The railway closed in 1929 and when the whole scheme was completed seven years later the village was sold off in lots over two days and dismantled. The canteen moved a few miles down the valley and still stands as Darley's Memorial Hall.

Walking down to Scar House Dam you can appreciate the sheer scale of the undertaking. Flanked by corporation-waterworks'-default-architectural-style castellated turrets, the dam was the tallest in Britain when it was built, standing more than 150 feet (45.7m) above the original river level. At over 500 yards (457m) in length, a walk along the dam road gives plenty of opportunity to look up the dale to the swelling crest of the Pennines beyond. The first hill to capture the attention is Little Whernside, with its bigger brother coming into view as you reach the far end of the structure.

I turned left on to the Carle Fell Road and walked, accompanied by a peewit chorus, above and alongside the reservoir and past the scant mossy remains of the ruined hamlet of Lodge. Here I followed the road uphill, alongside Shaw Gill, to the col between Dead Man's Hill and Little Whernside. The former recalls the discovery, in 1728, of three headless corpses. They were thought to be the remains of Scottish pedlars who had gone missing some years before. According to some tales the innkeeper from Lodge, one Maggie Thompson, and her daughter (or son, according to some versions) were suspected, as it was noticed that, as well as the fact that they had become unusually well off, there was an unaccountable number of Scottish ponies in the valley and many of the neighbourhood women were wearing plaids. However, the same accusation is made of Jenny Twigg, proprietress of an inn at Arkleside, over the moor, and her daughter Tib, who are recalled by the naming after them of two massive free-standing rocks on the fellside half a dozen miles away to the east-south-east. Then again Jenny Twigg's daughter might have been called Meg and they could have been witches. Tales don't shrink with the telling. Looking at the tumbled stones of Lodge it is hard to imagine the amount of trade, from cattle drovers, packmen and pedlars, that supported such places on the fringes of eighteenth-century civilization.

Until recently the Carle Fell Road of the pack horses and cattle droves was used by off-road vehicles and the steep section by Shaw Gill has been badly eroded. I thought as I walked up it that there didn't seem to be much evidence of recent use, only a couple of bits of broken plastic, and I subsequently discovered that a Temporary Prohibition of Motor Vehicles Except for Access Order had come into force in August 2010 and was due to run until February 2012. What I did find at the side of the road was litter. Plastic bottles and cans that had held energy drinks. Why do some people who presumably come to the countryside because they enjoy being there spoil others' enjoyment by leaving their litter behind? Or are the hills just another racetrack as the modern athletes pit themselves against nature in the raw? I wish they'd pit themselves against something else, like a rubbish dump, where they could pursue both their activities without upsetting anyone, except the gulls.

At the top of Shaw Gill I left the road and headed for Little Whernside, which I crossed on a dinky little path threading its way across the peaty top, following groughs and little sandy banks, using bits of broken fence as stepping stones and trusting in faith to see me safely over some particularly squelchy bits, to the cairn which may mark the summit. The wall and path drop away to Long Sike Head, where the ridge is crossed by another of those routes, between the valleys of Nidd and Wharfe, that is impossible to date but which may have been used for centuries if not millennia. On the descent to Long Hill Sike Head, I passed a boundary stone which proved undecipherable and then another, built into the wall on a minor top just above Nidd Head inscribed 'YB' on the path side and 'KB' on the other.

A couple of hundred yards down the fellside at the base of a peat hag is Nidd Head Spring. Towards the end of the driest March for nearly sixty years there was the tiniest dribble of water seeping out of the ground and trickling away past a few stones and clumps of moss to hide itself, as if embarrassed, among the rushes and sedge. Further down it reappeared, stronger now and audible, as its valley spread out beneath and it began to collect the numerous sikes and dikes which must have appealed to the water engineers of Bradford a century ago.

The lost village of Scar

It is possible to make a way back down beside the infant Nidd to where it joins Angram Reservoir and the track to Scar House, but I decided to return to the watershed and follow it round for a while longer and take in Great Whernside's summit.

I reached the trig point, standing among a cluster of rocks, and took out my camera.

'What is it?' demanded one of a pair of sandwich eaters ensconced on a boulder.

I feigned ignorance and looked at him blankly.

'What is it?' he repeated and the exchange continued for a few seconds. I pretended to catch on and studied the camera closely.

'It's a N—'

'I can tell it's a Nikon from here. What sort is it?'

'I don't know, I just take pictures with it. They're usually OK.'

At that he gave me a withering look and then turned to his companion and gave him a man-style look. Shortly afterwards they left. I can't say I wasn't pleased.

The extensive, flat summit is littered with large blocks of millstone grit looking as if they have been tipped from some giant's wheelbarrow, and the top itself carries a large cairn and the trig point with flush bracket number 2976 and a plaque. There is plenty of shelter among the boulders and crag and it is often needed. Certainly the original surveyors, Thomas Colby and William Mudge, must have been grateful when they set up their theodolite here in 1808, Mudge choosing the flattest rock he could find for the base of the instrument. Just by the trig point there is a flat rock, into which has been inserted a small, brass cylinder. Could this have been put there for the theodolite during that original survey or does it date from later mapping? The view is wide-ranging on a good day with several iconic northern hills – Ingleborough, The Calf, Pendle Hill and Ilkley Moor – all in range. On a really good day the lucky visitor may even catch a glimpse of Great Gable and the great gash of Mickledore, between Scafell Pike and Scafell, in the Lake District.

Staying on the watershed I went south and then east to visit one of my Nick Wright Tops.[15] Although it's no longer on anyone's list of summits, somebody loves this nameless collapsed-pudding-shaped brow, for it sports three cairns. I dropped down into the valley of Stone Beck, Nidd's first main tributary before both were subsumed into the Angram Reservoir. After the tussocks and groughs of the descent, it was pleasant to walk the last couple of miles on well-graded tracks beside Angram and Scar House back to the car park.

Wharfe
Farre in the North

WHARFE	
SOURCE	Oughtershaw, North Yorkshire
G.R.	SD 834 821
LENGTH	60 miles (96.5 kilometres)
TRIBUTARIES	Skirfare, Dibb, Washburn, Cock Beck
MOUTH	confluence with Ouse at Wharfe's Mouth near Cawood

Most authorites consider that the 60 mile (96.5km) long Wharfe is formed out of Oughtershaw and Green Field Becks at their meeting by the hamlet of Beckermonds, though Ordnance Survey 1:25 000 mapping shows the river's name on the first named above the confluence. The river flows through tightly constricted Langstrothdale as far as Hubberholme, beyond which the valley broadens out and becomes Wharfedale. In many people's eyes Wharfedale is the archetypical Yorkshire Dale; every yard of the valley is a delight as the river flows southwards past Buckden, Kettlewell, Grassington, Burnsall and Bolton Abbey. Turning easterly, the 'winding

15   Please see under Wear, pages 185–6, for a fuller explanation of this anorak aberration.

one' visits Ilkley, Otley and Wetherby before joining the Ouse south of York at Wharfe's Mouth near Cawood. Its headwaters rise above some of the loneliest valleys in the Dales and there's the added bonus of the Cosh Knott Well mystery.

Beckermonds, a scatter of a dozen buildings, lies in a sheltered hollow at the confluence of the river's two main feeders. To say that the few, small, haphazard, drystone-wall-enclosed fields, the graceful bridge spanning Oughtershaw Beck and the thin strip of tarmac edging its way gingerly between barn and byre to follow Green Field Beck beside limestone scars are what make up Beckermonds is like saying Turner's 1809 watercolour of Bolton Abbey is mostly pigment and paper. This beautiful little 'meeting of the streams' would still be discernible to the Norse settlers who came here in the tenth century, spreading from Ireland and Cumbria, while the yeoman farmers of the seventeenth and eighteenth centuries would easily recognize their homes. By a twist of local pronunciation Beckermonds became Beggarmonds and the road climbing over Fleet Moss and crossing the Wharfedale/Wensleydale watershed to plunge down to Hawes is called Beggarmans Road on its northern side.

From Beckermonds, you can follow the river by road, as Dales Way walkers do, to Oughtershaw, a curious place with its pretend Celtic cross celebrating Queen Victoria's Golden Jubilee, dry water fountain commemorating her Diamond Jubilee, Victorian Tudor-style hall and Venetian-inspired school. It was originally the 'outer wood' and at the end of the fifteenth century it comprised six tenements, which were all connected with the Langstrothdale Chase hunting forest stretching from Buckden to the head of the Wharfe. In the middle of the nineteenth century, the Oughtershaw estate came into the possession of Charles Woodd, son of a London wine merchant, who had Oughtershaw Hall and the school built. The latter, also used as a chapel, was probably designed by John Ruskin and was erected in memory of Woodd's first wife. Built from limestone and gritstone bands, its east end is a porch inside a massive rounded arch. Just below the Celtic cross the Dales Way, following Oughtershaw Beck, leaves the road and heads westwards to the Wharfe's gathering grounds, passing Nethergill and then Swarthgill farms. These are not as ancient as many others in the area, their meadows and pasture being reclaimed from the moor by Charles Woodd in the 1860s.

Swarthgill, a fine building with mullioned windows, stands at around 1,300 feet (397m) and is the highest house in the Wharfe's catchment, so it is not surprising that it needs its screen of trees. Beyond here the broad valley becomes bleaker as you near the vague watershed; clumps of sedge testify to the dampness of the place and the bright green of sphagnum tracks the stream channels. The grassy path crosses rills running down sharply incised little valleys falling off Oughtershaw Side, all headwaters of the Wharfe, and, just before aptly named Far End Barn, you meet a wall that just about follows the watershed. In wet weather a beck rising by the wall in the boggy bed of the lonely valley could lay a claim to be the Wharfe's source, as it rises furthest west, but a stream rising to the south and running down past a shooting box on the slopes of Oughtershaw Moss is longer, as is one to the north which springs out of the ground on the

Delectable upper Wharfedale

southern slopes of Dodd Fell, below a wall corner on Kidhow. Up there is the easiest approach to the Wharfe's gathering grounds, as a gated road, a section of the Roman Cam High Road, can be used as far as Kidhow Gate. A short walk down the hillside from the wall corner east of the cairn on Kidhow Pike brings you to the spring and gives good views over the various headwaters and down the valley of Oughtershaw Beck.

Back down in the valley and crossing the watershed into Ribble territory doesn't feel right, as the land ahead appears to carry on rising. Cam Beck's headstreams are mostly named on the map – Far End Gill, Cold Keld Gill, Pot Close Gill and Red Sike, for instance. Maybe the original surveyors stayed at Cam and were given all the local details. After the skeletal Breadpiece Barn, the path climbs to Cam Houses, one of the most remote places in the Dales and the nearest habitation to the source. At one time a little self-contained community of several farms where the children went to school in a small upstairs room with the master doubling as the doctor, Cam was often snowed in for weeks on end. Now Camm Farm provides spacious and luxurious self-catering holiday accommodation. Near by are eight patches of new native woodland created by the Yorkshire Dales Millennium Trust as a wildlife habitat. Also near by is the much larger area of coniferous forestry that stretches across Cam Rakes to Langstrothdale and Ribblesdale. The Dales Way and Camm Farm road both climb to join Cam High Road, which can be used, together with a track across Green Side, to reach the Oughtershaw Road and the descent back to Beckermonds and the confluence of Oughtershaw and Green Field Becks.

The Wharfe's second main headstream, Green Field Beck, rises on an ill-defined watershed in the midst of plantations between High Green Field Knott and Cam Rakes. Or does it? The 1:25 000 map is not too clear, as it appears to show a stream originating at Cosh Knott Well, three-quarters of a mile (1.2km) to the south-east and 500 feet (153m)

higher, flowing in *both* directions: west towards the Ribble and east to the Wharfe, after passing through a little round pool deep in the forest. The 1:50 000 sheet is no more helpful, as a forest track obscures the vital spot, while the 1:250 000 scale (quarter-inch to the ancients) indicates the stream flowing in only one direction – to Green Field Beck and the Wharfe! One to investigate.

The very minor road alongside Green Field Beck can be followed past little crinkled, grey limestone scars to just before Low Green Field, where a space by the start of a forestry track provides parking. The rest of the road, through High Green Field, where the tarmac ends, and the forest as far as the watershed and the boundary between Buckden and Horton-in-Ribblesdale parishes, is open to traffic but the far side of it, over Low Birkwith Moor to Sell Gill and Horton, is a bridleway only. A sign by the gate at Low Green Field is likely to put off most motorists and anyway it's only about 3 miles (4.8km) to the strange start of Green Field Beck along the quiet road. Ideal for an afternoon stroll and even better, as it swoops up and down through a drumlin-plastered landscape, for a bike ride.

One of the cottages at Low Green Field was for sale (£199,950, reduced from £235,000) as we cycled through the hamlet of five dwellings. The agricultural writer Arthur Young passed this way in the 1770s, noting that the farmer was reclaiming 'black moory land' by first burning it and then adding lime before sowing it with turnips and then grass. The bright green colour of some of the fields commemorates the original improver to this day. The present OS Explorer map indicates the fields just as they were when shown on a mid-nineteenth-century map; Pike Field still carries its original name, as does Ryegrass Field, though it now grows a different, woody crop. Writing about this stretch of upper Langstrothdale in 1980, F. W. Houghton[16] commented 'these new plantations do not yet obscure

16   F. W. Houghton, *Upper Wharfedale*, Dalesman, 1980.

Beckermonds confluence

the gaunt outline of the fells but thirty years hence the valley will present a very different prospect'. The present-day visitor will agree.

The road, passing a fine drumlin before reaching High Green Field, was earlier used by Fountains Abbey, which managed the valley as a monastic sheep grange. It was part of a packhorse route between Lancaster and Yorkshire and, after you enter the forest, a fine arched bridge crosses Green Field Beck, where a footpath leads off to Ling Gill in a former field that is now Cow Pasture only by name. Another half mile and you are at the watershed and a junction of the track with a forest road. Here is the little round pond, into and out of which flows the stream emanating from Cosh Knott Well, but which way does it then flow? The majority of the water heads off westwards, only to disappear when it meets the limestone near Old Ing, possibly re-emerging as Coppy Gill, which joins the Ribble near Selside, just below the confluence of Gayle and Cam Becks. However, a few yards down from the little pond, a side channel, about a foot (0.3m) above stream level, goes eastwards to cross under the forestry track in a pipe. Is it possible that in times of heavy rainfall the stream is deep enough for some of the water to be diverted this way and so join Green Field Beck, which is trickling away on the far side of the track? Is it possible that forestry operations have altered watercourses and diverted the stream from its original Wharfe-bound direction? I would like to think so, backing up the evidence of the 1:250 000 map with Yorkshire historian Harry Speight's assertion that Green Field Beck 'descends from Greenfield Knott'.[17]

Whatever: the climb to Cosh Knott Well is justified whether it is one of Wharfe's headsprings

17   *Upper Wharfedale*, Elliot Stock, 1900.

or not, as it is found in exquisite surroundings. Diverting on to a forest road ('No Unauthorised Persons') and dumping the bikes in a ditch, we made our way steeply up a forest ride to emerge on to the open moor, where we followed an electrified fence to the well. Once you are out of the woods the views are extensive, with Whernside, Ingleborough and Penyghent all in sight. A tiny train trundled over Ribblehead viaduct but human achievement is scaled down to N gauge in such surroundings. The water of Cosh Knott Well springs pure and sweet from among moss-covered boulders at the foot of a limestone knoll surmounted by a fine shepherd's cairn. A trig point crowns the next lump to the east. Penyghent and its supporter Plover Hill form the southern horizon, rising prominently above high, lonely moorland pocked by caves and shakeholes and crossed only by a single bridleway, the medieval Foxup Road. There is a fine sense of emptiness, wildness and tranquillity here of the sort not often met in England. And when you've taken in enough of the view there's the prospect of the ride back to Low Green Field Hill – it's downhill.

Aire

a real North country limestone fountain

One of Yorkshire's main rivers with an important role in the county's industrial development, the Aire flows south-east and then east for about 70 miles (113km) from its source near Malham in the Pennines to its confluence with the Ouse at Airmyn near Goole. In the meantime it has flowed through Skipton, Keighley, Leeds and Castleford. At one time it was very heavily polluted; it used to be said that the water changed colour every few days below the dye works in Saltaire from purple to yellow to blue. A few decades ago the river was largely dead below Keighley but improvements have seen fish returning and ten years ago porpoises were spotted in the tidal stretch.

The water that becomes the river Aire flows out of Malham Tarn but shortly after leaving the lake it disappears underground. Logic would suggest that the vanishing stream is the self-same water that re-emerges at the other end of a dry valley beneath the massive cliff of Malham Cove, but there's little logic with limestone and the Aire only sees the light of day again at Aire Head, a further mile (1.6km) to the south. The visitor clearly cannot pursue the hidden subterranean ramifications of the Aire's course so may as well follow an interesting route above ground.

Malham is one of the most popular spots in the Yorkshire Dales and its National Park Information Centre has a large car park. It is only a couple of hundred yards from there to the recognized source of the Aire. A footpath, signed Hanlith Bridge, leaves Chapel Gate and leads across fields, following Malham Beck and crossing a tributary by a footbridge before entering the fields where Aire Head springs rise. There are two main resurgences, one on either side of a wall, with a third, lesser one rising on its north side. The most southerly spring was liberally surrounded by butterbur, one of our earliest flowering plants. The spiky purplish-pink flowers were already fading and the leaves, which appear after flowering, starting to grow. They can reach a yard in diameter and their traditional use, for wrapping butter, gives the plant its name. The resurrected Aire runs into Malham Beck, the stream rising beneath Malham Cove, and the

AIRE	
SOURCE	Malham Tarn, North Yorkshire
G.R.	SD 893 667
LENGTH	70 miles (113 kilometres)
TRIBUTARIES	Otterburn Beck, Worth, Harden Beck, Calder
MOUTH	confluence with Ouse at Airmyn

combined waters soon meet Gordale Beck: the river is born and Airedale begins.

Walking through the village on a wet morning during the Easter holidays, we had plenty of company, mostly families rather than the A-level geography groups whose haunt this usually is, when we took to the popular path leading towards the cove. The smooth, well-engineered track, used here by the Pennine Way, follows Malham Beck almost to its rising beneath the sheer magnificence of the cove. The scenery around Malham is dominated by the Great Scar Limestone, composed largely of shell debris, which accumulated on the bed of a shallow tropical sea some 330 million years ago. The rock lies level in regular layers but vertical joints and horizontal bedding planes coursing through it are dissolved away over time by water, which then travels along them, underground, rather than on the surface. The limestone, over 600 feet (183m) thick here, is shattered by fault lines. One of these fractures, the Mid Craven Fault, forms the long scar of which the cove is the most dramatic feature. The rocks to the south have been lowered several thousand feet in relation to those now forming the cove, together with its hinterland of dissected and desiccated limestone plateau stretching as far as Malham Tarn. The great wall of rock, 260 (80m) feet high and over 300 yards (300m) across, gained its curved face at the end of the last Ice Age when meltwater from further north, a kind of proto-Aire, carved back the cliff as it hurtled over the edge in a great cascade. The water resurging as Malham Beck last appeared above ground at the Smelt Mill Sinks about three-quarters of a mile (1.2km) north-west of the cove.

There was the usual web of climbers on the cove and I found a dropped chalk bag, its contents turned glutinous by the rain, on the ground. Vertical dark streaks on the rock are formed either by lichen and mosses growing where water trickles down the face or by a falling chimney sweep, according to imagination. Charles Kingsley, staying at Malham Tarn House in 1858, suggested this explanation, which he developed by degree into *The Water Babies*. The rock climbers are not the only explorers, as several cavers are convinced that there is a big cave system just waiting to be found behind the cove. Divers and diggers have been searching, in some cases for twenty years, for the elusive master cave.

We had a Meldrew moment in Malham. Plaintive signs between Town Head Farm and the cove asked dog walkers not to leave their poo bags behind, as they are dangerous to the stock. This polite request had been ignored by some of the doggy fraternity. In fact there was even a little pile of them around one of the signs. I thought it high time for a lecture by Mrs Doasyouwouldbedoneby.

We found a footpath to the west of Malham Cove which led to Dean Moor, crossing into and out of the National Trust's Ewe Moor land through little gates atop the stiles and with views across to the Wild West landscape of Watlowes and Comb Hill. At a signpost we followed a broad green track to find Water Sinks where, in the space of a couple of yards, the infant Aire, newly released from Malham Tarn but already with a fine flow, just disappears. It sinks into potholes hidden by boulders and choked with gravel. We had reached the line of the North Craven Fault, where the stream-swallowing limestone is replaced by impervious Silurian Slate. The tarn is a natural lake, the highest in England, and was formed behind a bank of glacial moraine. It was raised by about 4 feet (1.2m) at the end of the eighteenth century by Lord Ribblesdale. It is, however, smaller than it once was, a large area in its north-western corner having been filled with debris washed down by streams running off Fountains Fell at the end of the Ice Ages. The truncated successor of one of these, originating near High Trenhouse and flowing across the extensive raised bog of Tarn Moss, could now claim to be the Aire's true source. Its higher stretches were dry, just a depression in a lamb-filled field, but it was visible enough in its deep and narrow little channel as it ran through

Tarn Moss, now a nature reserve with boardwalk paths. Some riders passed us as we made our way back to the tarn – limestone cowboys?

We returned to the cove along the Pennine Way, which first follows the line of the erstwhile river along a grassy dry valley with the limestone scars on either side growing ever higher before the path zig-zags its way down what can best be described as an 80 foot (25m) high dried up waterfall to join the lower section of the gorge, known as Watlowes. Towards the end of glacial times when the underground fissures were still filled with ice, any meltwater would have flowed over the surface limestone, carving out this spectacular canyon. Now the water has returned underground and the grassy valley is strangely quiet. A wall running along its bed marks the former boundary between land belonging to Fountains Abbey and Bolton Priory. Watlowes ends abruptly, on the limestone pavement atop Malham Cove, where we hopped gingerly across the clints, the blocks of rock, to avoid the ankle-breaking grykes in between them. This is certainly no place to spend a night, unless you possess magical powers.

On a clear day there is a splendid view from the edge of the cove to the fields, walls and buildings of Malham and on towards Aire Head and Airedale. It is a scene that people have been gazing at for the best part of seven thousand years and they have left reminders of themselves scattered around the

Malham Cove

landscape. Tiny flints shaped by Mesolithic hunters have been unearthed near Malham Tarn. An isolated stone hut, oval in shape, was excavated in the 1960s at Comb Scar, south of the Tarn, and identified as being from the Bronze Age. The limestone uplands to the north-east are littered with Iron Age settlements. The slight earthbank of a large Roman marching camp is still discernible on Malham Moor, probably built during the second half of the first century AD when a rebellion by the local Brigante tribe was being subdued. The village name itself was coined by Angles, who were Malca's people, and yet more tangible reminders of their presence, the lynchets, long agricultural strips or terraces, are still plainly visible in the more modern fields. Many local names were given by Norse shepherds who settled the higher lands on the Moor – Langscar, Janet's Foss, the becks and gills. The area is traversed by monastic roads and the remains of several crosses set up to mark them are still evident, while Monk Bridge was the original name of what later became New Bridge in the centre of the village. Sixteenth- and seventeenth-century yeoman farmers were able to own their land following the dissolution of the monasteries and, with increasing wealth, rebuilt their houses in fitting style. Eighteenth-century enclosures saw the seemingly haphazard pattern of fields established around the village and in the mid-nineteenth the drystone walls marched up on to the moor, as that too was enclosed in a more regular pattern. A period of mining activity has left the smelt mill chimney and disused shafts. More recent times have seen the building of car parks and the information centre.

When we returned to Water Sinks later on, after the heavy rain of the morning had stopped, I'm sure that the Aire was disappearing a good two yards further downstream than four hours earlier, before the deluge. However, as this was a rare day of rain during an extremely dry March and April, I think it unlikely that we'll see the Aire falling over Malham

Cove in a sheet of spray (as it reputedly did a couple of times at the beginning of the nineteenth century) any time soon.

Ribble
too few people know it

RIBBLE	
SOURCE	Jam Sike, North Yorkshire
G.R.	SD 813 830
LENGTH	75 miles (121 kilometres)
TRIBUTARIES	Hodder, Calder, Darwen, Douglas
MOUTH	Irish Sea, Lytham

The Ribble was one of the rivers of my childhood. Red Ribble buses were our inevitable form of transport, day trips to the Ribble Valley our relaxation. My local town team played in the Ribblesdale Cricket League and as folky teenagers we sang of Ribble's fair waters and took girls on walks to Dinckley Bridge. Like the Lune, the Ribble is another archetypal Lancashire river that has its source outside the county, in this case in Yorkshire.

Ribblehead is an evocative name, especially for students of Victorian endeavour. It is where the Pennines came close to breaking the Midland Railway's heart while it was building its spectacular Settle–Carlisle line in the 1870s. The southwest gales, squeezed between Whernside and Ingleborough and blasting up Chapel-le-dale, led to days when work on the mighty Ribblehead Viaduct simply could not progress. Men were blown from the structure and years after the railway's completion trains were halted by the force of the wind as they approached the viaduct. Ribblehead was the setting for a goldrush-type settlement when a couple of thousand navvies, wives, families and followers, tradesmen, cheapjacks and hawkers lived on the bleak moorland. And Ribblehead does not even hold the source of the river.

The location of the source has long been a contentious issue. As far back as the early seventeenth century, Michael Drayton, writing in his 30,000-line masterpiece *Poly-Olbion*, personified Ribble's beginnings:

> From Pengent's proud foot as from my
>   source I slide,
> That mountain, my proud sire, in height of
>   all his pride,
> Takes pleasure in my course as in his first
>   born flood,
> And Ingleborough, too of that Olympian
>   brood,
> With Pendle, of the north, the highest hills
>   that be,
> Do wistly me behold, and are beheld of me.

He placed the source in the right area, as did his contemporary William Camden, who in his topographical survey *Britannia* stated: 'This river, comming with a quick and hasty streame out of the hils in Yorkshire, taketh his course first Southward by three exceeding high mountaines, Ingelborrow hill at the spring head.'

Modern visitors might argue with the exactitude of the geography but Drayton and Camden were at least more precise than the earlier John Leland, Henry VIII's Royal Antiquary, who stated that 'Ribil riseth in Ribilsdale above Salley Abbey', a statement that is true but not very helpful, rather like saying the source of the Thames is above Oxford. Claims have been made more recently for a field called High Ribblehead, while Harry Speight, an indefatigable late Victorian Yorkshire walker and author, located a spring near Gearstones. Another spring near Ribblehead station has also been cited. Some authorities give the confluence of Gayle Beck and Cam Beck near Selside as the source but that is a couple of miles down Ribblesdale and below Ribblehead. That doyenne of Lancashire writers Jessica Lofthouse placed the source on Wold Fell above Newby Head while her Yorkshire counterparts, Marie Hartley and Joan Ingleby, believed it to be a matter of choice. Current choosing trends towards the spring at the head of Jam Sike, 4 miles (6.4km) north-east of Ribblehead, and situated conveniently near to a path. If this is accepted then the present-day seeker after Ribble's source has no excuses for not finding it, for a long-distance path, the Ribble Way, leads virtually to it. The idea for a Ribble Way grew up in the 1960s as a proposal by the Preston and Fylde group of the Ramblers' Association. An original route which would have used many private fishermen's paths along a mainly riverside route attracted much local opposition, so that the scheme did not come to fruition until the mid-1980s when an alternative, 73 miles (117km) long and using existing rights of way, was opened.

Although it is possible to visit the individual sources from various starting points, a round walk of about 12 miles (19km), starting from Ribblehead, has the benefit of off-road parking, the Station Inn and, usually, a snack van and takes you to many of the recognized sources. Part of the Ribble Way can be followed in a circular route which also uses sections of the Dales Way, the Pennine Way and the Pennine Bridleway.

Ribblehead must have seemed like the end of the earth to the Midland Railway surveyors who tramped out the route of the line. John Sharland, a Tasmanian who was one of the pioneers, found himself snowed up for three weeks at Gearstones, then an inn on the Ingleton–Hawes turnpike. The navvies who laboured here, some of whom had worked the world over, certainly agreed that this was 'one of the wildest, windiest, coldest and dreariest localities' anywhere. Not a trace remains at Ribblehead of the former shanty settlement of Batty Green. This took its name from a pothole existing at the time, Batty Wife Hole. One story tells

how Batty had fallen in love with a local girl, courting and eventually marrying her, but when he later went to the bad, his broken-spirited wife leapt to her death. Also in this area of limestone extravagance are Braithwaite Wife Hole and Tatham Wife Hole. I can see that a navvy might not have been the best of marital prospects, but surely they can't all have chucked themselves down potholes? The more prosaic view is that this is where the women took their washing. Looking out over this bleak moorland it is hard to envisage that during the 1870s the view would have included rows of timber and felt huts, a school, a library, a post office, a mission house and a hospital. Batty Green, together with the smaller encampments of Sebastopol, Salt Lake City and Jericho, witnessed some of the last flourishes of navvy culture before the mechanical excavators – steam navvies – took the hard graft out of digging. Herds of cattle were driven to Batty Green to feed the navvies' appetite for beef, drinking dens were quickly established and bare-knuckle fighting was a major Sunday distraction. Each shanty settlement would have its own 'cock o' the camp' who would fight the best the others could put up until an undisputed champion emerged. This hero might then battle against fighters brought in from other parts of the country. The fights were bruising, bloody affairs, only ending when one of the contenders was battered senseless.

Accidents and death were never far away for the work. Weather and smallpox all took their toll and the graveyard at nearby St Leonard's Church, Chapel-le-dale, had to be extended, while a memorial tablet inside the church commemorates the men who died during the construction of the line. Their true monument stands overlooking the tumbled ground of Batty Green. The first stone of the quarter-mile-long Ribblehead Viaduct was laid on 12 October 1870 and the last in 1874. The twenty-four arches carry the railway over 100 feet (30.5m) above the moor and each arch has a span of 45 feet (14m). The foundations for the pillars had to go down 25 feet (7.6m) through peat and clay to find solid rock. Every sixth pier is extra strong while all are made from huge stones. Some of them weigh 7 or 8 tons with the courses being over a yard thick. The arches are turned in brick and about 1½ million were used. The diesel loco and its train of eighteen massive goods wagons which crossed when I was tying my boots looked toy-like in the immensity of its surroundings.

Lying strategically in the midst of Yorkshire's famous Three Peaks, Whernside, Ingleborough and Penyghent, Ribblehead is a popular venue for a day out and there are usually cars, vans and minibuses with their cargoes of walkers pulling on boots, potholers pulling on suits and railway fans pulling out cameras. The Tea Van, known as the Fourth Peak, has been trading here since 1969 and, after a day up on the fells, down in a cave or wating at the end of the viaduct, is a welcome sight.

About two-thirds of a mile (1km) along the Blea Moor Road, on the way to Gearstones, a footpath to Gauber climbs over the wall by a steep stile to a stone barn. It is named as 'Ribble Head House' on the map and the spring which rises below it is, according to Harry Speight, the 'usually accepted source'. It certainly looks like his source, lying below a barn near two thorn trees and emptying into Gayle Beck just below. If the Glastonbury thorn, attacked by vandals in December 2010, and reported by all the papers to be 2,000 years old, is truly so ancient, then the ones at Ribble Head could surely be the same trees that Speight saw in the late nineteenth century. Gearstones, which once belonged to Furness Abbey and was later the location for a weekly market and regular fairs, was an inn until 1911, becoming a shooting lodge for some time after the Second World War. It later fell into disrepair before being bought by the people of Mirfield as an outdoors centre in 1972. It is now run by a charitable trust.

Very new lambs were just finding their feet in the fields at Far Gearstones. I had felt like a kind of ovine Pied Piper walking along the road, as the sheep on the unenclosed land seemed to think that I was about to feed them and came rushing towards me. As I left the road for a bridleway I was passed by a red-haired shepherd who cleared a whole fellside of sheep by the simple expedient of driving across it on his quad bike, pulling a trailer carrying a bale of hay and hollering at them.

Crossing Gayle Beck, the track climbs purposefully between Round Hill and Little Round Hill up to Cam End. This is the start of a glorious couple of miles' march along the Cam High Road, a route followed by Roman legionaries, eighteenth-century packhorses and coaches, and present-day Pennine and Dales Wayfarers. The High Road was part of the Roman road between Ingleton and Bainbridge, which follows a very direct route for much of its 19 miles (30.5km). During the second half of the eighteenth century it was incorporated into the Richmond-to-Lancaster Turnpike. From Cam End there is a retrospective view over Ribblehead to the valley stretching away between Ingleborough and Whernside. I passed a young couple who were walking the Pennine Way and later a vicar on the same mission, and thought back over three and a half decades to when Mike and I passed this way. We noted that the route was pretty crowded but at least it was still a beautifully turfed, soft-walking, green way in the most part. Tom Stephenson – who first proposed his Pennine Way dream in 1935, in

Bright red memories

a *Daily Herald* article headlined 'Wanted – a Long Green Trail' – certainly couldn't have envisaged the hard stony track built along this stretch to cater for modern economic interests, let alone the lengthy stretches in the Peak District and Cheviots that are now paved because of pressure of popularity. A felt-tipped note on the top beam of West Gate reflected the farmer's feelings on having had to mend it: 'New Post → Y.D.N.P. or timber workers sort it out – please send £175 – J E Beresford Thank you.'

Still, if the way underfoot has become harder the view is as engaging as ever, as an important watershed is seen if not quite crossed. Beyond the plantations of Cam Woodlands, a wall descending from the top of Cam Rakes and passing Far End Barn on the valley floor, before rising to just east of Kidhow Gate on the side of Dodd Fell, marks the approximate and undistinguished divide between waters draining into Cam Beck and the Ribble and the headstreams of Oughtershaw Beck, which becomes the Wharfe. A track leads down to the isolated hamlet of Cam Houses, where they used to fire a gun at nightfall to guide benighted travellers.

I left the vicar to continue on his way to Scotland and backtracked along a bridleway at Cold Keld Gate, where a fine gateway now marks the entrance to Camm Farm. For half a mile (0.8km) I was crossing the top of Grove Head, where a series of gills and sikes runs away to Snaizeholme Beck, Widdale Beck and the Ure at Hawes. At least this delightful path was how Cam High Road used to be. It follows a route where the surface reflects the rocks below as, paved in places with patches of fossil crinoids, it crosses above pale limestone scars surrounded by bright springy green turf, dotted with wild flowers, and looks down on dark peat groughs in a dun moor. In the Pennines the whole mood of the landscape is dictated by the rock beneath.

Larks larking and singing overhead added to the general joy as I descended to Gavel Gap and the current favourite for Ribble's source. The path crosses a wall at Gavel Gap, which formerly marked the boundary between Yorkshire's West and North Ridings. For a few years there was an ugly breeze-block barrier here but a gate now takes the Pennine Bridleway route up to the Cam High Road. The start of the Ribble is on the far side of the wall, just a couple of hundred yards further up the fellside. The source is a spring, sometimes a mere trickle, of clear water seeping from a low limestone scar not far from the top of Cam Fell to run away as Jam Sike, just one of the longest of several streams draining off Newby Head Moss and Gayle Moor. They all join together with Long Gill to become Gayle Beck, which runs south-westwards for a couple of miles before turning to flow resolutely down its dale at Ribblehead. The view from the source is impressive with Great Knoutberry Hill and Whernside prominent. Below here the track, improved recently for the Pennine Bridleway, descends alongside Jam

Ribblehead viaduct

Ribble Head House source

Sike and then Long Gill before cutting back to join the B6255 Ingleton–Hawes road at Newby Head. Walking down I briefly disturbed a frog orgy taking place in a trackside pond. All the frogs stopped while I passed, more out of fear of predation than modesty, I suppose. In 1795 the route of the turnpike was altered from the Cam High Road to the present way up Widdale from Hawes, crossing Newby Head before dropping down to Gearstones. This made the gradients easier and lowered the highest point by about 500 feet (152.5m). Newby Head Farm was also an inn for many years, closing in 1919.

Half a mile (0.8km) along the minor road to Dentdale, Black Rake Road, a former droving route and now a bridleway followed by the Dales and Ribble Ways, heads south across Stoops Moss to cross the head of Ouster Gill, another Gayle Beck tributary. It passes a little new plantation and a sign saying 'DEEP PEAT', which made me think of my tired calf muscles, before crossing a couple of sharp little dells and following the top of the intake above High Gayle and Winshaw as Ingleborough looms ever larger ahead. In the last few decades of the eighteenth century this route and the Cam High Road across the valley would have been noisy with herds of cattle on the hoof and strings of salt- and coal-laden packhorses before the present road, today echoing with the buzz of motorbikes, was even built. The path descends and makes its way boggily around Winshaw before meeting the road by Gearstones for a mile or so's walk along the verge back to Ribblehead and, with luck, a mug of tea at the Fourth Peak.

Eden

seek the river of the soul

The Eden flows for about 65 miles (105km) in a largely north-westerly direction from the heights above the Mallerstang valley in the Pennines to the Solway Firth. It has a catchment area of just under 1,500 square miles (3,885 sq. km) and its valley

EDEN	
SOURCE	Eden Springs, Cumbria
G.R.	SD 810 992
LENGTH	65 miles (105 kilometres)
TRIBUTARIES	Eamont, Irthing, Petteril, Caldew
MOUTH	Solway Firth

largely forms the divide between the Pennines and the Lake District fells.

On the village green of the Eden valley hamlet of Outhgill stands the Jew Stone. In 1850 an eccentric wealthy local solicitor, William Henry Mounsey, walked the length of the river Eden and set up a stone, made from Dent marble, to mark his achievement. It was inscribed with Greek and Latin biblical texts and the Star of David. Part of the Latin text read 'William Mounsey, a lone traveller, commenced his journey at the mouth and finished at the source, fulfilled his vow to the genius and nymphs of the Eden on the 15th March, 1850.' It originally stood by Red Gill on Black Fell Moss, near the source of the Eden, until in 1870 it was broken into four pieces by navvies working on the Settle–Carlisle railway who were apparently frustrated at not being able to understand what it said.

William Mounsey was born in 1808 in Rockliffe, on the Eden estuary, and joined the army as a young man. He served in the Middle East, where he became obsessed with all things Jewish. When he returned he dressed as a Jew and adopted the Jewish way of life, being known locally as the Jew of Carlisle.

During the Second World War Shalom Hermon, who had escaped from the Nazis in Poland, came to England, where he became an officer in the British Army's Jewish Brigade. Having seen 'Jew Stone' on a map of the Eden Valley, in 1984 he returned to the area and visited Hanging Lund, where he was shown the remains of the stone lying in a barn. He declared it to have Jewish connections and on his return home to Israel he began fundraising, with a view to restoration. The stone had begun to shale badly, so a replica was made instead. It was placed on Outhgill Green on 21 September 1989.

Some take the confluence of Hell Gill Beck and Ais Gill by Aisgill Farm, on the B6259 Kirkby Stephen–Hawes road, to be the official source of Eden, for this is where the name first appears on the maps. An even earlier visitor than Mounsey, Daniel Defoe, stated that the Eden rises on 'the side of a monstrous high mountain called Mowill Hill, or Wildbore Fell, which you please'. He was presumably referring to Ais Gill and, without the intervention of the Ice Ages, he might well have been right. However, having begun in the company of the Jew of Carlisle, we will follow Mounsey's lead and follow the principal feeder, Hell Gill.

Three and a half miles (5.6km) south of Outhgill as the Eden meanders, where the watershed of England drops to valley level, Aisgill is a good starting point for a walk to the source. Here, the Settle–Carlisle line of the former Midland Railway reaches its 1,169 feet (357m) summit as it crosses the watershed as well as the county and National Park boundary. Half a mile (0.8km) to the north, by Cotegill Bridge, also known as Wreck Bridge, there is parking space for a few cars. You might well wonder about the alternative name. This wild spot has seen more than its fair share of tragedy, for two railway accidents, one triggered by nature and the other by human failings, have occurred within a mile or so of the summit. On the last day of January 1995 a landslip above Hanging Lund caused a diesel multiple unit Super Sprinter to be derailed into the path of another train passing minutes later on the adjacent track. The conductor of the derailed train was killed and thirty passengers injured. Nature had little to do with the earlier, even more serious accident. Early in the morning of

the first day of September 1913, a heavy train came to a standstill half a mile short of Aisgill summit, south of Cotegill Bridge. With a tender load of poor steaming small coal and slack and a train 13 tons over the limit for its class, Midland Railway four-coupled engine no. 993 simply ran out of steam. The driver was confident that the train would soon be moving again, so the guard did not attempt to protect the train by placing detonators on the tracks behind. Meanwhile a following train, pulled by locomotive no. 446, was also steaming badly because of the small coal. However, with a lighter load she was still making better progress than 993. Just before Mallerstang the driver left his cab to oil some of the working parts of the loco while the train was in motion. This was a habitual and rather macho action, as by now lubricators were fitted, which made the procedure unnecessary. While the driver was away on the framing, the fireman was struggling with an injector and the water level in the boiler was dropping. When the driver came back to the footplate both men worked on the recalcitrant injector and got it working. However, by this time they had missed all the Mallerstang signals and a red lantern being frantically waved by the signalman in the Mallerstang box. At just turned three in the morning the express from Edinburgh ploughed into the rear of the stationary Glasgow–London express. Fourteen passengers were killed and many more seriously injured.

Even if Hell Gill Beck were not Eden's main headwater, it would be well worth exploring for its own sake. From Aisgill Moor cottages, old railway houses at the line's summit, a track leads over a railway bridge and across a field to the 25-foot (7.6m) drop of Hellgill Force. The fall shows the Yoredale rock strata clearly. The lip is composed of a thin limestone layer overlaying a rust-coloured sandstone band, lying on top of the undercut weaker shale beneath.

Hell Gill Beck's lower reaches are the best parts, for it has been over-deepened and has cut itself a fine, half-hidden gorge. In former times, before glacial action disturbed matters, Hell Gill Beck flowed into the Ure and it still seems to be heading in that direction for the first couple of miles of its course. Moraine dumped at the end of the last Ice Age diverted the stream so that it now turns back on itself and flows north to form the Eden proper after its confluence with Ais Gill. The drop down to Mallerstang is greater than the fall to the head of Wensleydale, so, ever since the end of the last glaciation, Hell Gill Beck has had to work hard, trying to cut down to the level of its adoptive river. The full reach of Hell Gill Gorge can only be explored by those willing to get very wet, for a through journey from top to bottom is possible only by following the beck itself, at times down waterfalls 6 feet (1.8m) high and through narrow passages which are almost cave like – an adventurous canyoneering expedition for a hot, anticyclonic summer's day when visibility on the tops precludes a good view. It is difficult to get a good view of the gorge from its edge, for trees growing alongside obscure the best portions, although a glimpse of its depths may be obtained from Hell Gill Bridge, just above the farm of the same name.

The old stone bridge used to carry the main road through Mallerstang, the High Way, until the present route was turnpiked in 1825. For a mile or so Hell Gill Beck forms the county boundary and it is said that Dick Turpin once leapt on his horse across the gill to escape from the wrath of the Westmorland magistrates. The same tale is told of a more local highwayman, John 'Swift Nick' Nevison, and unless leaping Hell Gill was some kind of regular sport for gentlemen of the road, it seems likely that some confusion has arisen.

Beyond the bridge and the gorge the beck is a delight to follow, and I was constantly changing sides up a tight little valley. On one visit a number of minor landslips testified to the high rainfall over the previous few weeks. You pass several sheepfolds and distant Whernside, and then Ingleborough appear down the valley.

Higher still the stream, now known as Red Gill, is joined by Little Grain and Slate Gutter and runs through a miniature gorge before the moor opens out into Black Fell Moss, where a peaty depression, Eden Springs just short of the ridge, marks the source of the river. In the course of several visits, I have met no genius and unfortunately no nymphs in the vicinity.

Long before William Mounsey placed his monolith here, there was another noteworthy pillar in the vicinity. Near the summit of Hugh Seat, overlooking Black Fell Moss, stands Lady's Pillar, a fitting topping to a hill with a history. Hugh Seat, most recently surveyed at 2,260 feet (689m), is one of many hills named after someone but one of the few where we know something about the person to be so honoured. Hugh de Morville was involved in the murder of Thomas Becket in Canterbury Cathedral in December 1170. He was not implicated in the actual death but rather held back the crowds at the entrance to the transept who might have attempted to save the martyr. Such was the enmity which people felt towards the perpetrators of the crime that Hugh and his companions are said to have hidden for a year in his castle at Knaresborough. Later, as a result of Hugh's involvement in rebellion, the de Morville lands were forfeited to the Crown but eventually were given back to the family. Hugh's sister, Maud, married into the de

Hellgill Force

Hellgill Bridge

Lune
not even a crushed blade of grass

LUNE	
SOURCE	Green Bell, Cumbria
G.R.	NY 699 007
LENGTH	45 miles (72 kilometres)
TRIBUTARIES	Rawthey, Leck Beck, Greta, Wenning
MOUTH	Sunderland Point, Morecambe Bay

Veteripont family and a descendant, Lady Anne Clifford, Countess of Dorset and Pembroke, who owned Pendragon Castle in the valley as well as those at Appleby, Brougham and Brough near by, built the stone pillar which stands near the summit. It is inscribed 'AP 1664' on one side and 'FHL' on the other. Pembroke was Lady Anne's married name. The cairn was no doubt set up by Lady Anne while she was staying at Pendragon, to mark the bounds of her land; indeed the fell top was known locally as Lady's Pillar. It was restored by a later lord of the manor, Captain Frederick Horner Lyell – hence the carving on the other face.

Two rivers with the name Lune are spawned in the hills of northern England. The less well-known eastern-flowing stream rises in a treacherous Pennine desolation of peat hag and mire, Lune Forest, on the southern slopes of mighty Mickle Fell, once Yorkshire's highest summit. Its topmost feeder, Connypot Beck, tributary of Lune Head Beck, seeps out of the eastern slopes of Little Fell, whose name must surely have been given as a joke, in the Little John sense. This 12 mile (19km) long Lune joins the Tees half a dozen miles north-west of Barnard Castle, between Middleton and Mickleton. The source is generally given as the confluence of Lune Head Beck and Cleve Beck near Lune Head Farm by the B6276 Brough-to-Middleton road and it is probably best to accept this, for to seek out the true source involves any amount of trespass, risk to life and limb, and a possible peppering of shotgun pellets, artillery shells and machine-gun bullets. Much of the Lune Forest lies within the Warcop Ranges, a military training area and firing range. Helpful signs give the comforting warning not to touch anything 'as it may explode and kill you'. It is also in the Upper Teesdale National Nature Reserve and is a top grouse-shooting moor. Having once blundered right through a shoot while walking in the area, I can only put my survival down to looking rather like a spectral gamekeeper because of the tweed deerstalker hat, sixty years old and just about worn in, which I was wearing at the time.

As Lune is derived from an old Celtic word thought to mean 'pure or clean', it is not surprising that more than one river bears the name. Big brother Lune's source, the one visited here, is 15 miles (24km) to the south-west, in the northern Howgill Fells, and although the river has indirectly given its name to the county through which it partly flows during its 45-mile (72km) journey to the sea at Morecambe Bay, its beginning is not in Lancashire. Its source is often given as Wath, in Cumbria, a hamlet situated by the confluence of Sandwath Beck (Dale Gill) and Weasdale Beck, but as usual the true source is a few miles away and a thousand feet higher. I know this is not quite in the Yorkshire Dales National Park and so, strictly speaking, shouldn't be in this chapter but I'm at a loss as where else to include it, so here it is. Anyway, there's talk of expanding the YDNP to include this chunk of land, so it might end up in the right place after all.

The Howgill Fells are a compact group of green rolling hills, lying between the Pennines and the Lakeland Fells, which are familiar to travellers on the M6 as it hurries through Tebay Gorge. The fells are virtually surrounded by the Lune and its major tributary, the Rawthey. Their smooth, rounded nature is a result of the Silurian rocks from which they are made. This slatey-grey sandstone, known as Coniston Grit, is older than the Carboniferous rocks of the nearby Pennine tops and has been smoothed off by aeons of ice and water. The highest point on the Howgills, The Calf, stands above the fine market town of Sedbergh but the source of the Lune is further north, on the slopes of Green Bell. The attractive village of Ravenstonedale makes an ideal starting point for a walk, taking in Snowfell End and Knoutberry before climbing to the source and the prominent little top of Green Bell.

From the village a footpath leads south-west past Kilnmire before descending to cross Wyegarth Gill. You will find a plethora of paths ascending

the open fell over Snowfell End and Knoutberry, the ridge here forming the watershed between the Lune and the Eden, and from the col between Knoutberry and Green Bell, a slight descent leads to the springs which mark the source. The highest spring is close to a ruined sheepfold and the infant Lune starts off by heading north down the valley of Dale Gill, tumbling after half a mile or so over a series of little waterfalls. There is little to detain you, no cairn, tablet or marker, so the climb to the summit of Green Bell will round off the walk neatly. Here will be found an Ordnance Survey trig point and, on a clear day, good views south over the Howgills to The Calf. For a return to the valley from Green Bell, you can pick up a good track running across the hill to the west of the summit. If followed all the way down this will lead to Newbiggin-on-Lune but it seems more appropriate to stay with the young Lune as far as the remains of old stone quarries on High Cocklake. Here may be seen half a dozen of the fell ponies that roam the Howgills. There is a lovely path from Greenside across the fields to Ravenstonedale, which crosses a fine old bridge before reaching Town Head. Here I opened the gate for the farmer's wife and young child on their quad bike. They were going to look at one of the cows to see if she had calved.

The walk described above is a little under 6 miles (9.6km) but there is ample scope to extend it and explore more of the splendid walking country which the Howgills present. No walls or fences break up the high fellsides, so the only limit to route finding in clear weather round here is imagination. A straightforward stroll of less than a mile from Green Bell over Spengill Head and across the little top of Stockless, which being occupied by two sheep rather belied its name the last time I passed, follows the Lune/Rawthey watershed to the summit of one of the Howgill Fells' 2,000-foot hills, Randygill Top. The Top's top is marked by a cairn that is fair sized considering the paucity of stone in the vicinity, and it gives excellent views, especially to the Lake District mountains away westwards. Ingleborough and Whernside, two of Yorkshire's Three Peaks, are visible southwards and Baugh Fell and Wild Boar Fell loom large across the Rawthey Valley to the east while Cross Fell, the highest in the Pennines, forms the northern horizon. The Randy Gills, of which this is the top, are to be found south of the summit. Great Randy Gill separates Randygill Top from Kensgriff and Yarlside, another 2,000-footer, while Little Randy Gill lies between the latter two. The return can be made down Bowderdale after passing the confluence of Randy Gill and Bowderdale Beck, one of the Lune's major early tributaries. Bowderdale is a long and lonely steep side-valley, rising to the heart of the fells and typical of the dales which have been etched into the northern Howgills. If you follow it to Bowderdale Foot there is an hour or so of walking along quiet lanes and field paths before you reach Ravenstonedale – time to reflect on the walk and the quiet, ancient landscape that you have traversed.

Just over the col at Bowderdale Head, headwaters of Cautley Holme Beck, one of the Rawthey's tributaries, coalesce to plunge over the dramatic Cautley Spout waterfall and a fine source walk can be taken from the confluence of the beck with the river, steeply up past the Spout and alongside Red Gill Beck to its source north-east of the summit of Calders. On the way you pass one of Andy Goldsworthy's *Sheepfold* sculptures, complete with a decorative corner cairn. One of a series of works throughout Cumbria, the artist's aim in rebuilding the derelict fold was to remind us that this is a landscape shaped by past and present usage. Constructed in 2002, it is also partly a memorial to the devastation caused by the foot-and-mouth epidemic that ravaged the area during the previous year.

Outside the scope of this book is the source of the Lune or Lhûn in J. R. R. Tolkein's *Lord of the Rings*. One of over sixty streams and rivers mentioned in the Middle Earth trilogy, this Lune rises in the Blue Mountains in the north of Eriador. Visiting literary sources is perhaps best saved for extreme old age or a period of extended drought.

Derwent

to Whinny-muir thou com'st at last

DERWENT	
SOURCE	Derwent Head, North Yorkshire
G.R.	SE 888 974
LENGTH	57 miles (92 kilometres)
TRIBUTARIES	Hertford, Rye, Bielby Beck
MOUTH	confluence with Ouse, Barmby on the Marsh

The Yorkshire variety of this riverine version of a BOGOF rises on Fylingdales Moor in the North York Moors National Park. Containing the largest continuous stretch of heather moor in England, this park covers 553 square miles (1,432 sq. km). Heading off resolutely towards the sea at Scalby near Scarborough, a distance of a dozen or so miles (20km), the Derwent is another Ice Age casualty, being blocked off from its original course by a detritus-laden tongue of ice which stretched down the North Sea basin. The melting ice dumped its moraine, blocking the eastern route, and river and meltwater together formed a lake in the Vale of Pickering which grew and deepened until, like bathwater overflowing, it cut through the lowest point on the rim at Kirkham, gouging a gorge through the Howardian Hills as it rushed away southwards. The 57 mile (92km) long Derwent now joins the Ouse at Barmby on the Marsh and its waters ultimately become part of the Humber.

It was our first visit to the North York Moors since crossing them on Wainwright's exquisite Coast to Coast Walk during a delightful Easter

Cautley Spout

fortnight over thirty years ago. That route had taken us close to the source of the Lakeland Derwent; this time on a much shorter excursion we would visit the Yorkshire version.

From a car park beside May Beck in the Newton House Plantation we followed a gang of lads who were on path maintenance duties into the depths of the forest. Plenty of rain during the previous day meant that the beck – not a Derwent tributary, as its waters eventually join the Whitby-bound Esk – was a chattering companion until we left it to head further into the woods and a junction with a forest road. Here we turned right, past a flooded linear quarry, following the road until a track went off on the left heading towards the remains of York Cross. The North York Moors are waymarked by many old crosses, now mostly just shafts and stumps, marking important crossings.

A look at the map reveals a line of quarries crossing the moors in a west-nor'-westerly direction here, with the track heading the same way. This is Whinstone Ridge and the hard volcanic rock, known to geologists as Dolerite, is part of the Cleveland Dyke which stretches from here for about 250 miles (400km) to the island of Mull. It was squeezed into the surrounding rocks nearly 60 million years ago and has been mined and quarried for roadstone and setts. A couple of miles along the ridge, on the far side of the main A169 Sleights–Pickering road, a line of shallow excavations stretches across the moor eventually to reach Cliff Rigg Quarry above Great Ayton, which provided the cobbles for many of the Victorian streets of Leeds.

We backtracked to take a path running up to Foster Howes, three Bronze Age barrows standing in a line along the ridge, and continued along to Ann Howe, another barrow with the base of a cross on top. The track was in very poor condition, wet and rutted, as it climbed gently across the heather towards the high point of this part of the moor at Louven Howe. Away to the west a thick mass of smoke showed where they were burning heather on Widow Howe Moor while a thin trail of steam marked the passage of a North York Moors Railway train heading for Goathland and Grosmont with its unmistakable, haunting, high-pitched chime whistle echoing round the hillside.[18] To the south RAF Fylingdales Early Warning Station stood out, looking for all the world like a semi-decommissioned nuclear power station. From other angles it resembles an incomplete ziggurat or even a sandcastle like the ones we'd seen on Scarborough beach the day before, while the radar mounted on each face of the truncated tetrahedron gives it the look of a giant loudspeaker cab that could give most of Yorkshire a gig to remember. The latest structure replaced the former trio of giant geodesic golf balls in the early 1990s.

Louven Howe is yet another Bronze Age round barrow, one of a series including those already passed, which is thought to have marked a territorial boundary. It is surmounted by a boundary stone marked with a cross and letter C, and is a few yards away from a trig point. There are wide-ranging views from here to the west over Goathland Moor and east across Fylingdales Moor towards the sea south of Robin Hood's Bay. Also near by stands a concrete-filled 4 foot (1.2m) high upturned drainpipe on a square base with a standard Ordnance Survey spider on top. Nothing to do with arachnology, this is a metal plate designed to hold a theodolite and the column was presumably installed in connection with surveying for the construction of RAF Fylingdales in the early 1960s.

Now that you have entered the Derwent catchment area, a short walk leads to Lilla Cross and views towards the upper valley. This is one of the finest of the North York Moors crosses, standing at

the boundary of four medieval parishes, marking the edge of the land belonging to Whitby Abbey and at the junction of important tracks. Long before that it was another Bronze Age barrow site, continuing the boundary previously noted. Near by stands a stone with a couple of plaques explaining all.

ERECTED ABOUT AD 625 OVER
THE REPUTED GRAVE OF LILLA,
AN OFFICER OF THE COURT OF
EDWIN, KING OF NORTHUMBRIA,
WHO DIED SAVING THE LIFE OF
THE KING. BELIEVED TO BE THE
OLDEST CHRISTIAN MEMORIAL
IN THE NORTH OF ENGLAND.
ORIGINALLY ERECTED ON MOORS
BETWEEN PICKERING AND ROBIN
HOOD'S BAY, RE-SET IN 1933 BY
THE NORTH RIDING COUNTY
COUNCIL, REMOVED IN 1952 BY
ROYAL ENGINEERS TO AVOID
DESTRUCTION FROM GUNFIRE ON
ARTILLERY RANGES.
LILLA CROSS WAS RE-SET HERE
IN 1962 BY 508 FIELD SQUADRON
ROYAL ENGINEERS TERRITORIAL
ARMY OF HORDEN, CO DURHAM IN
CONJUNCTION WITH THE WHITBY
RURAL DISTRICT COUNCIL.

The Lyke Wake Walk, a famous tough North York Moors challenge, passes Lilla Cross. This 40-mile (64km) walk is a complete crossing of the moor between Osmotherley and Ravenscar along the main west–east watershed separating Esk and Derwent. It was inaugurated by local farmer Bill Cowley and friends, who made the first crossing in 1955. The Lyke Wake Walk achieved great popularity during the 1960s and '70s, when erosion of the route became a problem. The walk's name comes from the Lyke Wake Dirge, one of Yorkshire's oldest dialect poems, which tells of the soul's passage

---

18   Gricer alarm: erstwhile London and North Eastern Railway A4 Class locomotive *Sir Nigel Gresley,* recently returned to service after lengthy boiler repairs.

through the afterlife. Anyone completing the route in less than twenty-four hours can apply to join the Lyke Wake Club and become a Dirger or Witch, depending on gender.

I took the track south from Lilla Cross, chanting 'This ae neet, this ae neet, Ivery neet and all, Fire and fleet and candleleet and Christ receive thy soul' to myself as I crossed the Lyke Wake route. The descent to Derwent Head, on the edge of Langdale Forest, is gentle and several headstreams pass under, over and, in at least one case, along the track. Derwent Head itself is a rushy morass just above the track. Near by stands a boundary stone erected by the Commissioners of the Wykeham enclosure in 1786. The little stream collects itself together to flow away down its wide, boggy valley, followed for a couple of miles by the forest fence.

From Derwent Head the most direct way back to the car park at May Beck follows part of the way-marked Moor to Sea cycle route, but those with a dislike of regimented trees or geographical puns can take the Robin Hood's Bay Road, a path which descends besides, or sometimes as part of, Blea Hill Beck on the east side of the forest. You can abandon this for an intermittent path which meets another near John Cross and make a descent across a field and then steeply down gorse and bracken-covered slopes to the road and car park. This walk provides good exercise but perhaps late autumn doesn't show the moors at their best and a visit during August when the heather is flowering would add to its attractiveness. Easier still, take a bike and cycle up from the car park.

Other ways of reaching Derwent Head can be devised. Anyone interested in gaining a close-up view of RAF Fylingdales can follow a bridleway from near the car park on the main road above the Hole of Horcum. This goes along Saltergate Brow before descending to Malo Cross and a forest edge track heading north past the early warning station on Snod Hill before trending east across Worm Sike Rigg and then north again to Derwent Head.

A direct ascent of the river itself from the south-east is not really practicable, being much complicated by fields, forests and bog, and it is in places like this that the British walker can only envy his New Zealand counterpart's Queen's Chain. Nothing to do with Windsor plumbing, this is a 22-yard-wide strip at the edge of rivers, lakes and the sea owned by the Crown or local authority and generally available to the public for recreation. Were it statutory in this country then it would certainly make looking for sources simpler. Although the river itself cannot be followed you can pick up a forest track after leaving the end of the road beyond Lownorth Bridge in Harwood Dale and descending to a ford across the Derwent. The track ascends through the trees to Derwent Head Rigg and the edge of the forest just above the source. A return can then be made via Lilla Cross and a bridleway, heading first east-nor'-east then south-east, past Brown Hill and Riverhead Farm on the way back to the start.

LAKELAND DIVERSIONS

Driving up the M6 I am always tempted to veer westwards to the Lake District, the perfect little mountain wonderland. Of the countless rivers, becks and gills rising among the fells in the wettest part of England, the sources of the Derwent and the Esk stand nearest to the heart of Lakeland in sight of some of the finest mountain scenery in Britain.

Derwent

make ceaseless music

	DERWENT
SOURCE	Sprinkling Tarn, Cumbria
G.R.	NY 228 091
LENGTH	33 miles (53 kilometres)
TRIBUTARIES	Greta, Cocker
MOUTH	Workington, Cumbria

It is by no means the highest nor the most remote; nonetheless, of all the river sources described here, that of the 33 mile (53km) long Cumberland Derwent has, in my view, the most perfect mountain setting. Sprinkling Tarn, reckoned by most authorities to be the river's birthplace, is set on the broad, high, knobbly ridge of Seathwaite Fell between the river's two main headwaters, Styhead Gill and Grains Gill. The fell itself rises to 2,073 feet (532m) and the tarn stands only slightly below the 2,000-foot (610m) contour. It is a delightfully shaped, angular piece of water with a large promontory and a small island. At its longest the tarn measures around 900 feet (275m) and its width is about half that. Lying on a high mountain ledge rather than being a corrie tarn like many others in the mountains, Sprinkling Tarn is fairly shallow, reaching only about 30 feet (9m). This means that it is quick to freeze over in the winter but can warm up in the summer, making it a bit more comfortable for a swim than some of the deeper tarns. All around are rocky outcrops and humpy moraines, boggy hollows and heathery banks. The great Lake District artist William Heaton Cooper counted Sprinkling Tarn as the 'most completely satisfying of all the tarns of Lakeland'. It has recently become a nursery for Britain's rarest freshwater fish, the vendace, a small fish with silver flanks and a bluish-green back that is a relic from the last glacial period. Threatened by pollution in watercourses feeding their spawning grounds in Derwent Water and Bassenthwaite Lake, over 130,000 vendace eggs were taken to Sprinkling Tarn in 2005. A further 25,000 newly hatched vendace made the journey in April 2011, this time being transported by llama.

The shelf holding the tarn is crossed by paths used by thousands of walkers each year making their way between the axial valleys of Wasdale, Langdale, Eskdale and Borrowdale, the Derwent's own valley, and heading for the highest and most rugged of Lakeland's fells. This in itself would make the source of the Derwent an exciting place to be but it is the surroundings, and especially the backdrop, that provide the majesty of the setting. Sprinkling Tarn lies at the foot of Great End, a mountain named with poetic simplicity, for it stands at the brink of the highest chunk of land in England. From

Styhead Tarn

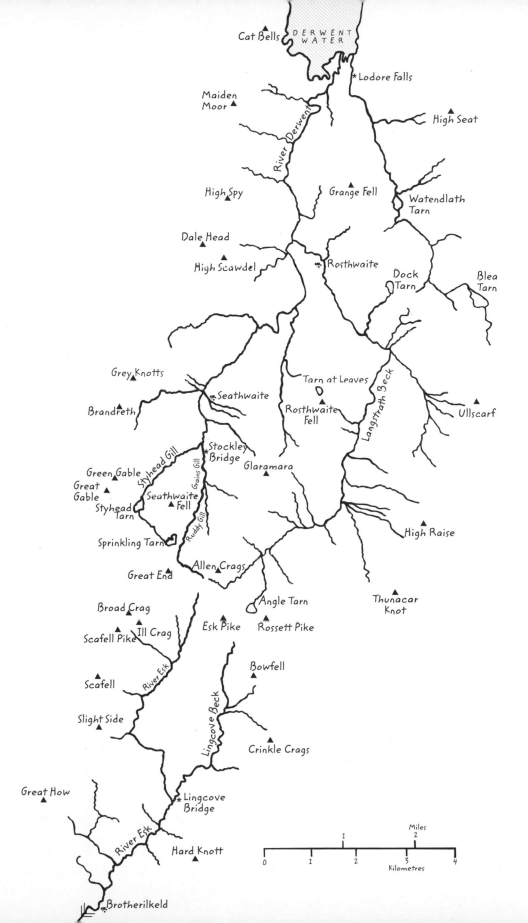

Sprinkling Tarn

Stockley Bridge

best winter climbing south of Scotland. Small runnels flow down from the crags and gullies, and the source seeker who is also a competent scrambler may spend a few happy hours poking about to find the highest.

The proto-Derwent, as yet unnamed, leaves the western end of Sprinkling Tarn to flow steeply down to Styhead Tarn, a fall of about 500 feet (152m) in half a mile (0.8km). Styhead Gill then flows north-eastwards for a further mile (1.6km), which includes the plunge over Taylorgill Force, before meeting Grains Gill. The waterfall marks the end of a hanging valley, a feature common among the glaciated mountains of the Lake District. During the last Ice Age a subsidiary glacier flowed down from the vicinity of Sty Head to join the main glacier in Grains Gill and Borrowdale. The latter, having more erosional power, deepened the main valley more than the side valley. After the ice had retreated the little stream coming down from Sty Head, a misfit in an ice-broadened valley, had to tumble over the step and has done so ever since. Many of Derwent's tributaries hurry-skurry down hanging valleys – that's why the water comes down at Lodore!

It could be argued that the meeting place of the two main headwaters, Styhead Gill and Grains Gill, just below Stockley Bridge is the real source of the river Derwent. It is certainly only so named on the maps downstream of the confluence. However, anyone accepting this would be missing one of the finest source walks in Britain.

The route starts at Seathwaite, first mentioned in the annals in 1292 and the wettest inhabited place in England. As this book is about river sources and as rivers depend on rainfall, this seems a suitable spot to mention the work of John Fletcher Miller, Victorian meteorologist, who discovered the pre-eminent wetness of the place. In 1844 Miller began to collect data about the rainfall of the area, using as many as thirty rain gauges and reaching from the valleys right up to the summit of Scafell. His expeditions to collect measurements from his

the summit of Great End, 1,000 feet (305m) above the tarn, you can walk to Scafell Pike, nearly 1½ miles (2.4km) away, without ever dropping below 2,500 feet (762m). Great End's glory is its magnificent north-eastern face, deeply gouged by plunging gullies tumbling down to the tarn. When these clefts are plastered with snow and ice they give the gauges were wonderful feats of walking and he once covered 70 miles during the course of a single trek. In 1848 he presented his paper outlining the results of his work to the Royal Society, which was staggered by his report that parts of the Lake District received more rain than tropical India. The average for Sprinkling Tarn was given as nearly 150 inches (3,810mm) a year and it had reached 180 inches (4,572mm). The highest monthly total had been greater than 30 inches (762mm), more than falls on many parts of eastern England in a year, and the maximum daily downpour had approached 7 inches (178mm). J. W. Fletcher, MP for Cockermouth, continued Miller's work, which had been received with scepticism by some of his contemporary scientists, and came up with even more remarkable statistics. In 1866 Fletcher recorded a total of 224.56 inches (5,704mm) at Sty Head.

In 1898 Seathwaite was almost destroyed by floodwaters and again, in the early 1950s, great damage was done to buildings, walls and the bridge carrying the road across the Derwent. The hamlet had long held the unenviable accolade of having had the wettest Lakeland day on record, when 8.03 inches (204mm) fell during 12 November 1897, but this was surpassed on 19 November 2009, when over 12 inches (316.4mm) of rain fell. Described by the Environment Agency as a once-in-a-thousand years event, this is a record for the amount of rain falling in any United Kingdom location within twenty-four hours. The Derwent and Cocker burst their banks, the main street in Cockermouth became a raging torrent, bridges were swept away and a police constable was drowned in Workington. Seathwaite now holds the records for the highest 24-hour, 2-day, 3-day, 4-day, 5-day, 6-day and 7-day rainfall in Britain, while Styhead claims the record for a calendar month.

A cluster of farm buildings and cottages stand around the farmyard, which must be one of the most tramped through in these islands. Passing the farm and heading up the valley a broad track runs between hummocks of moraine dumped here

by glaciers retreating to their final stronghold in the heart of the mountains at the end of the Ice Ages. Bank strengthening and protection work is in evidence along this stretch of the young river, dating from another serious flood in August 1966. One drumlin has been halved by the power of the stream.

Stockley Bridge, a fine packhorse bridge, is on the Sty Head route between Borrowdale and Wasdale and across it a path turns left to follow Grains Gill. It has been rebuilt and gives easy walking above the gill. Seathwaite Fell rises on the right and craggy Glaramara forms the left-hand skyline. A footbridge crosses the stream and the valley closes in. Ahead are the crags and gullies of Great End, completely dominating the view. Towards the top of the valley the stream, here known as Ruddy Gill, has etched a deep little ravine into the rock. The path joins the main Esk-Hause-to-Sty-Head track where the headwater of Ruddy Gill flows down from the south-east. The gill has taken advantage of a fault in the rock, which was later infilled by red haematite, thus giving its colour and name. The confirmed source seeker may wish to follow Ruddy Gill, as one of Derwent's main headwaters, to its ultimate source below Allen Crags and Esk Hause, on the far side of which the Esk rises, before returning to the path junction and continuing north-westwards over a broad ledge towards the – as yet – unseen Sprinkling Tarn.

It will be noted that Sprinkling Tarn does not feed Ruddy Gill – the barrier of moraine which caused the tarn to form here prevents that; rather this branch of the infant Derwent, unnamed as it leaves the tarn, runs down to Sty Head. The route follows the well-worn path downhill, past the outflow and with Great Gable rising starkly ahead, to Sty Head. Like the higher Esk Hause this broad ledge of land beneath the high mountains holds another important junction of paths and there is usually a little group of walkers clustered around the stretcher box in the lee of a large boulder debating where to go next. For the source walker the way leads down to the tarn and then alongside Styhead Gill and back to Stockley Bridge. A glimpse will be had, halfway down, of the fine plunge of Taylorgill Force.

Nothing remains now but to walk back along the broad track to Seathwaite, turning around now and again to look once more on Seathwaite Fell, wettest place in England and birthplace of the Derwent. The walk up Grains Gill to Sprinkling Tarn, returning by Styhead Gill, is about 5 miles (8km) if starting from Seathwaite. Four hours will provide time for dawdling and admiring the view but be warned: the lure of the mountains is strong and has been known to lead even the most dedicated of source seekers away from his or her goal!

Esk

their very fountains

ESK	
SOURCE	Esk Hause, Cumbria
G.R.	NY 232 079
LENGTH	16 miles (25 kilometres)
TRIBUTARIES	Lingcove Beck, Whillan Beck
MOUTH	Ravenglass, Cumbria

Esk is one of the more common river names and there are half a dozen or more river Esks scattered across northern England and Scotland. The name is probably derived from the British word *isca*, meaning 'water', and is related to Usk, Exe and Axe. One Esk rises in Scotland and, joined by the Liddel Water near Canonbie, marks the border for a few hundred yards before entering England proper to join the Solway Firth. The other Cumbrian Esk, described here, abbreviates all that is most appealing about British rivers into 16 or so magnificent miles (25km). It rises in the mountains, flows through the wild grandeur of Upper Eskdale, descends through the pastoral beauty of its lower valley and meanders its way finally to

Upper Eskdale from the slopes of Harter Fell

join the Irish Sea near Ravenglass. There are few places in England where the scenery can justly be described as awesome, but upper Eskdale is one of them. Samuel Taylor Coleridge, sitting on the top of Scafell, deemed 'the upper part of it the wildest and savagest surely of all the vales that were ever seen from the top of an English mountain, and the lower part the loveliest'.

I spent a night at Ravenglass, where the Esk, joined by its similarly economically lettered neighbours the Irt and the Mite, flows through a broad, sandy estuary to the sea. Ravenglass is one of those end-of-the-road places: a village street parallel with the wide beach with the shore side walls shored up and windows high. The conversation in the warm and welcoming Holly House Hotel was largely focused on the half dozen or so dogs populating the wood-beamed, stone-tiled, stove-heated, real-aled bar. Some resident, some visitors, they sat, lay and circled in a fine display of canine etiquette. Good beer, good food and everyone made welcome. A proper pub, and the dog owners real masters. Ravenglass has some of the highest Roman walls in Britain, just down the lane from the campsite. Up to 13 feet (4m) high, the walls of the bath house for the fort of Glannaventa, which guarded the harbour and one end of the supply route across Cumbria, provided some relaxation for the soldiers stationed here during the best part of three centuries. Standing in its own lake as a result of the recent rain, it was living up to its former usage.

The following morning I drove up the valley, with river and railway – the Ravenglass and Eskdale, built to carry iron ore and reflecting changing economics by now functioning as a popular heritage line – for company. Past La'al Ratty's terminus at Dalegarth station near Boot the valley constricts and the road girds its loins to climb Hardknott Pass. Just past the cattle grid at its foot there is parking for half a dozen vehicles and a stroll back down the road leads to a red phone box which you may well have seen, as it has featured in several adverts. My friend and walking companion Geoff once navigated his way back from the Scafells by the light in this phone box. A track leads to Brotherilkeld Farm. Brotherilkeld is from Old Norse, meaning 'Ulfketil's huts'. The farm was Buthcrulkil in 1242 when acquired by Furness

Abbey; perhaps the brothers provided the r but the pronunciation is still pretty much as it was in the thirteenth century. The footpath used to pass through the farmyard but is now diverted down to the river.

My old OS one-inch Tourist Map of the Lake District, with its black ink lines marking walks, shows many visits to and around upper Eskdale – I remember the time I'd set off to walk up by Cam Spout on to Scafell when I got only as far as Great Moss because it was just too hot, and another vertiginous scramble out of Little Narrowcove on to Rough Crag – but I'd never before set out to walk the length of it to Esk Hause. This is one of the delights of source seeking: finding new ways to familiar places. I'm glad I had been there before because the morning I chose, 'early mist and cloud clearing', turned out to be one of atmospheric obscurity which didn't break until early afternoon and my return.

Atmospheric obscurity

Walking through the Brotherilkeld inbye, where the clear-day visitor has a tremendous view forward to Bow Fell, the only clear thing I saw was the river water, its crystal clarity showing up every stone in its bed. On the right I was aware of the land rising to Hardknott with its Roman fort and couldn't help thinking that a couple of millennia ago this would have been a good day for a Brigantian attack.

Splashing through little tributaries while crossing a field of Herdwick sheep made me optimistic about finding water at the source and across the river I could just make out green paths through golden bracken beside Scale Gill with its white waterfall tumbling out of the mist. Last night's talk in the pub had turned to camping and rain, leading to inevitable exaggeration and tales of dragging sodden, collapsed tents across flooded campsites and through raging torrents. I climbed Ullscarf once on a day when I woke in the youth hostel and

the first sound I heard was the heavy artillery of rain against the window. It went on all day, mostly as a well-disciplined fusillade but very occasionally subsiding to a ragged sniping session. It was a day when so much rain fell continuously that the becks gave up their struggle to hold the deluge and abandoned it incontinently to the fellside. A day when there was little difference between path and torrent so that the one became the other. It was the kind of Lakeland day that everyone ought to experience at first hand. Once.

As I crossed the last stile the valley narrowed. I passed several solitary, riverside hollies, one full of berries and adding colour to the misty scene, before I became aware of the increasing noise of the river. The ground fairly trembled with the crash of the water as I passed Tongue Pot and Vicar Swa falls below Lingcove Bridge, where I sensed the clag thinning. Also known as Throstle Garth Bridge,

Seeing a bit more . . . near Esk Hause

'The kind of Lakeland day . . .'

the graceful stone arch spans Lingcove Beck by its confluence with the Esk, and was possibly built by the monks of Furness to reach their lands in Borrowdale.

Beyond the bridge the path climbs beside Esk Falls but a lower way, little more than a sheep trod, gives more intimate views of the falls. The river is in a narrow ravine here, with many cascades and pools, and is a popular summer swimming attraction. On this late winter's day it was the power of the water that grabbed my attention as it boiled and swirled down the gorge. I regained the path under the delightfully named but currently invisible Throstlehow Crag and, on a day when West Bromwich Albion squandered a three-goal lead, thought of Geoff, a long-suffering Baggies supporter. Emerging above the Esk gorge, I realized that my meteorological sense was letting me down, as the mist was thicker than ever. Here, I thought, I should be able to see the rocky upper few hundred feet of Slight Side, Scafell, Scafell Pike and its satellite Ill Crag, a glorious sight. The river makes an acute turn below the dark crags of Scar Lathing, and across from Green Crag, Eskdale's own miniature Half Dome, and I went so far as to take out my compass, just in case, even though I was wearing Ordnance Survey socks. One of the joys of Eskdale is that, because of its length and relative remoteness, it is not as popular a route to Lakeland's highest fells as the eastern valleys of Borrowdale and Langdale and the shorter western approach from Wasdale. This means that there is more of a sense

of solitude and not so much of a path.

I emerged on to Great Moss – the name says it all – and crossed the river where it spreads lazily and runs through a wide, stone-strewn channel. I followed the west bank past the imagined huge tumbled boulders of Sampson's Stones, walked without catching a glimpse of the white ribbon of Cam Spout and ambled beneath unseen Dow Crag and its rocky top knot, Pen. I was walking blindly through the finest natural amphitheatre in England. Still, at least it wasn't raining. Climbing up the Tongue I met a couple who were looking for a scramble on Ill Pike. 'You haven't got a 1:25 000 map, have you?' he asked. 'My 40 000 hasn't got the same detail.' We looked at my map and I said, 'That little knoll just down there's Skilling Crag. Oh, it's gone again.' Then it started to rain.

The path up the Tongue soon descended back to the river and climbed through another little rocky gorge, crossing and re-crossing the infant Esk until the slope became less steep, the stream became a trickle and, just above a bank of snow, a tiny spring emerged from the middle of a green mossy flush surrounded by pale grass. The source of the Esk. I looked back down the valley I had followed for the last three and a quarter hours and saw – nothing.

I decided that I might as well climb the remaining 500 feet (152.5m) to the top of Esk Pike, in case I came out of the cloud. So I did, but I didn't. But at least it was no longer raining. There's a decent bit of shelter just below the pale, rocky summit, a good place for lunch on a fine day. I could have carried on, down to Ore Gap, named after the exposure of haematite, a red iron ore, found there and returned down Lingcove Beck to the packhorse bridge but, as the cloud was at last lifting, decided to return the way I had come in the hope of seeing a bit more.

Of course, you could cheat and visit Esk Hause after going to Sprinkling Tarn and the Derwent's source, but that would be to miss one of the finest walks to any British river source – assuming, of course, you have a clear day.

HIGH PENNINES

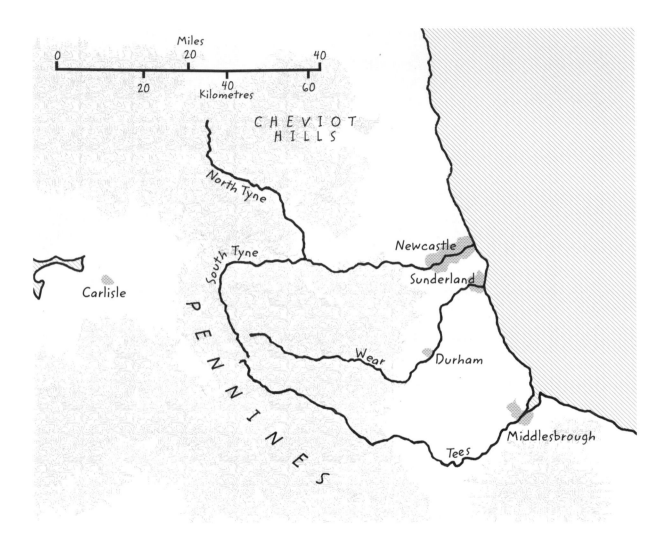

This area has been described as England's last wilderness and it certainly possesses a sense of remoteness more often associated with the next country up. The river sources here are all found on the high, sprawling, dissected uplands of the northern Pennines, except for the North Tyne, which almost requires a diversion over the border into Scotland. This is a region for long treks and long views. Standing on the top of Cross Fell, on a bright day in May, having followed the Tees for half a dozen miles, you might well wonder why you should ever wish to

go anywhere else. It's also another land where the past, in the form of old walking ways and the ghosts of former enterprise, is always quietly evident.

Tees
in tumult leaves his source

You could spend a week, some might say a lifetime, devising different ways of reaching the source of the 81 mile (130km) long Tees. The longest river in northern England rises, fittingly, on the slopes

TEES	
SOURCE	Tees Head, Cumbria
G.R.	NY 699 340
LENGTH	81 miles (130 kilometres)
TRIBUTARIES	Lune, Greta, Leven
MOUTH	Tees Mouth

of the highest hill in the Pennines, Cross Fell. It used to make its way untrammelled through the glories of upper Teesdale, tumbling over the rapids of Cauldron Snout and the falls of High and Low Force, a rowdy and rumbustious youth, before settling for a placid middle age once past Middleton and an industrious old age beyond Stockton. It was the hard-working lower reaches that robbed the youthful wilderness of much of its wildness with the construction of Cow Green Reservoir, built between 1967 and 1971 to supply the industries of Teesside with water. The scheme went ahead after a Parliamentary enquiry, in the face of much opposition from conservationists who wished to preserve the unique flora of the upper valley, and, as a sop, the area around Cow Green became part of the Moor House – Upper Teesdale National Nature Reserve and a car park and nature trail were developed. In a letter at the time to *The Times*, Professor Humphrey Hewer of the Council for Nature stated, 'What [Parliament] must decide is whether, to satisfy the demands of industry for a few years, it is prepared to give such an appalling example to the rest of the world.' As usual, it was. Like all reservoirs, it displays an ugly tidemark when not full and it has not enhanced one of the last remaining wild corners of England.

That said, the Cow Green car park makes possible one of the most memorable source walks in Britain which simply follows the river for 8 miles (12.8km) and through millennia of history. This is a walk to be tackled on the clearest of days but

not with the clearest of consciences, as it involves going to places where the pedestrian is not especially welcome even though it is now all Access Land. The Countryside and Rights of Way Act 2000 (CRoW) means that the public can now walk freely on mapped areas of mountain, moor, heath, downland and registered common land without having to keep to paths. These new rights, for which people had been campaigning for over a century, came into effect all over England on 31 October 2005. What isn't so generally crowed about is the fact that land managers are allowed to restrict or even exclude access in certain circumstances. In June 2010, for instance, several large areas of moorland around upper Teesdale, including a section of the route followed, were 'temporarily closed' for twenty days, only being open at weekends during most of the month. I was interested to find out what the 'certain circumstances' were and searched the Natural England website to find that the 'Purpose' of the exclusion was 'At Land Managers's Discretion' and the 'More Information' column was blank. I was lucky in my choice of date for visiting the area, though this was purely out of ignorance. I wonder how many visitors to Access Land think to check with Natural England before taking advantage of the 'approximately 865,000 hectares of land across which they can walk, ramble, run, explore, climb and watch wildlife as they are given the freedom to access land, without having to stay on paths'. Except when it's temporarily closed.

Across the reservoir rises Meldon Hill, while further north the Dun Fells and Cross Fell, the ultimate aim of this walk, look a long way away. An old mine track, Peghorn Lane, leads north-west from the car park, passing the remains of Dubby Sike, with its ore hoppers, and Greenhurth lead mines. Just beyond the buildings of Greenhurth the track heads north, away from the Tees, to join the tarmac at Yad Moss. I crossed to an old mine level and dropped down to the river, following it to Crookburn Foot, where the Tees idled through banks of pebbles and trout disappeared from view as soon as they were spotted. This is the point where the old counties of Durham, Westmorland and Cumberland met. The Tees marks another boundary here, for the river separates the Earl of Strathmore's estate to the south from the Raby estate of Lord Barnard with its white-painted farms and cottages to the north. There is much evidence of glaciation here, notably in the shape of the rounded hillocks of boulder clay and rock, and there are several islands in this stretch of the Tees. An extensive streamside area of gravel, sprinkled with leadwort, indicates another mining site and just round a bend, where the views open out to Cross Fell, you pass a gated level mouth in a limestone outcrop below Metalband Hill. The Metal Band vein may have been optimistically named as the mine, which worked around the middle of the nineteenth century, only produced around 120 tons of lead ore throughout its existence.

A track leads west from Metalband to join the one coming from the South Tyne valley at Troutbeck Foot. Here, hard by the confluence of the 4-mile (6km) old Tees and its first major tributary, Trout Beck, which rises to the east of Great Dun Fell and Knock Fell, is the first bridge across the river, Moorhouse Bridge. This carries the old London Lead Company track from the South Tyne valley on its way over the Pennine watershed to Knock and Dufton. A sign by the bridge marks the boundary of the Moor House – Upper Teesdale National Nature Reserve and tells walkers 'for your own safety keep to the waymarked routes – there are hidden mine-shafts in the area. The weather can deteriorate rapidly . . .' Ahh, Natural England, heir to Drake, Cook and Scott. Covering an area of 55 square miles (142 sq. km), the reserve reaches up from the hay meadows of the valley to the blanket bog of the high fells and encompasses a greater range of rare habitats than anywhere else in Britain. Many of the plants and creatures living here first colonized the area at the end of the Ice Ages and have survived ever

since. Moor House itself, by Moss Burn, less than a mile up the Trout Beck valley, was a shooting lodge belonging to the Earl of Strathmore, built in 1842. It was used as a study centre for the NNR from 1952 until 1979. When I first passed in April 1990 the house was derelict, though a few tins in the pantry indicated some transient habitation. It was demolished in 1999. Scientific research must be mainly digital these days and the view from the high Pennine ridge has lost a focal point.

The walk from Troutbeck Foot to the source, following the river and sometimes taking to the scalloped slabs of its bed, was a delight. The young Tees meanders its way across a gently sloping moor, passing more mine remains and flowing over stony flats and rocky little falls. Where it crosses limestone the water has eroded the joints to leave smoothed blocks full of potholes and in places the fossil stems of coral can be seen. Further up the valley, rushes and cotton grass take the place of violets and pansies, and there are deep beds of peat, cut through by the stream, lying on boulder clay left behind by the glacier that once flowed down here to meet up with the South Tyne ice before creeping to scoop out the hollow now occupied by Cow Green – a glacial lake only about 10,000 years too late. A fence descending from the north leads up to Crossgill Pants – and yes, it is, I've been there!

I lost count of how many times I crossed the Tees as the valley holding the peat-stained, deserted burn finally narrowed and steepened. Every little tributary passed – Fallcrag Sike, Crooked Beck, Swath Beck, Slate Sike – means there is less water in the channel and the roar of High Force and Cauldron Snout eventually becomes a chatter, becomes a tinkle, becomes a murmur, becomes a memory. The silence came just above the highest tiny tributary; there was still water but it was just a collection of disconnected little pools. Up yet another green bank and there was the boundary stone, traditionally reckoned to mark the source. It is inscribed 'B T', standing for Blencarn, a manor

Upper Tees

whose land reaches up from the Eden valley over the watershed, and Thanet (the Earls of Thanet held the neighbouring manor of Milburn from the seventeenth till the nineteenth centuries), on the downhill side, and 'F36', indicating the land ownership of a Mr Fleming and possibly the date, on the other. A fence follows the boundary just above the stone and a tiny pool on the uphill side of it stakes its claim as the real source. From here the Tees can be seen snaking down across the moors, a green channel through the brown peat and heather of the broadest view in England. In the far distance is Cow Green – do I really have to get back there?

Before the descent, it would seem churlish not to visit the highest spot in the Pennines half a mile (0.8km) and 400 gentle feet (122m) of ascent away. The summit, standing towards the western side of the great flat top, is marked by a large cairn and wall shelter 20 yards from the trig point. The top has seen its fair share of excitement from the visit of St Augustine, who is said to have planted a cross to rid the fell of demons, through the celebrations to mark the passage of the great Reform Bill of 1832 when fifty brass bands played on the plateau, to the night landings and take-offs by Lysander aircraft which pilots practised here during the Second World War as they trained for clandestine missions

in Europe. Now the cairn sees the passage of scores of Pennine Wayfarers and it is fitting that they should pause here at the apogee of their walk. But they shouldn't think it's all downhill from here. It is always worth having a walk around the shelter to see what's been left behind – a length of shock cord, a map, someone's butties. Mind, the sheep usually have them.

It is downhill, for a short while at least, for the walker who wishes to accompany the upper Tees watershed for part of the way back to Cow Green. The Pennine Way passes a 10 foot (3m) high cairn where it starts to descend from the Cross Fell plateau but the spring by the path is not a Tees tributary: Crowdundle Beck runs west to feed the Eden. I crossed the grassy mound of Little Dun Fell and the golf ball on Great Dun Fell, visible for much of the day so far, hoved into massive view. The 82-foot (25m) high radome, constructed for air traffic control purposes in the mid-eighties, replacing the four 60-foot (18m) timber lattice masts which had stood on the summit since the 1940s, dominates the scene. The one thing that can be said in its favour is that it provides accurate meteorological data. The records provide proof positive of the severity of the weather on these fells. Temperatures of -20°C and winds of 116 knots have been recorded, while sunshine amounts are as little as a quarter of those received in the surrounding valleys.

The Tees watershed carries on over Knock Fell and Meldon Hill, a walk I once made following ski tracks through melting snow; I ended up with feet so cold and wet that I swore I'd buy myself a really good pair of boots and really look after them. Well, I swore. The easiest way back from Great Dun Fell is to continue along the Pennine Way until it meets the track descending to Troutbeck Foot. I decided to follow the minor watershed, between the Tees and Trout Beck, which descends from Great Dun Fell over its eastern ridge, Hard Hill. I passed a fenced shaft and ruined building, old pits, acres of peat and cotton grass, an odd linear excavation and lots of cloudberry before I reached the trig point. Cloudberry, a member of the rose family, has a white or pink flower and produces orange fruit. We ate them once at a wedding in Sweden, ripe and creamy with a taste of yoghurt. When eaten fresh they have the tartness of most wild berries. The Hard Hill trig point, erected in May 1960, must be one of the remotest in Britain, giving long views under a big sky – and Cow Green still looks a fair way off. From the pillar you can follow Hardhill Hush or one of Trout Beck's little tributaries down to the bridleway. Hushing was a method of proving the ground for lead by damming a stream until a good head of water was let go to scour the vegetation and topsoil away and reveal, it was hoped, the veins in the rock beneath. The shallowness of Hardhill Hush compared with the 100 foot (30.5m) deep Dunfell Hush further up the valley and the lack of other mining remains in the vicinity may indicate that it was a hard hill indeed.

In places the track by Trout Beck had been undercut by the stream and collapsed entirely. From Moorhouse Bridge you can follow the Metalband track to where it peters out and cross a stretch of moor back to Peghorn Lane and Cow Green. I walked for the best part of eight hours, covering about 18 miles (29km), and, apart from along the Pennine Way stretch, I saw no one else except for two English Nature operatives sampling water from Trout Beck near Moor House. Either everyone else was following EN's advice or perhaps they shouldn't really have any need to worry.

One approach to Tees Head can be made from Dufton following 7½ miles (12km) of the Pennine Way past Dufton Pike to Knock Fell and then over the Dun Fells. The Teesdale Way starts at Dufton, although it avoids the source and first 10 miles (16km) of the river, instead following the PW as it makes its way across the watershed at High Cup Nick, a spectacular walk but hardly Teesdale, to join the river at Cauldron Snout. The Pennine Way route from Garrigill is 8½ miles (13.6km) of gentle

ascent, mostly along the old corpse road between Garrigill and Kirkland through a lead mining landscape. Another route from Garrigill could follow the South Tyne valley past the source of that river as far as Troutbeck Foot before ascending the upper reaches of the Tees. From the west, a bridleway heads straight up the scarp from Blencarn, over Grumply Hill and Wildboar Scar, before breaching the watershed at Crowdundle Head; or you could follow the corpse road from Kirkland until it meets the PW just north of Cross Fell. Yet another bridleway ascends from Milburn to Silverband Mine high on the western slopes of Great Dun Fell. The mine, originally worked by the London Lead Company, produced 215,000 tons of lead ore between 1939 and 1963. When it was later worked for barytes, an aerial ropeway and latterly massive lorries were used for transport and in the 1980s it was producing up to 10,000 tons a year. Following the closure of the mine much of the area has been landscaped. So, take your pick, but the royal road to Tees Head must be the one hugging the river.

Wear
I pray lend an ear

WEAR	
SOURCE	Wearhead, Co. Durham
G.R.	NY 857 394
LENGTH	66 miles (106 kilometres)
TRIBUTARIES	Waskerley Beck, Bedburn Beck, Gaunless, Browney
MOUTH	Sunderland

Asked to name a river in north-eastern England, for most people the Tyne and the Tees would probably spring to mind. Followed at a distant third by the Wear. Rising a Pennine ridge further north than its better-known neighbours, it was

Wearhead: the confluence of Killhope and Burnhope Burns

the longest English river to flow through just one county, Durham, until Tyne and Wear was created in 1974. Nowadays, although its lower reaches flow through the Metropolitan Borough of the City of Sunderland, the bulk of the 66 mile (106km) long river is still in the Land of the Prince Bishops. The Wear's headwaters rise in the Pennines, 10 miles (16km) east of the English watershed at Hartside Top. The three main ones, Killhope Burn, Wellhope Burn and tautological Burnhope Burn, drain a large stretch of soggy moorland between the summits of Killhope Law and Burnhope Seat. The river proper is said to start at the confluence of Burnhope and Killhope Burns in Wearhead. In this part of the world 'hope' is a valley.

A commodious car park in Cowshill, just off the A689 road between Alston and Stanhope, is a good starting point for a visit to some of the Wear's sources. A display board provides interesting information about the area's history and a map which,

incidentally, names Killhope Burn as 'River Wear'. Is this a dastardly attempt to wrest the source away from Wearhead, less than a mile down the Killhope valley? At Cowshill I joined the 77 mile (124km) long Weardale Way, which starts at Killhope Lead Mining Museum and ends up on the coast at Roker.

The Way makes its way through flower-spangled meadows to Wearhead until it crosses Westfall Bridge to join the main road through the hamlet. Standing at a height of over 1,100 feet (335m), Wearhead is one of the largest places in upper Weardale. It had a population of 116 in 1881 but 12 of its 46 houses were unoccupied, a reflection of the decline of lead mining in the valley brought about partly by cheap imports from Spain and partly through the intransigence of the mineral rights owners, the Ecclesiastical Commissioners. This little settlement was the terminus of one of the most far-reaching of Victorian railway tentacles, the Wear Valley Extension Railway, possessing a station, together with an engine shed, goods warehouse, turntable and signal box. Passenger services operated from 1895 till 1953 and the line closed entirely in 1961. After a long period of decline, which perhaps culminated in 2005 with the closure of the Co-op and the Methodist church, now things are maybe looking up and there is a village store, while a craft shop and café occupy the old Co-op building. Wearhead United's football ground is reckoned to be the highest in use in England.

Crossing the first bridge over the Wear I took the path through a field to the official start of the river, at the meeting place of Killhope and Burnhope Burns. A little light trespassing is necessary to reach the actual confluence, shaded by trees, where the two burns coalesce but I daresay the local kids find the spot often enough. The path follows Burnhope Burn until it joins a road leading up to Burnhope Reservoir. Built by the Durham County Water Board between 1931 and 1937, the reservoir drains a catchment area of over 10,000 acres (4,047ha). Looking west from the dam, Burnhope Seat – I was going to write 'dominates', but that's not really true of these rolling fells; let's say it builds a backdrop to the 103-acre (42ha) sheet of water. We once crossed the dam at the end of an early March day after a walk around the local tops just as the sun dropped behind Burnhope Seat. The fells were a black slash between a sky and lake of gold.

Walking up the couple of miles of Grasshill Causeway, the highest public road in England and much loved by the four-wheel-drive community, gives ample time to reflect on local place names. Ahead is High Field, a.k.a. Great Stony Hill, and first summit of the day on a walk around a fair part of Wear's watershed. As befits a hill in a lead mining area there are plenty of hushes – Milburn made one, as did Smith, but I wonder who Em was. She or he had an eponymous hush that is shown on the map to this day. And who was A'uld Will? He had a 'Cot' on the west side of the hill in an area of old workings associated with the former Ashgill Head

mine. Did he offer lodgings to miners? If not there was always Coldberry Shop or Hawk Sike Shop to provide shelter. At least one of the local mines was mechanized to some extent, if Mill Sike is anything to go by. Peat Fell tells us of another aspect of the local economy but fuel seekers presumably kept well clear of the Quicksands near by. What are we to make of Battle Spots on the south side of Burnhope Reservoir? Was this the site of some ancient skirmish between local farmers and raiders making their way up Weardale; or could it have been where the navvies employed on the works settled their differences after a night in Cowshill or Weardale? In the early nineteenth century there actually was a battle, down the valley at Stanhope, between local lead miners and the Bishop of Durham's agents over the rightful shooting for food, or poaching, of grouse depending on point of view. The bishop's men were bloodily defeated by the miners and the whole event commemorated in verse – 'The Bonny Moor Hen'. Down in the Burnhope valley is Redan, a tiny ruined shooting hut mentioned by that lover of these lead valleys W. H. Auden, in a play, *The Dog Beneath the Skin*, while on the heights above, a little enclosure is called the Malakoff, seemingly dating its construction to the time of the Crimean War. Back on the road, Causeway Foot and Causeway Head mark either end of the steepest section and Cutthroat Meas suggests the road had a bloody past. Was this moss, at the top of the track, a good spot for a highwayman to lurk? Galloway Hill reminds us of its use as a packhorse route. Nowadays the visitor is more likely to find 4x4s and trail bikes than ponies and the stony track shows evidence of their passage – bits of red plastic, unidentified lengths of cable, engine blocks, chassis units; well, the first two anyway. Although we did once come across an entire vehicle stuck in a snowdrift. There were no miners, peat diggers, navvies, drovers, highwaymen, poets, off-road fanatics or anyone else for that matter as I reached the summit of the Causeway at 2,212 feet (675m).

A fence leads off towards the cairn and trig point on High Field and follows the treeless watershed over Langtae Head to Scaud Hill. At Langtae Head, where pale rashes of excavated stone show up against the dun and green surroundings, a paternal grouse hopped and fluttered along, distracting me from the chicks, which had bulleted into the air at my approach. Some patches of green are very green and crossing them is like walking on a waterbed. When Nick Wright passed this way in the early 1970s while researching his *English Mountain Summits*, he noted that Scaud Hill's summit cairn consisted of nine stones. It has more than doubled since then. The watershed continues over Redgleam before descending to Scraith Head, one of the main sources of Burnhope Burn, where stands a restored boundary stone inscribed 'EC, DC and GH' and dated 1880. On earlier visits this had been broken in two and lay on the ground. It was good to see it standing once more. 'EC' stands for Ecclesiastical Commissioners (on behalf of the Bishop of Durham), 'DC' for the Duke of Cleveland and 'GH' for Greenwich Hospital, mineral royalty owners on these moors.

There were mine workings at the bleak head of Scraith Burn and fifteen men were raising ore here in 1830. The mine produced 7,705 tons of lead concentrates between 1818 and 1847. Climbing away from the peaty morass, you soon reach Burnhope Seat, the highest summit on the ridge between Weardale and Teesdale. The trig point on its

Summit of High Field

concrete base marks the old County Durham top – since boundary changes in 1974 Mickle Fell, formerly the Yorkshire summit, has been the highest point in the county. It doesn't, however, mark the top of the hill, which lies 100 yards (91m) beyond the fence in Cumbria, née Cumberland. The trig pillar's base does give the only dry place to sit down and provides a fine view down Burnhope, over hedgeless country, the source of streams, to the reservoir and Weardale.

A faint fence-following path crosses Burnhope Head and descends to another black waste, where one more of Burnhope's headstreams rises – another peat-stained, deserted burn – around Sallygrain Head, before climbing to Dead Stones and the ridge that forms the minor watershed between Burnhope and Wellhope. I reflected that the old fence posts now used as stepping stones across the bog might have been the very same ones that the fence builder with his Swedish caterpillar-tracked vehicle was putting in new when I walked along here a quarter century ago.

Approaching Dead Stones, I spotted two figures, silhouetted like matchstick men, beside the tall cairn, the first people I had seen since leaving Wearhead. Then followed one of the coincidences of my peak-bagging life and, dear reader, I crave your patience while I indulge in a little anorak wafting. The two chaps turned out to be 'doing the Nuttalls' and were down to their last eight or nine. John and Ann Nuttall's two-volumed *The Mountains of England and Wales* lists and describes walks to the summits that are higher than 2,000 feet (610m) and have a minimum of 50 feet (15m) of ascent on all sides. There are 190 in Wales and 253 in England, and climbing them all is a fine achievement. We had a chat, comparing notes, as I'd finished my final few Nuttalls the previous year, after having completed three rounds of the Bridges. George Bridge published his *The Mountains of England and Wales* in 1973 and he listed 408 summits. The discrepancy in numbers can largely be explained by advances in cartography over the years rendering some of Bridge's tops, taken from the old one-inch OS maps, redundant, while others have been promoted. A few minutes later, descending through the peat groughs north of Dead Stones, I met two more blokes. 'Crowded today,' I said, explaining that I'd met the two others at the summit. We got talking of hills and tops and one of them came out with his trump card. 'I bet you've never heard of Nick Wright.' Oh, but I had. His 1974 book *English Mountain Summits* was based, like Bridge's, on the one-inch OS maps but Wright listed all the tops in England that were enclosed by an individual contour ring. This threw up some oddities like the five 'summits' of Tynehead Fell, which, as anyone who has ever been there will agree, is nonsense. The modern map shows three tiny eminences on the fell rising above 610m, the nearest metric equivalent to 2,000 feet, but the hill no longer appears in the lists, as the dip between it and Bellbeaver Rigg is negligible. This may be all far too nerdy, but having walked for decades rarely meeting any other self-confessed 'bagger', to meet four in the space of ten minutes, the only other walkers I saw all day, on one of the most remote tops in England was decidedly spooky. Incidentally, Nick Wright lists 345 English summits and another four shared with Wales. I still have eleven of them left to walk, and even though accurate modern surveying proves that some of them don't actually exist, I still intend to visit them.

Continuing over Nag's Head and Knoutberry Hill, where stretches of peat render the boundary wall intermittent, I crossed another minor watershed, between Wellhope and Killhope Burns, and reached the road at Killhope Cross. A fitting end to the day would be to carry on along the watershed up over Killhope Law and Stangend Rigg before dropping down to Cowshill but, remembering another occasion when I'd squelched my way up through the slough to the Law and then across the seemingly never-ending tussocks to the Rigg, I wimped out

and took the easy way down the valley. The road is not too busy and in places there are flowery verges to follow. Looking across to Killhope Law there was so much cotton grass in bloom that it looked like snow in June. A mile or so past Killhopehead Bridge, the road passes the North of England Lead Mining Museum, where they were still finishing the building work planned for the winter but delayed because this year we had had one. L. S. Lowry came this way in the early 1960s and sketched the wheel, standing in a bare landscape before the plantations of conifers now surrounding the site appeared. For anyone with an interest in this area or mining history, Killhope is a must. The centrepiece is the 40-foot-diameter wheel. Built in the 1870s to power a plant for crushing and separating lead ore from the Park Level, the wheel ceased turning at the beginning of the twentieth century. It was due to be cut up for scrap during the Second World War, but the destruction never happened: the man with the torch never arrived. It was taken over by Durham County Council in 1968, and restoration began in 1980 and continues.

Beyond the museum a path leads down past an old quarry to Killhopeburn Bridge, and the confluence where Wellhope Burn joins. The route back to Cowshill follows the burn closely across meadows and crosses Heathery Bridge on the way. I had determined to treat myself to a pint at the Cowshill Hotel when I returned and had wondered what local real ale would best fit the occasion. It was shut, a circumstance that seemed to reflect the bleak philosophy of northern ridges.

Tyne
all mine, all mine

The Tyne has two branches, North and South, which converge between Warden and Acomb, a mile or so west of Hexham in Northumberland. The length of the conjoined river from there to the sea is about 34 miles (54km). The two main feeders are remarkably

TYNE	
SOURCE	South Tyne
	Tynehead, Cumbria
	North Tyne
	Deadwater Rigg,
	Northumberland
G.R.	NY 753 351
	NY 606 978
LENGTH	74 miles (118 kilometres)
TRIBUTARIES	South Tyne
	Allen, Nent
	North Tyne
	Kielder Burn, Rede
	Tyne
	Derwent, Team, Don
MOUTH	Tynemouth

consistent in length; South Tyne runs about 40 miles (64km) from its source in the Pennines to the confluence while its northern brother travels virtually the same distance from the Scottish border. Although the Tyne is primarily thought of as an industrial river through its shipbuilding and coal-carrying past, this is only true of the lower reaches and most of the river is delightfully rural. Historically the Tyne formed the boundary between County Durham and Northumberland.

The drive over Hartside Cross on the A686 between Penrith and Alston is one of the finest watershed-traversing routes in Britain, climbing steeply up the zig-zags of the western Pennine escarpment before descending across miles of dipping moorland. I once had to push start my motorbike in a blizzard up at Hartside but today, in mid-June, all was benign, the café at the summit was flourishing and two dozen or so bikers were enjoying the view westwards towards Lakeland. Leaving the main road a couple of miles short of Alston, I joined the South Tyne valley at Leadgate and drove through

Garrigill to the end of the tarmac just beyond Hill House.

Looking east from here you can see a typical north Pennine panorama to good effect, with the bulky Burnhope Seat rising across the valley to separate the Tyne's headwaters from those of the Wear. The flat tops and bench-like features on the slopes reveal the bones of the landscape, for these hills are composed of alternating almost horizontal layers of limestone, shale and sandstone. The benches are made of the harder limestone and sandstone while the less resistant shales have been eroded to form the risers between them. The variety of rocks has helped give rise to the fine assemblage of flowers found in the area and more famously across the watershed in upper Teesdale. Splashes of yellow and purple, pale blue, white and mauve decorate the riversides and grasslands while the lower meadows are golden with buttercups and the higher moors whitewashed with cotton grass.

The track, part of a drove route from Scotland which saw thousands of cattle being herded to southern markets in the sixteenth and seventeenth centuries, passes above the remains of Dorthgill and below the ruin of Cocklake with its intake – fields hard won from the moorland and now reverting – before dropping down to cross the river by a modern barn. As it climbs higher, the remains of the Calvert mine and the ruins of cottages at Calvertfold and Shelwell point out the long lead-mining history of the valley. The starry little white and yellow flowers of spring sandwort, commonly called leadwort because of its ability to thrive in these toxic soils, brightened the spoil heaps while fragments of galena and quartz sparkled in the sunshine. A track crossing the infant Tyne makes its way to the former workings just up the hill. Lead was mined around here from the twelfth century and many miners had smallholdings where they would grow potatoes, turnips and oats and keep a few cows, sheep and poultry. Trees were grown to provide shelter and in places the moorland edge was pushed back to nearly 2,000 feet (610m). I once spent a night camping at the confluence of the South Tyne and Calvert Burn, with only the chattering water, the sheep and the ghosts of miners for company. The latter would have tramped this way early each Monday morning to spend their working week at a mine. I woke up the following morning to a mist so impenetrable that I failed to find any of the tops of Tynehead Fell and only realized where I was when I hit the tarmac on the other side.

The South Tyne narrows as you approach the watershed and the location of the source was never too clear in an area where several small streams emerge. The last stream that the track crosses before the Tees watershed was usually given the accolade and on one previous visit it sported a small cairn. In 2002 this was confirmed by the unveiling of a monolithic sculpture by Gilbert Ward. A vertical slot carved through the stone enables you to focus on the actual source itself, below the cairn a few yards higher up the fellside, where the Tyne trickles into daylight from a secret, peaty hollow. The work was one of many pieces of artwork commissioned in the north-east in the two decades around the millennium, and local people, farmers and walkers helped develop it with the sculptor. It will certainly last longer than the fifteen sheep that had one word from a poem sprayed on to their fleeces so that viewers on a platform could observe 'both the random movement of the animals and a new poetic format'. Wool, full, yes, baa, any, sir, have, three, black, sir, baa, you, yes, bags, sheep?!

Of course, the true source of the South Tyne is 150 feet (46m) higher, on Tynehead Fell, the north-western slopes of Bellbeaver Rigg, whence the rain percolates down through limestone layers before emerging at its spring. There are tributaries, like Pether Sike and Allen's Cleugh, whose waters see daylight at a greater altitude than the main river, and a walk over the fell is more interesting than re-tracing footsteps back down the valley, on a clear day anyway. On a claggy day it may well be even

more interesting, but not especially enlightening. As you walk up the hillside above the source sculpture, you pass a cairn near a shakehole and a concrete-slab-capped shaft. From here are immense views over the upper gathering grounds of the Tees to the high Pennine trio of Great and Little Dun Fell and Cross Fell. You can cross a fence to reach the two cairns standing on the top of Bellbeaver Rigg. The nearer, western, cairn marks the summit while the further one gives views over upper Teesdale to two more Pennine prominences, Mickle Fell and Meldon Hill. Just south of here rises Tynegreen Sike which, rather confusingly, joins the Tees. Turning north, you cross, somehow, a sporting area of peat and sphagnum which spawns Seavy Sike, a serpentine stream seaming along a bright green channel before disappearing underground for a while, to a fence corner. I followed the fence, or rather a broken line of posts, downhill, sparring with Pether Sike, to rejoin the track by the bridge at the foot of Allen's Cleugh.

A lead smelting mill stood here. It was built around the end of the eighteenth century and was said to be producing 8,000 pieces of lead in 1796. The South Tyne Trail leaves the track here and follows the river downstream, where it has cut through the columnar volcanic rocks of the Whin Sill to form the attractive pine-tree-framed, two-tiered Dorthgill waterfall. The area around the fall is rich in wild flowers, with the Teesdale violet and the insectivorous butterwort, bird's-eye primrose, mountain pansy and orchids growing on the grassy slopes. A blissful spot. Further along the path I passed the Sir John's Mine level, with its grassed-over spoil heaps and ruined buildings. The level, driven from the east bank of the Tyne, worked lead ore that was particularly rich in silver. During the 1850s, 158 tons of lead concentrates were extracted from the level, yielding 40 ounces of silver per ton of lead. The mine was re-worked during the Second World War in a search for the Great Sulphur Vein for iron sulphide. The 8 mile (12.8km) long vein, one of the biggest in the north Pennines, is 100 yards (91m) wide in places and was known by the old miners as the 'backbone of the earth'.

Lapwings were swooping overhead as I approached Tynehead, now a single dwelling but once a hamlet with its own Lord of the Manor. It seems that the South Tyne Trail is not overly used. The fencers whom I met seemed unaware of the trail they had blocked until I told them about it – 'Looks like we'll have to put a stile in, like.' The trail continues downstream to Garrigill and through Alston to Haltwhistle, a couple of dozen miles away, but I crossed the bridge and walked up the track, part of the old pre-turnpike road between Alston and Middleton-in-Teesdale, back to the end of the tarmac. Daisies are our silver, buttercups our gold, as the old hymn has it. In this silver-lead-rich valley it was the gold of the meadows that will stay in my memory.

Forty miles (64km) to the north-north-west, the North Tyne rises on the less than invitingly named Deadwater Rigg, hard by the Scottish border and with a history of lawlessness and tales of raiding and reiving. A tiny stream, in less than a mile it is joined by the more powerful Deadwater Burn and 2 miles (3.2km) later it flows into Kielder Water, the largest artificial lake by capacity in the UK. Emerging from the reservoir a proper river, the North Tyne flows east and then south-east, through Bellingham and Wark, to join its southern brother.

Kielder Castle has a fine reiving ring about it but, unlike other Border castles, bastles and peels, this stone tower saw no raids, sieges or knives in the dark. It was built in 1775 as a hunting lodge for the 1st Duke of Northumberland. Now the informative Kielder Water and Forest Park Visitor Centre, it makes a good starting point for a walk to the source. I walked down the hill to the Anglers Arms, close to the confluence of the North Tyne and Kielder Burn, and along a riverside path through the campsite, which led to the road to Scotland. From here there is a glimpse of Deadwater Fell and its clutter of air

traffic paraphernalia. A short walk back towards the village and then, opposite a row of neat forestry houses, a track leads uphill to cross the old railway by a well-preserved platelayers' hut. Here I joined the trackbed of the former Border Counties Railway as it made its way through the forest, and there was plenty of opportunity to play at trains along shallow, curving cuttings and through a pair of old bridge abutments before emerging by the roadside near Bells Burn. An avid trainspotter in my early youth, I put my interest in hills and mountains partly down to the frustration of not having spotted all of the British Railways London Midland Region steam locomotives before they were scrapped. Some years later, exchanging Ian Allen's lists of locos for George Bridge's lists of mountains, I knew I was on to a good thing: they can't scrap mountains and I was eventually able to tick off the lot of them.

The old railway continues beyond Bellsburnfoot towards Scotland, crossing the North Tyne and then Deadwater Burn on double-arched bridges. This section of the Border Counties Railway opened in 1862, through some of the emptiest country in England. Originally planned to transport coal from Plashetts Colliery on the other side of Kielder, the 42-mile single-track line ran between Hexham and Riccarton Junction, where it joined the North British Railway's Waverley route from Carlisle to Edinburgh. Deadwater Station, now a house, opened in 1880 to serve a nearby quarry. It can have generated little passenger traffic in such a remote spot but was staffed until 1955 and closed three years later, together with the rest of the line.

The North Tyne, which flows across the gently sloping meadows of Deadwater Lakes a short distance to the west, was disturbed by the building of the railway and runs in a rushy ditch parallel with the track as far as the Scottish border. Here, where a sign reads 'WELCOME TO SCOTLAND', then 'End of waymarked cycle trail' and then 'Return the way you came', the stream runs down the side of a patch of forest from the road, also on the border. Up

Dorthgill

there the sign announced 'SCOTLAND WELCOMES YOU' while another one informed drivers that the road was soon to be closed for three days. This is the first bridge over the North Tyne, a culvert really, and the source is in the field above, a spring in the side of the little valley, a hundred yards or so above the road, where the forest fence curves round to the left. This is stated on the authority of Mr J. B. Jonas,[19] who spoke to the farmer who has lived all his life at Deadwater and was shown the source by him. Now, I am not generally averse to a spot of trespassing but as the farmer was gethrin' his sheep in the self-same field, I didn't wish to disturb this important activity and anyway, after the driest spring for eighty years, there was no evidence of the Tyne above the road, the first water being a muddy puddle on the west side of the bridge.

19 *Walking the North Tyne*, Ramblers' Association, 2005.

Like its southern twin, the North Tyne has tributaries that rise at a greater altitude than the main source, which is a good excuse for a sally up on to these border hills. Walking along the road away from Scotland, I passed Boarstone House and Deadwater Farm and crossed the Deadwater Burn. There is a Bore Stone on the fell above and the name is possibly derived from 'border stone', while Deadwater refers to the flat area of rushy ground at the head of North Tynedale, a valley which suggests by its broad bottom that it once held a glacier. A forest road soon leads off to the left and climbs north above Deadwater Burn before descending to cross it. Where the track peters out, a faint path follows a grassy ride north to a broken stone wall at Rushy Knowe. Here a sign proclaimed that I was on the Kielder Stane Walk. Following the wall and fence, which here demark the border, I soon reached the edge of the forest and the steep pull up Peel Fell gave many opportunities to pause and inspect the surroundings. With the blessing of a clear day and the use of a good map, you can pick out the Anglo-Scots border line as it crosses the landscape, though it follows a contrary route to the west of the valley, ignoring the watershed and zigzagging across Bells Moor, seemingly as undecided about its course as the water that will eventually become the English Tyne or the Scottish Liddel. The area around Deadwater was marked as 'disputed ground' on maps as late as 1769.

Below can be seen great blocks of conifers, some recently felled, which are part of the massive, 250 square mile (650 sq. km), Kielder Forest. Planting began during the 1920s following the post-war establishment of the Forestry Commission to oversee the creation of a strategic timber reserve for the nation. Forestry is still Kielder's key function, with not far off half a million cubic metres of timber being produced each year, but currently there is greater concern about the environment and tourism. Although three-quarters of the planted area is still the regimented coniferacy of Sitka spruce, more native trees are now grown, straight lines have been blurred and visitors are encouraged to walk and cycle, stay and spend.

Off to the west, hidden in the plantations on the far side of the Liddel Water valley, lay Riccarton Junction, meeting place of the Border Counties Railway and the North British Railway's Waverley route, Victorian engineering's high road to Scotland. In its heyday Riccarton had a population of over 100, an engine shed, a railway station that served as a village hall and post office and a refreshment room acting as the local pub. The village also boasted a school and a branch of the Hawick Co-op. Special trains took residents to church on Sunday, alternately to Newcastleton and Hawick, for there was no road connection from Riccarton Junction to the outside world until 1963, when a forest track was built. In a fine display of Victorian hierarchy the schoolmaster's detached house had three bedrooms and an inside toilet, the stationmaster's house was also detached but had its toilet outside, while everyone else lived in terraced housing and quite possibly shared. For a century it was a totally self-contained railway community. Riccarton was no longer a junction after 1958, and the line closed entirely early in 1969. The subsequent squabbles between different factions of would-be preservationists prove that the border mentality is alive and well in these parts.

Continuing to the summit of Peel Fell, amid bilberry and cloudberry, you may or may not see feral goats, or they may turn out to be boulders that look like goats from a distance. The top is flat with a peaty tarn and the summit is marked by a cairn. This (1,975 feet/602m) is the highest point in the Borders south of the Coquet and is said to give views across England from the Solway Firth to the North Sea. I am unable to confirm this but at least saw The Cheviot rising hazily 22 miles (35km) as the peregrine flies to the north-east. A mile or so to the south is Deadwater Fell and the high land curves around over Mid Fell between the two. Here rise the headwaters of Deadwater Burn. After you have followed the border fence for 250 yards (230m), a sign points in the direction of the Kielder Stane, the way to which tracks another tributary of the North Tyne, which becomes Scaup Burn. The Stane is worth visiting both for its geography – it is a 1,500-ton chunk of Carboniferous fell limestone, much grooved and scoured by weathering – and for its history. It was used as a kind of post box during the border troubles, and one of its recesses now holds a plastic container with a log book begun in April 2003. What tales it could tell if it had been started seven centuries earlier! This was another area of disputed ground and it was not until 1778 that the Duke of Northumberland and Archibald, Earl of Douglas, finally agreed that the border should pass through the stone, thus ending an argument which had stretched back to the 1330s. Among other graffiti carved into the stone, and on numerous boundary stones along the border to the east, are the letters N and a reversed D; some put this down to an illiterate mason who used the stencil backwards but others say it was done purposely to annoy the Earl by the Duke, who'd had to pay for the work.

Returning over Mid Fell with its chambered cairn and Reivers Cross, I reached Deadwater Fell, topped by a battered trig point, radar installations, sheds, towers and arty mountain-bike shelter, and followed forestry tracks back down to the valley. Adventurous mountain bikers can follow difficult and severe trails and Nanny has provided useful information boards giving the locations of the nearest casualty departments and mountain rescue. On the way down there were views to Kielder Water and I wondered if the volume of water in northern Europe's largest man-made lake was greater than the volume in the rest of the Tyne or even, given that the water in the reservoir was really part of the Tyne anyway, if the river was actually the greatest in England or even Britain, Europe or the world. Then I decided it was definitely time to visit the Anglers Arms.

SOUTHERN UPLANDS

Often passed through at top speed by Sassenachs making for the Highlands and not overly visited even by Scots, the sparsely populated, rolling Southern Uplands reward the visitor with a sense of peace and quiet in a land where raiding and reiving history is ever close to the surface. According to local lore, three out of the four streams in this chapter rise on the same hillside, which should make finding them easy enough, but as ever with rivers, it's not as simple as that. To find the fourth source I took some Glaswegian advice: 'On yer bike, Jimmy.'

Tweed and Annan
this blessed, honest-smelling hill country

According to an old Borders rhyme, 'Annan, Tweed and Clyde a' rise oot o' ae hillside'. Although this is not strictly topographically correct, the Tweed and the Annan certainly rise on opposite sides of a broad ridge, followed by the boundary that used to divide the counties of Peebles and Dumfries and is now the line between the Scottish Borders and Dumfries and Galloway. This ridge, culminating at 2,650 foot (808m) high Hart Fell, effectively forms

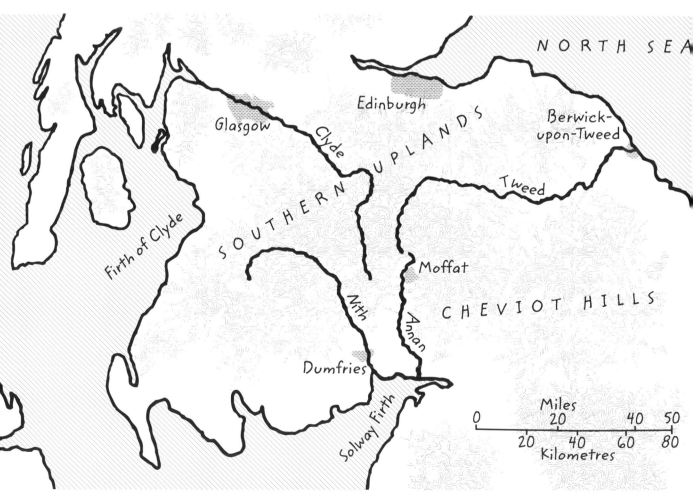

TWEED	
SOURCE	Tweed's Well, Scottish Borders
G.R.	NT 053 146
LENGTH	97 miles (156 kilometres)
TRIBUTARIES	Ettrick Water, Leader, Teviot, Till
MOUTH	Berwick-upon-Tweed

the watershed between streams flowing to the Irish Sea via the Annan and the Esk and those bound for the Tweed and the North Sea. The Tweed makes its way, north-east and then east for 97 miles (156km) and in its lower reaches forms the border with England for 18 miles (29km) before – rather like Berwick, the last town it passes through – deserting the land of its birth entirely and running for a couple of miles wholly in England.

The source, Tweed's Well, is one of the easiest to find; which was just as well the first time I came here, as I'd sprained a calf muscle the previous day and could barely hobble. Half a dozen miles north of Moffat on the A701, a lay-by has been created, complete with four marked parking bays and a sculpture which explains all. The red sandstone block is carved with scenes from the river's course, showing birds and plants, monks and travellers, bridges

Tweed's Well sculpture

and towns as well as verse. It gives views across to the enclosures where, among pools and trickles in the wet ground, the river begins. As Valerie Gillies' poem puts it:

The moor is an open hand,
The palm lined with streams.
In winter, on the frozen land,
Tweed's Well shows up as green.

In summer when the upland dries
The source is flowing free,
A clear spring will always rise
While Tweed runs to the sea.

Above the boggy hollow once stood Tweed's Cross, a pre-Reformation landmark which guided travellers from one monastery to another. Although there is no trace of the cross now, there are several other stones, markers and monuments in the vicinity. By the side of the road near its summit 1 ⅓ miles (2km) back towards Moffat is the memorial to the driver and guard of the Dumfries-to-Edinburgh mail coach that was caught in a severe blizzard on the first day of February 1831. The coach's guard, James MacGeorge, driven by duty even though conditions were bad enough to warrant staying in Moffat, insisted on continuing through the storm. When the drifts became too great for the coach to continue, guard and driver John Goodfellow removed the horses from their traces, loaded the precious mail sacks on them, and led them up the hill. They must have soon realized that the horses could not break through the drifts and so shouldered the bags themselves. It seems that the two men eventually accepted the futility of their efforts, for the following day the bags were found tied to a post. MacGeorge and Goodfellow perished while trying either to carry on to Tweedshaws or to return to the coach. A sense of melancholy still seems to hang around this spot by the headwaters of Cross Burn, a feeder of Evan Water which joins the Annan south

The Devil's Beef Tub

of Moffat. The gloominess is encouraged by the dark plantations covering the surrounding hills.

A further half mile (800m) and you reach the Devil's Beef Tub. This dramatic deep basin, hemmed in by Ericstane Hill, Annanhead Hill, Peat Knowe and Great Hill, was originally the Corrie of Annan, a truer description of its glacial origin. It changed its name in the sixteenth century when it was used by the Johnstones, whose cattle-reiving antics earned them the devilish nickname among their many enemies, to herd the beasts captured in raids and became known as the Devil's Beef Tub or the Marquis of Annandale's Beef Stand. Another memorial, to John Hunter, a Covenanter, shot by pursuing Dragoons in 1685, stands on the lip, as does a toposcope.

A fine round trip, visiting headwaters of the Annan as well as a couple of the Tweed's highest feeders and Tweed's Well itself, can be made from the car parking pull-in above the Beef Tub. Annan is a forthright stream in its upper course, flowing determinedly southwards from its sources on the rim of the corrie. Longer streams, rising on the southern slopes of the ridge as far away as Hart Fell to the east, all have their own names – Pot Burn, Auchencat Burn, Lochan Burn, Tweedhope Burn – before they join the Annan, so the stream that rises below Annanhead Hill and actually runs through the corrie can be said to be the Annan's true source. I followed the Annandale Way, a 55-mile (88.5km) long-distance path opened in 2009, over the hill, which is crowned with a trig point. As I walked beside the watershed wall with a brilliant cock wheatear zig-zagging in front of me, the ridge was rich with the white bobbing heads of cotton grass. I soon reached a cairn marking the northern extremity of the Way. This stands on the col at the head of Tweedhope Burn between Chalk Rig Edge and Spout Crag and is one of a pair. The southern cairn is on the Solway coast. Built by a local sculptor, Max Nowell, they are made of a colourful collection of local stones, including one from the locality of the other to represent the endless cycle of the river. There are long views down the green corridor of the Annan valley from many places along the roller-coaster ridge.

The crowd of young trees seen on the slopes around the cairn mark the efforts of the Border Forest Trust, which purchased the land at Corehead, the highest farm in Annandale, in 2009 and has set about restoring the landscape to its former native-woodland-cloaked self. The trust plans to use traditional farming practices and ecological restoration techniques to create and improve hay meadows, wetlands and heather moorland habitats on a holding which stretches from the Devil's Beef Tub as far as Hart Fell. The farm is of great historical and cultural significance, for it is said that William Wallace gathered men from the Border clans and Ettrick Forest at Corehead Tower, which belonged to his brother-in-law, Sir Thomas Halliday, before he led his first attack against the English in 1297.

The Annandale Way heads off to the south, following Tweedhope Burn and then the river itself. A continuation of the path northwards, part of an old drove route, is shown on the map but is less obvious on the ground. Crossing Whitehope and then Powskein Burns, I made my way to the summit of Crown of Scotland, an intriguingly named hill but one with only the vaguest of views as the clouds, threatened on the forecast, poured in from the south-west. At this place in 1306, Robert the

Bruce, having murdered his rival the Red Comyn in Greyfriar's monastery in Dumfries, made an alliance with James Douglas that resulted in Bruce becoming Scotland's most renowned ruler.

Descending Killiecrane Hill I passed the third slender mast of the walk. These masts are survey masts for a proposed wind farm. I reached the ruins of Earlshaugh, its sparse screen of trees just coming into leaf a good month later than back at home, and crossed the stream a few yards up from the vehicle ford, where the water was less deep and wide. Following a new fence I crossed Cor Water, one of the Tweed's highest tributaries, and followed the track heading south-westwards past a large enclosure, a small plantation and a fold. The clag was thick enough to blot out all but the nearest views but a decrease in speed announced an increase in altitude as the track crosses the minor watershed between Cor Water and the Tweed. The path improves just before you reach a forest corner at the site of Tweed's Cross and it then descends to join another track running north to where the map shows 'Tweed's Well (Source of River Tweed)'. Several springs exist in the vicinity, some on the slopes of Corse Dod and Foal Burn Head, but the favourite is found in the valley. Just inside a large, angular enclosure, a spring rises and flows away to join the waters of Corse Burn. Bright yellow splashes of marsh marigold decorate the pool formed from the spring as the water trickles away through the bog.

Walking back up to the track by the long fir wood, I rejoined the Annandale Way just by the main road less than three hours after I'd started. I had met no one, was chased by no aircraft, there was no road mender working when I returned to the van and no Marmaduke Jopley in his fine new car. Later on I got some dinner in a humble Moffat public house and thought of John Buchan, who took the title Viscount Tweedsmuir on his appointment as Governor General of Canada. Writer, politician, war correspondent, poet, lawyer, Member of Parliament, he is, of course, best remembered as the author of *The Thirty-Nine Steps*, in which his

hero Richard Hannay is chased around these rolling hills. He took his title from the name of the highest village on the Tweed.

Hilaire Belloc wrote of a Scotsman, James Bruce, who claimed he had discovered the sources of the Nile and was ridiculed for comparing them to the sources of the Tweed, Clyde and Annan which 'rise in one hill; three rivers as I now thought, not inferior to the Nile in beauty'. Belloc argued that he was right, for that greatest source, sacred to him, reminded him of the sacred places at home. Arguments about the source of the Nile and its discoverer have echoed down the centuries from Herodotus and Pliny the Elder, through Bruce, Speke and Stanley to the present day. In March 2006, the Ascend the Nile team of a Briton and two New Zealanders reached what they claimed was the true source, a muddy hole in Rwanda's Nyungwe Forest. However, as Juan Jose Valdes, a National Geographic Society senior cartographer, was quick to point out, 'The concept of a river's source is not a clearly defined one and is open to a number of interpretations. In the case of the Nile, as with the Amazon, the enormity and complexity of the river system make the use of the term "source" a troublesome issue.' Still, in a world surveyed by satellite and gauged by Google Earth, it's good to have some uncertainties left.

Clyde
bonnie banks

Scotland's third river is officially formed near Watermeetings, at the confluence of Daer Water and Potrail Water, in a broad strath between the little rounded tops of Brown Hill and Doddin and overlooked by the current farm and the former bastle of Glenochar. As with many other major rivers, though, it's not so simple. The old local verse which gives three streams one birthplace makes a reasonable rhyme but not necessarily good geography. John Wilson, scholar and poet, wrote in his 1764 work *Clyde*, an epic almost as long as

CLYDE	
SOURCE	Daer Head, South Lanarkshire
G.R.	NS 969 013
LENGTH	98½ miles (158 kilometres)
TRIBUTARIES	Douglas, Avon, Kelvin, White Cart
MOUTH	Firth of Clyde

the river itself, agreeing with the old established belief that 'From one vast mountain bursting on the day, Tweed, Clyde and Annan urge their separate way.' Being later offered the post as master at Greenock Grammar School on condition that he gave up 'the profane and unprofitable art' of writing poetry, Wilson apparently burnt his unfinished manuscripts and never wrote another couplet. The traditional source, Clydes Burn, certainly has the name and it does rise on the forested slopes of Clyde Law within a couple of miles of Tweed's Well and Annanhead, but perhaps the name of the first farm on the stream, Little Clyde, is more appropriate, for the burn is both shorter in length and smaller than the currently accepted headstream.

Daer Water has already flowed for over 10 miles (16km) and has been joined by two dozen tributaries before it meets Clydes Burn above Elvanfoot, a scattered hamlet standing where the A74, its motorway offspring and the West Coast Railway line clatter into Clydesdale. A visit to its source is an excellent way of exploring some of this pensive Southern Upland landscape.

A minor road leads off the A702 Carronbridge–Elvanfoot highway and, crossing a couple of really laid-back bridges over Potrail and Daer Waters, makes its way alongside the latter, to rise through forestry and pass the Daer Reservoir dam. The reservoir was inaugurated by the Queen in 1956 and supplies water to the central belt of Scotland. I parked the van at the foot of a forest track just

before Kirkhope Cleuch and set off alongside the reservoir, entertained by lapwings and gulls striving to outdo each other vocally. Just beyond the strangely suburban, brick-built and plastic-windowed bungalows of Crookburn and Kirkhope, the tarmac ends and the track climbs around the lower slopes of Ewe Gair and Little Hill and past a flurry of folds to pass above the deserted steading of Daerhead, surrounded by a huge bowl of hills. Had the Brontës been Scottish, Daerhead would have been Wuthering Heights, or maybe Watherin' Heets. From the broken-down house, which showed signs of recent if sporadic occupation, I made my way up the boggy slopes, decorated by the light mauve flowers of lady's smock and guided by intermittent quad-bike tracks and an infallible wall, to the col at Daer Hass. The name is pronounced 'Dar', but given local weather conditions, on many days it could well be 'dire'. Hass is related linguistically to the Lake District hause, 'a pass or low point along a ridge', and an old route across the hills between Elvanfoot and Thornhill certainly came this way.

The stream rises just before the wall and new fence running along the watershed. There are several other little channels in the vicinity, any of which could make a claim to be the source. All of them are narrow enough for you to be able to claim to have stood astride the Clyde. One particularly strong one was tumbling over a miniature waterfall on its way down from the slopes of jaunty little Earncraig Hill.

As I debated what to do next, a tiny vole disappeared into its hole in the grass at my feet and I realized I'd lost my compass. It had been in the same pocket as my notebook and must have been dislodged when I scribbled some *bon mot* or useless bit of information. Unbelievably, I was carrying a spare. I remembered shoving it into my rucksack after finding it in a drawer at home. It's the Silva Starter model I bought for my son, Rob, about twenty years ago. Most of his expeditions these days are around eighteen holes but his little compass did take him up Pic d'Aneto and a few more worthy mountains.

Daer Hass

The cloud was flirting with the summit of Earncraig Hill and maintained that 2,000-foot (610m) level for most of the rest of my walk, which was a shame as most of it was above 2,000 feet. I had decided to visit some nearby Donalds[20] and look for a few more sources. First I went up the steep little slope on to Earncraig Hill, which gave ample opportunity to study the pale violet mountain pansies speckling the grass. These close-ups were certainly better than the view from the summit, which afforded an impressionist glimpse of the reservoir through the cloud. Returning to the Hass I made my way up Gana Shank, where a solitary deer dashed up the slope ahead of me, to the summit of Gana Hill. In the cloud I was glad of the fence running along the ridge for, apart from a couple of cairns at either end, Gana Hill is fairly free of features of interest to anything apart from sheep and grouse. So free that the Ordnance Survey nominates both 'cairn' and 'pile of stones' to a couple of heaps of rock at the other end of the summit bulge that are about a yard apart.

It wasn't pouring down but the fine persistent rain was of that particularly annoying kind that clouds both sides of the lens. No one who doesn't need glasses can even start to appreciate the frustrations of navigation in cloud and rain which have to be tolerated by the bespectacled so, not surprisingly, Five Wells, a line of springs claimed by some to be another Clyde source, proved elusive in the clag. Maybe the post I found at the head of the meteorologically appropriately named Thick Cleugh was the one mooted by others to be the source. In clearer conditions the Wells show up as green patches among the dun grass of their surrounds and Thick Cleugh certainly carries more water at its meeting with Daer Water than its confluee. Wedder Law gave the same view as the other summits visited but has a beautifully soft, mossy top. A track, heading down to Smuring Hags, looked to give a better route to the next top, Scaw'd Law, than the fence which appeared, from the map at least, to run through the worst of the bog along the ridge, above Carsehope Middens. There are many other evocative names around here. Within a couple of miles of the top of Gana Hill you'll find Haggie Hill, Foxes Shin, Brandy Holes, Pettylung, Glenimp and Smurn Gutter.

Just as I reached the gate in the fence that would lead me up to Scaw'd Law, I heard a chugging sound and discerned, through the mist, an approaching quad bike. It was a very smart Honda affair with a dashboard that wouldn't have disgraced a transatlantic jet, and was the steed of the

20 Anorak alert: Donalds are hills in the Scottish lowlands higher than 2,000 feet and are so named after Percy Donald, who first collated them.

local gamekeeper. I opened the gate for him and he stopped for a chat. The track had been here for about eight years, he told me, and was part of an attempt to develop grouse shooting. He reckoned there would be lots more such tracks in a few years' time when the moor prospered. His take on the blocking of drainage ditches was one I hadn't come across. Re-bogging the moor encouraged crane fly, which the adult grouse eat to supplement their diet of heather and which are an important food source for the young during their growth phase. With a last comment on the weather where he'd come from, 'It's lovely and sunny down that way,' we parted and I made my way up on to Scaw'd Law, its twin tops unmarked, not especially lovely and certainly not sunny, until the wall met a fence heading off to the north-east. This crosses Ballencleugh Law, with its fasces-like summit cairn of old bundled fence posts, and wanders off northwards to Comb Law. I continued, fenceless over trig point-topped Rodger Law, before dropping down off Watchman's Brae back to the road at Kirkhope Cleugh, the waiting van, a change of clothes and a cup of tea.

It is possible to carry on along the wall, over Little Scaw'd Law and Durisdeer Hill, to drop down to the watershed where it is crossed by the Roman road between Nithsdale and Clydesdale running north-east from Durisdeer. Now known as the Well Path, this was the original route through these hills, tramped by legionaries and later followed by travellers making the pilgrimage between Edinburgh and Whithorn, site of the shrine of St Ninian and the first Christian settlement north of Hadrian's Wall. Traversed by Scottish monarchs from Robert the Bruce, dying and carried on a litter, to Mary, Queen of Scots, this is a high way with a history. James IV covered the full 160 miles (257km) route in eight days during 1507. It subsequently became the turnpike to the capital and it was used until a new road was constructed through the lower and more westerly Dalveen Pass in the early nineteenth century. A Roman fortlet still stares out over the

best part of two millennia on the Durisdeer side. Just to the east of the wall, here marking the border between Strathclyde and Dumfries and Galloway, rises one of the headstreams of Potrail Water. Joined by other Sikes and Grains rising high on the slopes of Durisdeer Hill, Scaw'd Law, Ballencleugh Law, Hirstane Rigg and Comb Law, it flows 5 miles (8km) from here to join with Daer Water and form the Clyde proper. A late summer evening stroll from the main road near Trolloss farm to the head of the Well Path can surely, according to company, encourage the gentle singing of 'roamin' in the gloamin", though a similarly timed walk in winter could possibly lead to unorchestrated manoeuvres in the dark.

Nith

with trees on either hand

	NITH
SOURCE	Prickeny Hill, East Ayrshire
G.R.	NS 550 061
LENGTH	70 miles (112 kilometres)
TRIBUTARIES	Euchan Water, Scar Water, Cluden Water
MOUTH	Solway Firth

The Nith probably doesn't feature highly on most people's lists of well-known rivers. In our Anglo-centric kingdom, few people south of the border have probably even heard of the river, and fewer still would be able to place it on a map. Yet the Nith is the seventh-longest Scottish river and is just outside the top twenty longest in Britain, surpassing the much better-known Forth, Exe and Dart as well as all the Derwents. About 70 miles (112km) in length, the river rises in East Ayrshire, in the Carsphairn Hills, about 4 miles (6.4km) east of Dalmellington, and heads north to New Cumnock only to swing east then south-east along Nithsdale before flowing through Dumfries to join the sea in the Solway Firth.

The river was written about poetically and approvingly by Robert Burns, who lived 'by the sweet side o' the Nith' for much of his life, but another couple of authors were less than enthusiastic about it. Francis H. Groome in the *Ordnance Gazetteer of Scotland*, published between 1882 and 1885, describes the upland stretches of the Nith as 'one of the most cheerless of streams, sluggish and shallow, seldom more than 15 feet wide, deeply tinctured with moss and rarely graced with plantation, greensward or even a bold bank to relieve the dreary monotony of its moorland landscape'. Groome would be surprised to see it now, as far from the Nith being 'rarely graced with plantation', its source is in the middle of one. William Scott Douglas,[21] writing in 1874, was even wrong about its source, writing that the 'Prickeny and Powkelly burns unite to form the infant Nith'. Powkelly Burn is a Nith tributary but Prickeny Burn, although rising within yards of the Nith, joins the Water of Deugh, itself a tributary of the Galloway Dee, and joins the Solway Firth 20 miles (32km) west of the Nith, at Kirkcudbright.

I have never enjoyed walking through forestry. The regimented rows of plantations always seem to deaden the landscape and confuse the contours. A study of the map shows that the 'Source of the Nith' is in the col between Enoch Hill and Prickeny Hill, modest heights rising to around 1,800 feet (549m), and that a forest track, Prickeny Road, leads almost to it. When I arrived at the glass-spattered lay-by, on the B741 New Cumnock-to-Dalmellington road, next to the start of the forest track, it was misty and raining, so I decided to take to two wheels and pedalled off into the woods. It was a pleasant enough ride, though I would have been glad of some gladsome plains; this stretch of track is all up and down.

Forest tracks have two sides, where the wheels of the vehicles run, with a humpy bit in the middle. One side of the track always seems smoother than the other and it's inevitably the one you're not riding on. If you cross from left to right then the smoother bit magically transfers to the left.

Eventually, after passing several junctions and a number of small former quarries, the track crosses Powkelly Burn and starts to climb alongside the little Nith valley. Down below, on an unplanted stretch of ground, a redundant circular sheepfold stands by the confluence of the infant river and Loup Burn, its highest named tributary. It's quite a pull up the last three-quarters of a mile or so, past another quarry, to the junction of Prickeny Road and Maneight Road, another track, which runs down to the source. When I say 'quite a pull' I really mean quite a push, as I was out of the saddle for most of the ascent.

At a boggy little plain where a break in the trees allows the diminutive river to trickle away down its valley, the track crosses the tiny stream at what is the first, plastic-pipe, bridge across the Nith. The true source lies a few score yards away from the other side of the path, beyond the blank, green wall of conifers, deeper in the close-planted forest, a stinging push through sharp-needled branches, the collected rainfall of the previous half day at last freed to drip, trickle and then pour malignantly through once waterproof clothing, a hot, sweaty, midge-disturbing, immeasurable period of time spent tripping and tumbling over half-seen tussocks, glasses steamed up and useless, to find a soggy little depression, one of hundreds hidden in the matted undergrowth of this green hell of the north, where the Nith springs to life. At least, that's how I imagined it. I was back on the bike and whooshing away down the track. I fully embrace T. S. Eliot's maxim that 'old men ought to be explorers, here or there does not matter', but this is one that I gladly leave to somebody else. You explore here, I'll find somewhere there – preferably half a country further north.

---

21 In *Ayrshire: A descriptive picture of the County of Ayr with relative notes on interesting local subjects, chiefly derived during a recent personal tour.*

HIGHLAND SPRINGS

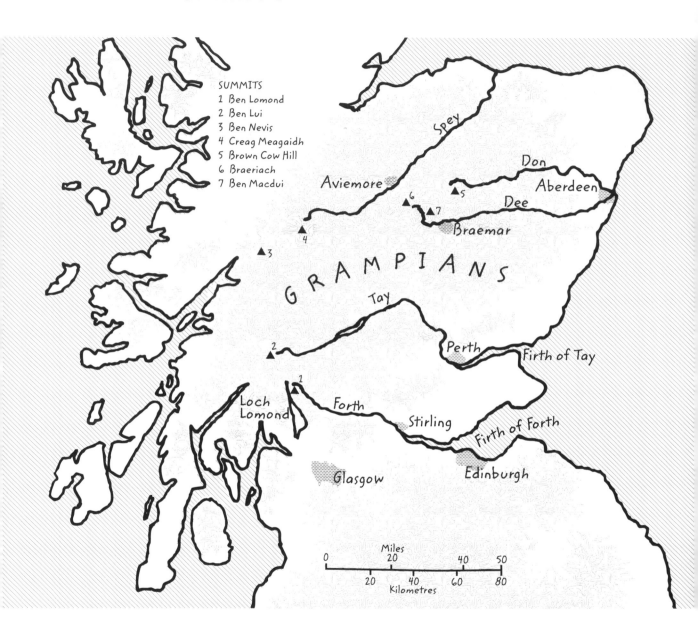

SUMMITS
1 Ben Lomond
2 Ben Lui
3 Ben Nevis
4 Creag Meagaidh
5 Brown Cow Hill
6 Braeriach
7 Ben Macdui

The sources of the five monosyllabic rivers here invite the visitor into some of the most remote places of Britain. They are all distinguished rivers and their risings should be approached with an air of reverence. Although sometimes thought of as being one homogeneous mass, the Scottish Highlands hold a great variety of landscapes, ranging from the sharp, rocky peaks of the west to the sprawling semi-arctic massifs of the east. All of it is beautiful and by visiting these sources one experiences a superb cross-section of the scenery. The walks tend to be long and sometimes lonely, involving a lot of ascent, and one of them, to the Wells of Dee, really justifies a night out.

Forth

a sapphire of the elements, an entity of blue

FORTH	
SOURCE	north of Ben Lomond, Stirling
G.R.	NN 353 069
LENGTH	64½ miles (103.5 kilometres)
TRIBUTARIES	Goodie, Allan Water, Teith
MOUTH	Firth of Forth

One of the best-known rivers of Britain, the Forth begins in two streams rising high in the mountains of south-west Perthshire. Duchray Water and Avondhu make their separate ways through the Loch Ard Forest to meet at Milton a mile or so west of the quiet (off-season)/hectic (on-season) village of Aberfoyle. Thereafter the Forth meanders sluggardly across the plains of Flanders Moss and Drip Moss to be joined by its major tributary, the Teith, just before Stirling, where it becomes tidal. Below here it transforms into the Firth of Forth, which broadens out into the most substantial estuary along the east coast of Scotland. Its length has been calculated at anywhere between 39 and 116½ miles (63 and 187km), depending on where its beginning and ending are reckoned to be.

On a day when the forecast speaks of heavy showers, you can expect a drenching. I drove out from Aberfoyle, past Loch Ard and through woods carpeted with hosts of Scottish bluebells, along the road that goes to Stronachlachar and Inversnaid, and parked by little Loch Dhu. The Water of Chon flows out of the loch before entering Loch Ard and emerging as the Avondhu. Walking up the track towards Loch Dhu House I was sluiced from a puddle by a vehicle haring down in the opposite direction; not quite the drenching I was expecting but as my bandmate Brett once said, 'It's wet in Scotland even when it's not wet.'

I had bumped into an old walking pal in town a few days earlier. 'How many have you got left, Ron?' 'Only sixteen, but they're spread out all over the place.' One of the reasons I have never tried to do the Munros[22] is all the travelling involved from the English Midlands. So, when I was getting around to the last few, Scottish, sources I planned an expedition that would visit several of them. I had the space of a couple of weeks when other commitments allowed me to nip off in the van. Of course, after weeks and weeks of dry, sunny weather, this window corresponded with the following forecast on the very useful Mountain Weather Information Service (MWIS) website. 'Low pressure will often be resident off northern Scotland over the next week or so. This will lead to widely cloud on most mountain areas, especially on western mountains in Scotland, where summits will almost always be cloud covered. All areas will have further rain, often falling as heavy showers, and particularly across Highland Scotland, frequent windy, with upland gales for periods.' I rather think the person who typed that had had something planned too but it made me keen to see 'widely cloud'. All this, of course, at the same time as hosepipe bans, standpipes in the streets and rocketing food prices were being predicted south of the border. As one radio presenter calmly put it, 'I don't want to be negative, but what's the worst-case scenario?'

Next to Loch Dhu House stands the eponymous Cottage, built in 1890, whose access gates tell that it was built in connection with work on the great Glasgow Corporation waterworks scheme. This massive undertaking involved building and blasting a 34 mile (55km) long tunnel and aqueduct to carry water from Loch Katrine to the city. A shaft by the track just above Loch Dhu House shows where the water passes underground on its way south.

The track crosses a forested low ridge, the minor watershed between the Forth's two major

---

22 Scottish mountains of over 3,000 feet, named after Sir Hugh Munro, who compiled the original list and published it in 1891.

The road to Comer

headstreams, before dropping down into Gleann Dubh, the valley of Duchray Water. Just off the track are the remains of Stronmacnair, a tumble of walls that's easy to walk by without a second glance but another place with a story to tell. Near the ruins of a cottage probably dating back to medieval times, there is a burial ground, inside an enclosure of turf and boulders, which includes unmarked headstones and slabs. Below the burial ground are the remains of bloomery mounds, sites that show evidence of iron working dating from the seventeenth or eighteenth centuries. The place was marked on General Roy's map of 1747–55, produced after Bonnie Prince Charlie's Jacobite Rebellion. The oldest map I have of the area, a one-inch OS sheet of the mid-1950s, shows the place to be whole and as yet unafflicted by afforestation but by 1993–4 the cottage had fallen into such a poor state that the roof was removed and it has continued to deteriorate since. Its remote and eerie location (locals have called it the most haunted place in Scotland) led Stronmacnair to be featured in several scenes in *The Last Great Wilderness*, a rather oddball feature film, with a nod to *The Wicker Man*, made in 2002.

I had passed several signs pointing the way to Comer, which was just as well as, in this maze of forestry, that was the next destination. Having descended into Gleann Dubh, the track follows the valley north-westwards, crossing under power lines marching resolutely in the same direction, and

leaves the forest. The passage of several heavy, blustery showers meant that taking photos was a case of whipping off the rucksack, taking out the camera, turning round quickly and snapping, but as I made my way past Loch Dubh, the grey mass in front of me gradually decided to let me see that it actually was Ben Lomond and by the time I reached Stùc a' Bhuic I could almost see the summit towering grandly above the last farm in the valley, Comer.

Like most glens in Scotland, this place looks very different from how it would have appeared three centuries ago, when it would have supported a number of small farms, like Stronmacnair, and families, before being sold for sheep grazing. Later forestry interests took over much of the valley, leaving just one productive farm. The Comer estate, stretching from the valley floor to the moorland and steep rocky slopes of the enclosing mountains, is now owned by the Aage V. Jensen Foundation, whose objective is to contribute to the preservation of nature in all its diversity and encourage the public to see what nature has to offer. The foundation bought the estate in 1987 and still work it as a farm, though it has encouraged the development of a wider diversity of habitats. Certainly you will walk past recently planted areas of native woodland, which make a change from the acres of conifers of the Loch Ard Forest recently left behind.

At Stùc a' Bhuic, currently an outdoors centre with an excited school party just arriving as I passed, the track climbs northwards, giving glimpses of a fine waterfall on the Abhainn Gaoithe, as this furthermost Forth feeder is now called, and passes several wooded areas. Gleann Gaoithe was living up to its name with a lively westerly pushing through the valley. Meteorologists use the Beaufort Scale as a measure of wind strength. Rear-Admiral Sir Francis Beaufort developed his scale, observing the effects of the wind at different forces on sea conditions, in an attempt to standardize what had hitherto been a fairly subjective area. It still can be: one mountaineer's 'It was a bit fresh' is another's

'It was blowing a hooley up there'. I often don my deerstalker when walking in Scotland, as effective an anemometer as any. It usually sits on my head quite neatly with the flaps up but if I have to tie it under my chin then I know it's really windy.

The track, its verges decorated with little clumps of vivid blue heath milkwort and pink lousewort, has by now lost the power lines which disappear north over to Loch Katrine. It runs above the stream, which here and there performs two-dimensional acrobatics to produce some wonderful meanders. One was so close to being beheaded that I almost expected to see an oxbow on my return. As you approach the col the valley opens out into a broad strath before suddenly tumbling away over the watershed, steeply down to Loch Lomond. Just about on cue the cloud-wreathed mountains across the loch revealed most of their glory and the summits of Ben Vorlich, Ben Vane and Beinn Narnain came and went in the 'widely cloud'. As I looked down, Loch Lomond stretched away, steely blue water below dark green wooded sides. It is the largest sheet of fresh water in Great Britain, one of the most attractive and certainly one of the most popular. All around is the country of Rob Roy McGregor, a more solid character than the Robin Hood to whom he is sometimes likened but another who fought against changing times with mixed success. Jacobite, outlaw, hero, blackmailer, cattle dealer, cattle thief, patron of the poor and sometime cave-dweller, he was immortalized by Sir Walter Scott and his greatest contribution to his nation is the untold thousands of dollars his tale attracts to the Trossachs.

All that remained was to locate a likely source from the scores of little streams that coalesce to make up Abhainn Gaoithe. I found one close by the watershed running between the rounded tops of Cruachan and Cruinn a' Bheinn and somewhat higher than the track. A trio of boggy little channels united to run away and meet many more before heading off down the glen to join water pouring in tumult into Abhainn Bheag high on the northern flanks of Ben Lomond. These two meet up by Comer to become Duchray Water. I stood for a time among the wiry heathpacks and flitches of fern, looking across from the source to the rounded pile of Cruinn a' Bheinn and the more pointed top of Ben Lomond beyond. The mountain is the most southerly of Scotland's Munros and one of the most popular. It has a commanding position on the edge of the Highlands and long-ranging summit views on a clear day. I heard a cuckoo and wondered if it was the same one that had accompanied the beginning of my walk by Loch Dhu. After one more glance around at the wildness and wet I turned and walked back down the track. A few days later as I drove across the Forth Road Bridge and looked over to the cantilevered steel tracery of the railway bridge, I wondered how many out of the millions who had crossed these mighty structures had ever thought about where it all began.

Many streams rising in, and a couple just above, the Loch Ard Forest, flow into Loch Chon, to form the Avondhu, a.k.a. Water of Chon, the Forth's other main feeder. One of the highest rises in Lochan Mhaim nan Carn below the eastern slopes of Beinn Uamha. The river is unusual, as more of its length is made up of lochs than running river. Where it meets Duchray Water near Milton, it is noticeable that the latter is the larger river and thus the prime Forth headwater.

Glossary

Abhainn Bheag: little river

Abhainn Gaoithe: windy river

Avondhu: black river

Beinn Narnain: notched hill

Beinn Uamha: hill of the cave

Ben Vane: middle mountain

Ben Vorlich: hill of the bay

Cruachan: bold hill

Cruinn a' Bheinn: crown of the hill

Gleann Dubh: black valley

Inversnaid: Snaid Burn confluence

Lochan Mhaim nan Carn: lake of the cairned breast-
   shaped hill

Stronachlachar: point of the wild ducks

Stronmacnair: Macnair's point

Stùc a' Bhuic: buck hill

Tay

most beautiful to be seen

TAY	
SOURCE	Allt Coire Laoigh, Stirling
G.R.	NN 274 245
LENGTH	120 miles (193 kilometres)
TRIBUTARIES	Earn, Isla, Tummel, Almond, Lyon
MOUTH	Firth of Tay

The longest river in Scotland, at about 120 miles (193km), and sixth longest in Great Britain, the Tay originates high on the slopes of Ben Lui in the Southern Highlands in a trio of headstreams: Allt Coire Laoigh, Allt Coire Ghaothaich and Allt an Rund. A serial name-changer, it is soon the river Cononish; next it becomes Fillan and then Dochart, until it joins Loch Tay at Killin. From there it's Tay all the way, silvery or not, until, east of Perth, it broadens out into the Firth of Tay, which stretches some 25 miles (40km) north-eastwards to the North Sea. According to a display in Perth Museum it takes 440 days for a drop of water falling on Ben Lui to reach Dundee; 420 days are spent getting through Loch Tay. How do they work out such facts?

Western Scotland in July can often mean midges but I felt that the masks, like bee-keepers' hats but with presumably a finer mesh, worn by a couple of German walkers on the By The Way campsite in Tyndrum were a little extravagant. There were midges around but they seemed relatively benign compared with some previous 'I was driven out of my mind' experiences. Leaving the campsite, on the site of former railway sidings and now next to the West Highland Way, I followed the latter through woods and across a piece of bare ground, relic of Tyndrum's lead-mining past, to where it met the track to Cononish. Just before the junction I passed the Loch of the Legend of the Lost Sword. Few lochs beside long-distance paths can be with-out their legend. This one concerns Robert I. The fleeing Bruce, routed by the English at Methven and being pursued north, suffered another defeat, by the MacDougalls of Lorne, here at Dalrigh. In order to hasten their escape, the Bruce told his men to lighten their loads by throwing their heavy weap-ons into the lochan, setting an example by hurling in his own great sword, reputed to be over 5 feet (1.5m) long. One for the Time Team, I think, unless the tatters have got there first.

Passing under a railway bridge, Ben Lui came into view, a distant, clouded peak. It is one of the finest mountains in Scotland, rising to a sharp double summit above the arms of a great scalloped corrie. The track passes the farm and bright green barns of Cononish and one branch heads off to a disused gold mine, which is always rumoured to be about to re-open any day. Allt Eas Anie, a Cononish tributary, tumbles impressively down the crags above the workings and gives a popular winter ice climb. Further up the glen and Coire Laoigh runs ruler straight down from its bealach between Ben Oss and Ben Lui while the latter looms ever closer. Just before a crossing of Allt an Rund the track ends and the collar work begins. A path, not too vis-ible from a distance but obvious enough underfoot, starts beside a rectangular sheep fold and climbs steeply, following Allt Coire Ghaothaich up to its sources. Bands of steeply folded mica-schist rock are crossed, glittering and plunging down into the roots of the mountain while the stream launches itself over a succession of slides and falls.

Looking back from the foot of the corrie the

Coire an Lochain

superiority of Allt Coire Laoigh as the main Cononish feeder is apparent, for it carries more water than the other two combined. Still, Allt Coire Ghaothaich has a more dramatic birth, up here in the giant scoop where its headstreams gather themselves after emerging from fans of scree and myriads of tiny springs up to a height of around 3,100 feet (945m), the Tay's highest sources. This is a magnificent mountain setting with the rocky ramparts of the jagged corrie rim ahead, but it is also fine in detail with clumps of purple saxifrage among the flowers speckling the grass as they have since the end of the last Ice Age. A little path slants off to the right to head for an obvious notch in the ridge. There was no one in sight and no sounds except for my breathing and running and trickling water. Looking back towards Ben Oss, though, I could see a stern face framed with flowing locks, picked out by the sun, Mount Rushmore-like in the side of the corrie wall. Perhaps he is some long-forgotten

Gaelic chieftain waiting like King Arthur, to spring back to life at his nation's call. I studied the map carefully to see if he was named but only discovered that the stream flowing from the corrie is one letter different from the name of the great bowl itself. Some quirk of Gaelic or perhaps copying.

Crossing Ben Lui's north-east ridge, Stob Garbh, I descended into Coire an Lochain, where various headstreams of Allt an Rund run into and out of a complexity of lochans lying at over 3,000 feet (915m). This is the most western of Tay's headwaters and as such has been described as the true source, rising only 5 miles (8km) from salt water on the west coast. Making my way up in cloud through the ice-axe-and-crampon-scratched rocks to the summit cairn, I was reflecting that it would have been good to have seen the view but that some things ought to be left for heaven when, for just a few seconds, the wind tore aside the veil and I had a momentary full-length view down the Cononish glen.

Ben Lui

At 3,707 feet (1,130m), Ben Lui, the first Munro of my source-seeking walks, is twenty-eighth on the list in terms of height and one of the best in terms of interest and enjoyment. On a clear day the view from the summit is wide ranging from the Arrochar Alps in the south to Ben Nevis to the north.

I made my way down Ben Lui's broad southeast ridge to the wide and damp, lochan-spattered bealach separating the mountain from neighbouring Ben Oss. Here Allt Coire Laoigh, longest and largest of the Tay's three headstreams, rises, over 600 feet (183m) lower than the others. Water flows both ways from the col; in fact it flows both ways from some patches of bog, feeding both the Tay and (via Allt nan Caorainn, the river Falloch, Loch Lomond and the river Leven) the Clyde at Dumbarton. Allt Coire Laoigh flows straight and true down its valley to join its brothers and become the river Cononish. Although, in view of its greater length and volume of water, it was given the accolade of true source by the Tay Western Catchments Project[23] in September 2010, the boggy risings of Allt Coire Laoigh are rather a disappointment after the dramatic surrounds of Coire an Lochain and particularly Coire Ghaothach, and I left undisturbed the time capsule buried at 'the source' by the project's surveyors.

On the climb to Ben Oss's summit, two streams falling to join Allt Coire Laoigh have sources which gave dramatic views across the deep glen to the almost perfect pyramidal peak of Ben Lui, while from the cairn I had the briefest view of a walker silhouetted on the skyline, the only other person I saw all day. I decided that I might as well take in the top of Beinn Dubhcraig, a quick and easy walk from the col above Loch Oss. From the cairn I could see the ridge, cloudy again, below Ben Lomond, where I had found the Forth's source, and then the rain set in. The inimitable Munroist and author Ralph Storer describes the path back to Dalrigh as 'bog. Not just any old bog. We're talking Slough of Despond.' Being out of necessity something of a student of mire and morass, I couldn't resist it. It was bad in patches, but not as bad as Ure Head or the upper reaches of the Tywi or the crossing of Waun y Griafolen. Anyway, the path had the consolation of passing through a beautiful pine wood in its lower stages, one of the few relicts of the Caledonian Forest in the Southern Highlands.

Back at Tyndrum after nine and a quarter hours on the hill, there was no worry about midges. The rain saw to that.

Glossary

Allt Coire Ghaothaich: windy corrie stream

Allt Coire Laoigh: stream of the calf's corrie

Allt Eas Anie: possibly a corruption of Eas Aonaidh – waterfall of the steep brae

Allt nan Caorainn: rowan tree stream

Bealach: col, pass

Beinn Dubhcraig: test your Gaelic[24]

Ben Lui: Beinn Laoigh, mountain of the calf

Ben Oss: elk mountain

Coire an Lochain: lochan corrie

Dalrigh: king's field

Stob Garbh: rough point

Tyndrum: house ridge

---

23   Commissioned by the charity Scottish Native Woods.

24   Black crag mountain.

Spey

home of the pike and the dipper

SPEY	
SOURCE	Loch Spey, Highland
G.R.	NN 413 948
LENGTH	98 miles (157.5 kilometres)
TRIBUTARIES	Tromie, Feshie, Dulnain, Avon
MOUTH	Spey Bay

A couple of miles short of the hundred (157.5km), Spey is Scotland's third-longest river (after the Tay and the Clyde), although some authorities place it second, there being only about half a mile between the Clyde and the Spey. It is in the top ten of longest British rivers. Rising in the Central Highlands, between the eastern end of Lochaber and south-west of the Monadhliath Mountains, in a lonely, wide and boggy glen, the river runs east and north-east through Badenoch, passing Newtonmore, Kingussie and Aviemore, where the valley becomes Strathspey. It then meanders from Grantown-on-Spey to Spey Mouth, situated on a broad bay between Lossiemouth and Buckie. The river is noted for its salmon fishing while the valley is renowned for whisky distilling.

Lower Speyside is home to more than half of Scotland's distilleries, featured in a popular Whisky Trail, but the higher parts of the valley are less well known; indeed the source of the Spey lies in the centre of what the Scottish Mountaineering Club Guide describes as 'that vast, desolate tri-angle with its base Glen Spean and Loch Laggan and its apex Fort Augustus'. Amazingly, then, it is possible to drive to within 3½ miles (5.6km) of the recognized source, Loch Spey.

I was blissfully unaware of this as I parked the van at Garva Bridgeafter driving along the single-track road through the broad Spey valley stretching away westwards into the hills from Laggan on the

A86 between Spean Bridge and Newtonmore. As a through route it is deceptive, for it does not lead directly to the Great Glen as might be thought but rather to the headwaters of the Spey and, across the watershed, into Glen Roy, which turns southerly and back to Glen Spean. The only way out to the Great Glen is to branch north, over the high, steep and, in winter, often impassable Corrieyairack Pass. This route, used by drovers and travellers for centuries and developed by General Wade as one of his military roads in 1731, makes a grand approach towards the head of the Spey.

Garva Bridge is gated and, according to several books I had read, the end of the road for vehicles, as the surface deteriorates badly thereafter. The first few hundred yards, climbing up to a forest, looked reasonable but I had already decided to unship the bike and pedal as far as Melgarve, where the path to Loch Spey deserts the military road. With a fresh westerly blowing I knew I could look forward to an easy ride – on the way back. The bridge is a fine ex-ample of General Wade's thoroughness; its double-arched structure, massively buttressed on the up-stream side, is like two bridges joined together, the central pier standing on a rocky island. Completed in 1732, it is in remarkably good condition, having been repaired some years ago. Wade himself, proud of his first double-span bridge, named it St George's Bridge but, unsurprisingly, the name didn't make its way into the local consciousness.

The gradient of the hill and the oncoming wind made it into mine as I cycled, mostly uphill, along the dead-straight lengths of Wade's road. This is a huge landscape, dwarfing the pylons and power lines that parallel the track. After forty minutes' pedalling I reached Melgarve and found half a dozen cars. I could have driven after all. I'd cer-tainly noticed nothing wrong with the road, which must have been resurfaced. Still, I thought, as I chained my bike to the sign which currently said nothing but presumably once indicated the weak-ness of the bridge beyond the end of the tarmac, at least I had the moral satisfaction of having reached this remote spot under my own steam. Walking up the stony track, which now looked something like it must have done in George Wade's time, I passed a gate with a 'ROAD CLOSED' sign on it. Although pedestrians and intrepid cyclists can still follow the General's road for a further 13½ miles (22km) to Fort Augustus, vehicular transport is now banned. An abandoned Wade bridge crosses Caochan Riabhach, a Spey tributary, just before the bothy at Melgarve, where the path to Loch Spey abandons the military road, leaving it to climb its numerous zig-zags (originally eighteen, later reduced to thirteen) to the summit of Corrieyairack Pass at about 2,500 feet (762m).

The track to the head of the Spey descends past a cottage called Drummin, where a few young trees flourish, surrounded by high wire deer fences. The numerous fords along the track have been replaced by bridges and the track is in good condition as far as the lonely cottage at Shesgnan, in the throes of renovation when I passed and sporting a notice on the door reading 'Rome was built in a day'. Along this stretch the Spey runs lethargically, meandering and braiding as it attempts to fill a valley much too big for itself. Across the strath to the south the land rises to culminate on 3,700-foot (1,128m) Creag Meagaidh, which has an extensive summit plateau. There were still a few patches of snow visible which added interest to, from this side, a fairly level stretch of mountain but only the outthrust Càrn Dearg really caught the eye. Bonnie Prince Charlie crossed this high ridge just a few days before he reached the coast and the French ship that was to take him into exile at the end of his desperate five-month-long game of hide and seek across the Highlands and islands.

I was following occasional quad-bike tracks along this highest stretch of the Spey valley and in places was just wading through the bog until I suddenly came upon Loch Spey. Standing at 1,142 feet (348m) above sea level, the loch is about three-eighths of a mile (600m) long and about 200 yards

(182m) across. It stands in a wide boggy sweep of ground surrounded by a few outcrops of rock and piles of moraine. Just to the west, over the complex watershed, the ground falls away into Glen Roy with its Parallel Roads, real-life contour lines that are the remnants of the shore lines of an ice-dammed lake that filled the glen 10,000 years ago. The upper 'road' marks the highest shoreline, cut by frost weathering and wave action, while the lower ones were formed as the lake level fell and then stabilized for a time. The limiting factor was the height of the cols, over which the water could flow as the ice retreated. The current watershed between Spey and Roy is over 1,150 feet (350m) and is actually named 'Col' on OS maps. The 'roads' are more prominent when viewed from the open end of the glen but, given the right lighting conditions, the eye of the faithful can discern part of the highest one from the col, while piles and ridges of moraine speak of the glaciers that carved out the broad valleys on either side.

The watershed is vague and, from higher up the slope, the burn which can claim to be Spey's source, rising about three-quarters of a mile beyond the loch on the south-eastern slopes of Creag a' Chail, appears to travel uphill in places. At least from the boggy head of the unnamed stream Creag Meagaidh was visible, its top dusted with recent snow like icing on a cake. I had crossed the path over the col while climbing to the source, which at least meant I wouldn't have to paddle back through the bog on

Melgarve

my return down the glen. The path stays quite high, giving long views of the Spey meandering down the valley. Cycle tracks in the mud made me think of the Rough Stuff Fellowship, that intrepid bunch of mountain bikers from the days before mountain bikes. Founded in 1955, the RSF hard men went off road on bikes that were basically on road machines, with steel frames and hub gears, often carrying full camping kit. The fellowship continues to get off the beaten track and, although drop handlebars are still to be seen, they're quite happy to accept mountain bikers these days.

I had noticed two walkers on the path while I was ferreting around looking for the source of the headstream and I caught them up at Shesgnan Burn. They were doing it by the book, taking off their boots and socks and wading across. My feet were already wet enough for me not to bother and I found a spot where the burn was a bit wider and walked through. I was soon unchaining the bike and thoroughly enjoyed my ride back to Garva Bridge. Nearly entirely downhill, with a following wind, long, straight stretches and definitely all smooth stuff.

Glossary

Badenoch: drowned land

Caochan Riabhach: brindled streamlet

Càrn Dearg: red cairn

Corrieyairack: *coire dheirg* – red corrie

Creag Meagaidh: crag of the bog

Melgarve: *meall garbh?* – rough round hill

Monadhliath: grey moor

Shesgnan: the bog reed

Don

How now?

Scotland's sixth-longest river and comfortably inside Britain's top twenty, Don runs for about 80 miles (129km) from its source north-west of Brown Cow Hill in the eastern Cairngorms to the North Sea at Bridge of Don by Aberdeen. The city takes

DON	
SOURCE	Well of Don, Aberdeenshire
G.R.	NJ 195 067
LENGTH	80 miles (129 kilometres)
TRIBUTARIES	Deskry Water, Water of Buchat, Kindy Burn, Mossat Burn, Ury
MOUTH	Bridge of Don, Aberdeen

its name from the river that runs its entire course through the county of Aberdeenshire except, curiously, where it flows through the city which, thanks to the vagaries of local government, is no longer part of the county.

The river gains its name below the confluence of Allt Tuileach and Allt Veannaich, which have already been known as Fèith Bhàit and Meikle Caochan Odhar, and is definitely the river Don as it flows beneath Cock Bridge on the A939 Tomintoul-to-Ballater road. This largely follows the route of the Old Military Road built after the 1745 Jacobite Rebellion. A couple of miles north of here is the Lecht pass, its untidy tangle of ski tows and cables witness to its popularity as a winter sports centre. The road is notorious as the first in Britain to be blocked by drifts and there are permanent snow gates on either side of the highest section. There was no prospect of snow when I set off to find the Don's source from the car park below Corgarff Castle by Cock Bridge, but the forecast was for heavy rain later and I was still thinking of the epigraph I had read on a monolith in a lay-by just up the road which gave glorious views of the upper Don – 'Take a moment to behold as still skies or storms unfold'. I had a shrewd idea of which was the more likely today. Apart from my van there was just one more vehicle in the car park, a Dutch camper van, but the castle warden was arriving in his Land Rover to open up as I left.

The superbly restored castle, first built around

the middle of the sixteenth century as a tower house, has been much altered over the centuries. In 1571 it was lived in by the Forbes family and attacked by Adam Gordon of Auchindoun during one of those incessant feuds that burn through Scottish history. In this case literally. Finding the laird of Corgarff to be away but his family in residence, the Gordons demanded the castle's surrender. Doughty Margaret, a Campbell and Forbes's wife, refused them entry. Shots were fired and one Gordon was hit in the knee. His fellows piled timber against the walls and set the place alight, burning Margaret, her children and servants to death. Twenty-seven people died in the conflagration. Corgarff was burned again, by Jacobites in 1689, by Hanoverians in 1716 and once more in 1746. Two years later the government bought the place, remodelled the tower and added the star-shaped outer walls. It was used as a barracks following the Jacobite Rebellions and later as a base in a campaign to stop illicit whisky distilling and smuggling until being abandoned in 1831. It was last occupied by the Ross sisters, known locally as the Castle Ladies, until they left in 1912. After the Second World War the surrounding Delnadamph estate, purchased by Sir Edmund and Lady Stockdale, used the curtain walls as shelter for occasional shooting lunches. The castle was taken into state care in 1961 with financial assistance from the Stockdales and has since been splendidly restored by Historic Scotland.

In view of the forecast 'I hauld it time to ga" and so set off along the track beside the Don that leads to the head of the valley. The river meanders extravagantly over a flat floodplain above which rise rounded hills. The lower slopes are patterned with geometric blocks of forestry with the moorlands beyond tartaned by strips and blocks of burnt heather. With the bright May morning sun shining between the clouds, the effect was to produce an iridescent landscape like something out of a kids' cartoon and I wouldn't have been surprised if Tinky Winky and Laa-Laa had lumbered across the track beneath a flock of hovering Tittifers.

Down by the river and just beyond the apparently empty cottage of Badochurn, an oxbow, cut off by the river's convolutions, is still crossed by a redundant footbridge. I soon passed Delnadamph, where only the cottage remains of a lodge, built around 1860. It was one of the highest shooting lodges in Scotland and had twelve bedrooms. Delnadamph is now part of the Balmoral estate and the lodge was given by the Queen to Prince Charles around the time of his marriage to Lady Diana Spencer. Apparently Princess Diana did not enjoy the remoteness of the place and it fell into disrepair, being demolished by the Territorial Army in 1988. Further along the track is a fine building with a large rear door; is it an outdoors centre or the estate office building, or could this be the large garage and chauffeur's restroom said to be ripe for conversion into a summer house for Prince Charles and Duchess Camilla? I wonder if they sell *Hello* magazine in Tomintoul?

The track soon crosses Allt Veannaich and I found myself in the unwished for position of sheep herder. The side valley is quite narrow and all the sheep grazing its grassy banks decided to follow one ewe towards the bridge along the track in front of me. I had no desire to herd them all across but also knew there was no way I could overtake them and cross first, so I took to the water and paddled through the fortunately shallow stream some yards upstream as they all stared pityingly at me from their vantage point on the bridge. The valley here, deepened and widened by glaciers, is plastered with piles of glacial and fluvial deposits cut through by the streams. All around are banks and terraces and on top of one mound of outwash material stands Inchmore bothy, the highest building this side of the watershed, now used as a shooting cabin. There was a farm here and even a mill but little trace now remains apart from stones.

The path continues to wend along an increasingly desolate strath, its broad floor leading up to heathery moors. A shooters' track leads up into the Corrie of Culvachie and a fence climbs the nose of a wide ridge – covered in heather and bilberry and with a few cloudberries showing sparse flowers in mid-May – descending northwards from Cairn Culvachie. Both of these can be used to gain the high ground above the Well of Don. Alternatively you can follow the track round, giving good views across the deep gash of Strath Avon and into the upper reaches of the glen, to a track junction above Lagganauld. From here you can follow the stream up to its source at Well of Don but it is worthwhile walking down to the abandoned farm and looking down into Glen Avon first.

Lagganauld was once visited by Queen Victoria who 'lunched in a splendid position' before continuing her journey to Balmoral by way of Brown Cow Hill. A rocky little valley falls from the old shieling down to the Avon, evidence that water from the present Don catchment once flowed powerfully in the opposite direction. Looking around it is amazing to imagine this place, now with its broken walls and deserted buildings, busy in the summer months with families looking after the flocks and herds brought up to these summer pastures to feed on the rich hill grasses, a result of an exposure of limestone and lime-rich schist in the vicinity. There is even a map, of 1840, in the Scottish National Archives, showing 'arable land of Laganauld and Inchrory'.

Upper Strath Don

The landscape in the upper Don valley is odd. The Fèith Bhàit wanders lethargically through an outsize valley and it was thought by geologists that the upper section of the Don was long ago – before the Ice Ages – captured by the Avon, which has since over-deepened its valley to form the dramatic glen we see today. More recently others have pointed to the formation of a series of south–north breaches eroded during the glacial era. One of these may have carved out the valley, now occupied by Builg Burn and the Avon, which runs so dramatically just west of the watershed and nearly 200 feet (60m) beneath it, beheading the Don and robbing it of a dramatic source in the heart of the Cairngorms. Below Lagganauld the tiny Allt Roderick can hardly have been responsible for the gorge it runs through down to the deepened valley below. Perhaps a remnant of the ice dammed the upper Don valley until the hemmed-in water took the easiest line of escape, biting into the rock as it poured down to Inchrory. The latter is a shooting lodge *par excellence*, a palatial affair extensively refurbished in 1996 and 1997 and said to be owned by foreign grandees – Malaysian businessmen or their ilk.

In mist a line of old, bent and battered metal fence posts leading across the highest ground falling from Cairn Culvachie before rising to the minor top of Druim na Fèithe is a good guide. The Well of Don lies a few yards down the slope from the col, where water trickling through a series of pools forms the Alltan Mhìcheil before becoming the Fèith Bhàit. From the Well the eye is led more towards the deep hollow of Strath Avon than the broad reaches of the upper Don but the sheer remoteness of the spot is a tonic.

Rather than reverse my route I decided to stay with the high ground and walk over the rounded top of Brown Cow Hill, a Corbett[25] but possibly the least exciting of over two hundred in Scotland. As I wandered over Little and then Meikle Geal Charn, my

---

25   Obsession alarm: Corbetts are Scottish hills of a height between 2,500 feet and 3,000 feet with a drop of at least 500 feet between each listed hill and any adjacent higher one. Named after John Rooke Corbett.

deerstalker told me it was very blustery but at least the wind was strong enough to hold off the rain. The view from the quartz-covered top that gives the hill its name was worth the effort. The eastern high Cairngorms, around bulky Ben Avon, were visible below a glowering band of dark cloud, its granite tors like warty protuberances breaking through the plateau top while patches of snow still decorated the higher slopes. I saw hares and snipe, as well as the grouse, which is a mainstay of the local economy, on the hill but definitely no brown cows. The western top, Cairn Sawvie, is not marked but the real summit (2,721 feet/829m), a slight swelling in the middle of the broad 1½-mile-long ridge, has a cairn and there's another one at the eastern end. Brown Cow Hill feeds three rivers: water draining from the north side ends up in the Don, the southern slopes feed the river Gairn, a Dee tributary, and a couple of streams at the western end flow into the Builg Burn which joins River Avon and ultimately the Spey.

From the eastern cairn a vague path passing through peat groughs in places joins a track leading down from Carn Oighreag and this takes you down to Corgarff Castle. I passed the warden's Land Rover and wondered if he'd had any visitors during the four and a half hours I'd been away walking. I had certainly met no one, apart from the Dutch couple. As a bonus, the promised rain held off until I was removing my boots in the car park.

Glossary

Allt Tuileach: stream of the hollow of the horse

Allt Veannaich: stream of the crow

Carn Oighreag: cairn of the cloudberries

Delnadamph: stag's field

Druim na Fèithe: boggy ridge

Fèith Bhàit: boggy thicket?

Inchmore: big meadow

Lagganauld: stream hollow

Lecht: cairn

Meikle Caochan Odhar: big dun-coloured stream

Meikle Geal Charn: big white top

Dee

water is speaking

	DEE
SOURCE	Wells of Dee, Aberdeenshire
G.R.	NN 938 988
LENGTH	86 miles (138 kilometres)
TRIBUTARIES	Lui, Clunie, Gairn, Muick, Tanar, Feugh
MOUTH	Footdee, Aberdeen

At around 86 miles (138km), the Dee is Scotland's fifth-longest river and a noted salmon stream, its course runs entirely through Aberdeenshire except, like the nearby Don, for the last couple of miles, which are within the city of Aberdeen. Rising at over 4,000 feet (1220m) in the heart of the Cairngorm Mountains, its traditional source is at the Wells of Dee between the tops of the third- and fourth-highest mountains in Great Britain, Braeriach and Cairn Toul, from where it tumbles over the Falls of Dee into Garbh Choire. The highest source of water joining the Dee, the Allt a' Choire Mhòir, rises on a gently sloping boulder field at nearly 4,150 feet (1,265m) on the western slopes of Ben Macdui, second-highest mountain in Britain, on the far side of the great glacial gash of Lairig Ghru. Another headstream, March Burn, descends from a broad, high col at about 3,750 feet (1,143m) a mile north of Ben Macdui before disappearing into a welter of boulders. Its waters later emerge from below the Pools of Dee to join the main stream in upper Glen Dee, from where the river flows south-eastwards to the waterfalls and pools of Chest of Dee and the dramatic gorge of Linn of Dee. After all this excitement the river calms down and flows through the beautiful valley of Deeside before it eventually meanders across the lowlands to reach the North Sea.

The key to finding the Dee sources is the Lairig Ghru, a mighty and magnificent mountain pass that cleaves through the Cairngorms. Fewer than seventy English and Welsh mountain summits would rise above the head of the Lairig Ghru, which lies at 2,733 feet (834m), while the Wells of Dee are another 1,250 feet (381m) above that. The pass has been used as a route between Deeside and Strathspey since people started to travel; raiders passed this way, and later drovers. Up until the 1870s, men from Rothiemurchus at its northern end cleared the track each spring of the boulders that had fallen on to it during the winter while their womenfolk carried baskets of eggs through to sell in Braemar. Modern traffic now uses Drumochter Pass on the A9 to the west or the more easterly Lecht on the A939 and the Lairig Ghru is the domain of walkers. Mind, they have to be prepared to walk. The entire route, from Aviemore to Braemar, is around 27 miles (43km) and even by starting at Rothiemurchus and finishing at Linn of Dee, where there are car parks, it is not far off 20 miles (32km). In winter this can be a fearsome place and even halfway through May, when I walked in from the north to visit the Pools of Dee, I encountered a snowstorm in the pass and the tops all around were dusted white.

I started from the splendid campsite at Rothiemurchus. It is situated in the centre of an estate stretching from the Spey to the summit of Braeriach, which has been stewarded by the Grant family for eighteen generations. The first four miles took me through magnificent Scots pine forest. Covering over 10 square miles (25 sq. km) and thought to contain over 10 million trees, Rothiemurchus is one of the largest surviving relics of the Caledonian Forest, which once covered huge areas. Colonizing the British Isles at the end of the Ice Ages, the pine forests retreated to Scotland as the climate warmed and encouraged other species to grow further south. Rothiemurchus and other remnants such as nearby Glenmore and Ballochbuie on the Balmoral estate probably make up about 1 per cent of the original Caledonian Forest. Many of the Rothiemurchus pines are over a hundred years old and some of them were seedlings before Bonnie

Prince Charlie was born. The way through the beautiful mature pine woods is on smooth tracks, popular with cyclists. The Am Beanaidh is crossed at the Cairngorm Club Footbridge, built in 1912 when John Clark was chairman and a no doubt fretful T. R. Gillies was treasurer. A mile or so further and you reach a path junction at Piccadilly, possibly named by soldiers training here during the Second World War. A path, signed 'Lairig Ghru', heads uphill through the thinning forest, climbing parallel with and high above the Allt Druidh, to emerge on to a heather moor, dotted with trees.

The eye is drawn to the great U-shaped trench ahead, which you will reach after a climb by the stream through a confusion of moraine and boulder patches. A memorial plaque on a rock stands where a path descends from the Chalamain Gap, a rough, boulder-strewn ravine on the approach from the Allt Mor car park at Glenmore.[26] The plaque is not far from the site of the Sinclair Memorial Hut. A small, concrete-block-built bothy, this was built in 1957 in memory of Angus Sinclair, who had died on Cairngorm three years earlier. The hut was removed in 1991, partly because of vandalism but also because it was thought to encourage a false sense of security in individuals or parties visiting these potentially dangerous places.

The path, made of stone blocks in parts, continues upwards through the narrow stream valley and another built path soon climbs away to the right. A continuation of the route through the Chalamain Gap, this leads up on to Sron na Lairige and the Cairngorm plateau. A climb up to Braeriach's cairn can be followed by a descent to the head of the Falls of Dee on the plateau edge. From here it is a case of following the stream up to the Wells of Dee. This is a grand, if long, walk in clear conditions in summer. In mist or cloud, navigation is tricky on the plateau and it is worthwhile looking up in the

---

26 At about 8 miles (12.8 kilometres), this route gives the shortest access to the Wells of Dee from a tarmac road but it needs to be remembered that it is also 8 miles back with a total of over 4,000 feet (1,220m) of ascent and that the path, through the Gap, is not always easy underfoot.

glossary below the meaning of Coire Bhrochain. In winter the whole basin around the Wells is likely to be filled with snow.

Back in the Lairig Ghru, the declining Allt Druidh is now on the left with the great wall of Lurcher's Crag looming above as the valley continues ahead. There were several small groups of walkers in the distance. I had noticed a few of them on the campsite the previous evening, some of them arriving very late, and when I stopped to talk to a guy with a large pack who was having a rest in the boulder fields that carpet the highest reaches of the pass, I suddenly remembered. It was May. They must be on the TGO Challenge. Originally known as the Ultimate Challenge, this was the happy inspiration of mountaineer and writer Hamish Brown. The idea of the challenge, started in 1980 and now supported by *The Great Outdoors* magazine, is to cross Scotland from coast to coast, choosing your own route and style of doing it. Individually or in groups of up to four, most folk fill it out to a fortnight, though it has been done in three and a half days.

Looking back towards Aviemore from near the top of the pass, the Lairig Ghru's stark U-shape speaks of its origin, as did the sudden blast of winter that turned the scene white. Glaciers sometimes created new glens by carving breaches through watersheds existing before the Ice Ages. Here ice spilled northwards when its outflow to the south was blocked by greater glaciers along the Dee, carving out a trough that was later deepened by ice streams travelling north across the Cairngorms. In the process about 750 feet (228m) of granite was removed from the northern end of the Lairig Ghru.

Cairns mark the top of the pass and the boundary between Strathspey (formerly Inverness-shire) and Deeside (Aberdeenshire). The aptly named March Burn can be seen tumbling down from the plateau on the left while precipitous slopes climb to Braeriach opposite. A tiny pond below the col and two larger ones a couple of hundred yards further down to the south are the Pools of Dee. Although believed by some to be the source of the river, no

stream actually emerges directly from them. Their modern name seems to be a fabrication rather than a translation, as the old name was Lochan Dubh na Lairig. Water seeps silently into and out of the pools beneath the rashes of boulders surrounding them, and they have no obvious inflow or outflow, though it is the March Burn water that presumably fills them. Even with their isolation trout are supposed to live in one of them. Just south of the largest pool, at the foot of a scree, rises Allt na Lairig Ghru which joins the Allt a' Gharbh-choire a mile or so downstream to form the river proper.

Looking south from the pools the two summits of Cairn Toul and the Devil's Point rise prominently, but I decided to leave those for another day and turned north to cross, once more, the top of one of the most awe-inspiring pedestrian passes in Britain. On returning to the van, I reflected on 15 miles (24km) of walking in nearly eight hours, and I hadn't even got within 2 miles (3.2km) of the source. I also reflected that I was one of the few walkers without poles. I used a pole, carved from a branch, on several long-distance paths years ago, but found it to be more encumbrance than aid. I daresay increasing decripitude will lead me to take them up sometime but for now I'll subscribe to the idea that if God had meant us to walk with poles he wouldn't have let us invent pockets.

A night spent out in the mountains is something every walker should experience from time to time. A splendid solitary Snowdon summit sunrise and a night on top of Cadair Idris with a radio ham for company spring to mind, and to appreciate the Wells of Dee fully there is nothing to beat a walk up the upper reaches of the river and a night out.

The tarmac ends at the Linn of Dee, 6 miles (9.6km) west of Braemar, where the river flows and falls through a 300 yard (275m) long rocky gorge surrounded by Scots pines. A track follows the river, already broad and a dozen miles (20km) from its source, westwards along a wide strath to its confluence with Geldie Burn at White Bridge, which was mostly red when I passed. You pass the scattered stones and walls of Dalvorar and Dubrach, Tomnamoine and Tomnagaoithe, former townships. One wall still standing to a height of about 8 feet (2.4m) is thought to be part of a sheep farm which was built after the Clearances and which was subsequently abandoned in the 1830s when the land was turned over for hunting. At White Bridge I left the track and took to a path gradually swinging round to the north, following the braided river and passing the watersteps and pools of Chest of Dee. There is a rare scatter of natural trees here, birch and aspen while the heather is enlivened by the pale pink flowers of heath spotted orchid and the yellow stars of bog asphodel. The valley gradually narrows and the land begins to rear up, stretching wide across the field of vision on either side until, crossing a small rise, the southern end of the Lairig Ghru appears, the pass dwarfed by the mountains towering above. In the distance appears a pale speck in a vast landscape, Corrour bothy, a welcome sight, for there I could rid myself of some of the weight I'd been carrying, just over three hours after leaving the Linn of Dee.

Crossing the metal bridge over the young Dee, built in 1959 by the Nature Conservancy, I reached the bothy. Corrour had the reputation of being little more than a midden but today it was pleasantly clean, tidy and homely with a stove and sleeping platform inside the stone-built hut. By way of a trial, it has acquired a composting toilet housed in a jaunty wooden extension. Standing beneath the dominating slabs of the Devil's Point, Corrour was originally constructed by the Mar Lodge estate in 1877 to shelter a deer watcher during the summer months before becoming a walkers' bothy in the 1920s. It was rebuilt in 1949 and its loo added in early 2008. Knowing I wouldn't be back here for several more hours and reckoning that the sleeping space would be occupied by then, I pitched my little tent outside and set off up the path behind the hut.

I had decided that I would gain the plateau and enjoy a little Munro-bagging on my way to the Wells of Dee instead of following the river further

Chest of Dee

Southern end of the Lairig Ghru

up the Lairig Ghru. The purist could follow in the footsteps of the Revd George Skene Keith, who traced the river to its source in 1810 thus recording one of Scotland's first rock climbs as he exited the wild Garbh Choire Dhaidh up the cliffs over which the infant Dee plunges. However, unless you wish to 'climb among huge rocks, varying from from one to ten tons, and to catch hold of the stones or fragments that projected, while [ascending at] an angle of 70 or 80 degrees', you will find an easier route. A steady walk up a well-engineered path beside Allt a' Choire Odhair brought me to the plateau edge. The Devil's Point, after all its dominance of the scene during the walk in, rises surprisingly gently to the south, while the stony slopes of Stob Coire an t-Saighdeir climb more steeply to 3,950 feet (1,204m) northwards. Allt a' Choire Odhair, an early Dee tributary, gathers its strength from a fan of tiny streams and springs in this broad col before sliding and tumbling down to Corrour. On the boulder-strewn climb to Cairn Toul, most pointed of the Cairngorm summits, the Dee, which had by now become a silent silvery streak in the depths of the Lairig Ghru 2,500 feet (762m) below, intruded on my consciousness again and I could hear the stream plunging over the corrie edge at the Falls of Dee, nearly 2 miles (3.2km) away as the eagle flies. Standing by the summit cairn of Scotland's fourth-highest mountain, I could see the third, Braeriach, across the great gash of Garbh Choire and the second, Ben Macdui on the far side of the the Lairig Ghru. I barely dipped below 4,000 feet (1,220m) as I made my way over to the Angel's Peak and then, past a herd of grazing reindeer, to the wide, bare summit of Carn na Criche.

I walked down into a vast upland bowl of semi-arctic tundra and sheets of granite gravel, striped in places by frost heave. Little clumps of moss campion

gave a brighter pink contrast to the pale grey-pink of the grit. This is about as remote as it gets in Great Britain; one of those rare places where you hear nothing but nature. The water rising from moss and rock is cold and perfectly clear, and I drank a couple of pints of it to go with a piece of my home-made waybread. From the highest source of the Wells of Dee it looks as if the water cannot escape from the broad basin, but it finds its way through a shallow saucer, losing its voice as it spreads out into a grassy bog and disappearing altogether in the gravel flats before re-emerging, stronger and noisier, 200 yards further down. The Dee is joined by other trickles and streams rising from the slopes of Einich Cairn and Braeriach and is already 8 feet (2.4m) wide before it gathers speed to rush and then plunge headlong over the Falls of Dee.

Standing on the rim of the cliffs I could hear but not see the young Dee as it drops in a succession of cascades over the ice- and water-smoothed rock to

Above the Falls of Dee

the corrie floor 500 feet (152m) below. Viewed from the crag edge on the climb to Braeriach the Dee scores a green braid through the granite-pink screes of the corrie, disappearing at times among the boulders and spreading itself into shallow pools. I sat by Braeriach's cairn, eight hours after I had left the Linn of Dee, gazing out over arguably the finest upper-river view in Britain. Seen between two ribs of crag, stony Coire Bhrochain forms a giant step below which the mountainside plunges once more to the Lairig Ghru floor. The two major headstreams of the Dee, Allt a' Gharbh-choire and Allt na Lairig Ghru, meet in a mêlée of meanders, channels, cut-offs and islands in a broad, boggy strath before finally merging to flow resolutely southwards. If the subject of the picture is commanding then the frame is even more so with Cairngorm, Ben Macdui, Carn a'Mhaim, Cairn Toul and the Angel's Peak projecting above the valley, their ancient bones exposed in the crags and their upper slopes dandruffed by scree and boulders.

The walk between Cairn Toul and Braeriach has been described as one of the finest high-level walks in Scotland, so I mostly returned the way I had come, and took in the Devil's Point for its glimpses into upper Glen Dee and the confluence with meandering Geusachan Burn. Cloud was gathering on Braeriach and just touching Cairn Toul and to the west a pink glow was illuminating range after range of mountains as I made my way back to the path to Corrour and my little tent. It doesn't go properly dark in high summer in the high mountains in the high latitudes, so it was light when I fell asleep and light when I woke up. Light and decidedly chilly. I was up and off just after half past five on a brilliant morning with the sun glinting on the crags of the Devil's Point and illuminating the dew on myriad spiders' webs which shone in the heather like old-fashioned gas mantles.

Arriving back at the Linn of Dee twenty-four hours virtually to the minute after I had left, I was spared tramping the 6 miles of metalled misery

back to Braemar by dint of hitching a lift from an Aberdonian Munroist from Slovakia who was dropping off two of his cycling compatriots before driving round to Glen Shee for a walk. We talked of mountains, in Scotland and in Slovakia, where they are twice as high as anything we have. 'And tell me, is there any other walking in Great Britain?' Luckily for him we arrived at the campsite before I had time to start.

Glossary

Allt a' Choire Mhòir: stream of the big corrie

Allt Druidh: stream of the oozing

Ben Macdui: hill of the sons of Duff or of the black pig

Braeriach: dappled hill

Cairn Toul: hill of the barn

Carn a'Mhaim: cairn of the breast-shaped hill

Carn na Criche: boundary pile of stones

Chalamain Gap: Eag Coire na Còmhdhalach – ravine of the corrie of the assembly

Coire Bhrochain: corrie of porridge. Local tradition speaks of some cattle that fell from Braeriach here. That's what they ended up like.

Corrour: from Coire Odhar – dun corrie, of which it lies at the foot

Devil's Point: Bod an Deamhain. Quick thinking by Queen Victoria's ghillie resulted in this name when HM enquired; in Gaelic it's the Devil's prick.

Drumochter: ridge of the high ground

Garbh Choire: rough corrie

Geusachan Burn: stream of the little pine wood

Lairig Ghru: pass of oozing water

Lochan Dubh na Lairig: black tarn of the pass

March Burn: Allt na Criche – burn of the boundary

Rothiemurchus: the place of Murchas's fort

Sròn na Lairige: point of the pass

Stob Coire an t-Saighdeir: point of the soldier's corrie

Tomnagaoithe: windy knoll

Tomnamoine: peaty knoll

Quotations

I have started the description of each source with a quote. Most of them are from literature of one sort or another but a couple I've included because they tickled me and some I've just made up. In case any reader is interested I include a list of them, together with their origin or explanation, below.

Peninsular Perusals
Tamar, Torridge *and Turner?* A reference to the painting discussed in the section.

Exe *marks the spot* Well, what else could it be?

Dartmoor Days – Dart, Taw, Teign, Tavy, West Okement *sound of slow trickling* Henry Williamson, *Tarka the Otter*, a powerful tale of struggle for survival. Tarka visits the high moorland where these streams rise.

Jordan *what did I see?* From the song 'Swing Low, Sweet Chariot', an African-American spiritual written by Wallis Willis sometime around 1860.

Piddle *tiny streams in a land of giants* A reference to the nearby Cerne Abbas Giant and my meeting with Long Distance Walkers Association folk.

Stour *genius of the place* Alexander Pope's *Epistle IV, to Richard Boyle, Earl of Burlington*, in which he laid down his ideas for landscape architecture, which are epitomized at Stourhead.

Valleys Broad and Fair
Thames *in paradise* 'Waterloo Sunset' by Ray Davies, the greatest songwriter of my generation.

Avon *smooth runs the water* William Shakespeare, *Henry VI Part 2*: it has to be the Bard for the Avon.

Great Ouse *Say it. Ouse. Slowly.* Graham Swift, *Waterland*, a novel, concerned with the importance and nature of history, based in the Fens.

Nene *royal road* Part of a Jean Plaidy novel title, *Royal Road to Fotheringay*, recalling times we moored on the river by the castle remains.

Witham *haunts of coot and hern* Alfred Lord Tennyson, 'The Brook'. The poet was born in Lincolnshire and the Sculpture Trail inspired by his work follows part of the river.

Medway *a mere trickle still* Tracie Jenkins, 'O Medway' in her collection *57 Poems about the River Medway*.

Bristol Avon *all my worries far behind* J. J.Cale, *Ride the River*, which remembers a narrowboat cruise between Bath and Bristol Harbour.

A Welcome in the Hillside
Taff *at the top* Sorry!

Usk and Tawe *lift your eyes where the roads dip* T. S. Eliot, 'Usk'.

The Welsh Desert
Severn *a silence in the hills* Alfred Lord Tennyson, *In Memoriam*, XIX.

Wye *or why not?*

Teifi *from out the store-house of the sky* Dafydd ap Gwilym, the greatest of all Welsh poets, who is said to be buried at Strata Florida Abbey.

Tywi *A step, methinks, will pass the stream* John Dyer, 'Grongar Hill'.

Quietest under the Sun
Teme, Onny and Clun *Far in a western brookland* A. E. Housman, *A Shropshire Lad*.

Snowdonia Wanderings
Dyfrdwy *where Dee unmix'd doth flow* Michael Drayton, *Poly-Olbion*.

Dyfi *king of rivers* George Borrow, *Wild Wales*.

Conwy *one of the famous rivers of the world* George Borrow, *Wild Wales*.

A Great Divide
Trent *a day's march* Arnold Bennett, *Clayhanger*, Book 1, chapter 2: 'Geography had been one of his strong points . . . But he had never been instructed for five minutes in the geography of his native country. He could have drawn a map of the Orinoco, but he could not have found the Trent in a day's march.'

Don *shimmer through this valley* Chris Jones, 'Meadowhall', included in *At the End of the Road a River*, a sequence of poems about the Don in Sheffield.

Derwent *out past the mill* Robert Louis Stevenson, 'Where Go the Boats?'

Calder *Castleford lasses must needs be fair, for they wash in the Calder and rinse in the Aire* Traditional.

Urban Interludes
Tame *damp tips of . . . weak headwaters* Roy Fisher, 'Birmingham River', from *The Long and the Short of It: Poems 1995–2005*.

Stour *how calm and clear it flows* Edward Caswall, 'St Kenelm's Well' in *The Masque of Mary and Other Poems*.

Mersey *water is life and heaven's gift* On the steel fence at the confluence of the Goyt and the Tame in Stockport.

Yorkshire Dales and Moors
Swale *this dear spot* Song of Swaledale, traditional.

Ure *a trickle in the grass* Ella Pontefract, *Wensleydale*.

Nidd *nothing could be serener* A. J. Brown, *Moorland Tramping in West Yorkshire*.

Wharfe *Farre in the North* Chaucer, *Reeve's Tale*, 'were they both that highte Strother. Farre in the North can I nat tell where', believed to be a reference to Langstrothdale.

Aire *a real North country limestone fountain* Charles Kingsley, *The Water Babies*.

Ribble *too few people know it* Hilaire Belloc, 'On the Sources of Rivers' from *First and Last*, a book of essays.

Eden *seek the river of the soul* William Mounsey, inscription on the Jew Stone.

Lune *not even a crushed blade of grass* A. Wainwright, *Walks on the Howgill Fells*.

Derwent *to Whinny-muir thou com'st at last* 'Lyke Wake Dirge', traditional.

Lakeland Diversions

Derwent *make ceaseless music* William Wordsworth, 'The River Derwent'.

Esk *their very fountains* Samuel Taylor Coleridge, *Letters*.

High Pennines

Tees *in tumult leaves his source* Sir Walter Scott, *Rokeby*.

Wear *I pray lend an ear* 'The Bonny Moor Hen', trad.

Tyne *all mine, all mine* Lindisfarne, 'Fog on the Tyne'.

Southern Uplands

Tweed and Annan *this blessed, honest-smelling hill country* John Buchan, *The Thirty-Nine Steps*.

Clyde *bonnie banks* Sir Harry Lauder, 'Roamin' in the Gloamin''.

Nith *with trees on either hand* Robert Louis Stevenson, 'Where Go the Boats?'

Highland Springs

Forth *a sapphire of the elements, an entity of blue* Craig Walton, 'Reflections of the River Forth'.

Tay *most beautiful to be seen* William McGonagall, 'The Railway Bridge of the Silvery Tay'.

Spey *home of the pike and the dipper* Nat Hall, 'On the Trail of the Erne'.

Don *How now?* Refers to the proximity of the source to Brown Cow Hill.

Dee *water is speaking* Nan Shepherd, *The Living Mountain*.

Select Webliography

Websites seem to appear and disappear as some river sources do. I've included a few that I have found to be useful and interesting.

www.mwis.org.uk/index.php
   Mountain Weather Information Service and much more
www.ordnancesurvey.co.uk/oswebsite/getamap/
   Ordnance Survey
www.legendarydartmoor.co.uk/
   Dartmoor history, legend and archaeology
www.ordnancesurvey.co.uk/oswebsite/freefun/didyou-know/placenames/docs/welsh_guide.pdf
   Ordnance Survey Welsh placenames guide
www.welshicons.org.uk/main/
   Welsh icons with a useful rivers section
www.scottish-places.info/ Extensive Scottish gazetteer
www.taywesterncatchments.blogspot.co.uk/
   Much information about the River Tay
www.theuplandofmar.squarespace.com/
   Detailed site on Cairngorm topography and etymology

Bibliography

First and foremost
Ordnance Survey maps. I've used about four dozen 1:25 000 Explorer and Outdoor Leisure sheets during the course of preparing this book. The best maps there are.

General
Bridge, G., *The Mountains of England and Wales*, Gaston's Alpine Books, 1973
Hewitt, R., *Map of a Nation*, Granta, 2010
Nuttall, J. & A., *The Mountains of England and Wales Vol. 1: Wales*, Cicerone, 3rd edition, 2009
Nuttall, J. & A., *The Mountains of England and Wales Vol. 2: England*, Cicerone, 3rd edition, 2008
Owen, S., Pooley, C., et al, *Rivers and the British Landscape*, Carnegie, 2005
Russell, R., *Rivers*, David & Charles, 1978
Wright, N., *English Mountain Summits*, Hale, 1974

Peninsular Perusals
Bingham, A., *Dorset Landranger Guide*, Ordnance Survey, 1987
Crossing, W., *Guide to Dartmoor*, David & Charles reprint of 1912 edition, 1965
Harvey, L. A., & St Leger-Gordon, D., *The New Naturalist Dartmoor*, Collins, 1977
Howden, N. J. K., et al., *Hydrology: Science and Practice for the 21st Century*, Proceedings of the British Hydrological Society International Conference, 2004
Powell, A. B., *Stealing Away, Like Time*, Wessex Archaeology, 2005
Thurlow, G., *Dartmoor Companion*, Peninsula Press, 1993
Williamson, H., *Tarka the Otter*, Puffin Books, 1962
Woodbridge, K., *The Stourhead Landscape*, National Trust, 2002
Worth, R. H., *Dartmoor*, David & Charles, 1967

Valleys Broad and Fair
Gibbings, R., *Sweet Thames Run Softly*, Dent, 1946
O'Neil, H., & Grinsell, L. V., *Gloucestershire Barrows*, Transactions of the Bristol and Gloucestershire Archaeological Society, 1960
Pritchard, M., & Carpenter, H., *A Thames Companion*, OUP, 1981
The Thames Path, Aerofilms, 1993

A Welcome in the Hillside
Brereton, J. M., *The Brecon Beacons National Park*, David & Charles, 1990
Davies, M. (ed.), *Brecon Beacons National Park*, HMSO, 1978
Mason, E. J., *Portrait of the Brecon Beacons*, Hale, 1975

The Welsh Desert
Bick, D. E., *The Old Metal Mines of Wales Part 4: West*

Montgomeryshire, The Pound House, 1977

Cliffe, J. H., *Notes and Recollections of an Angler: Rambles Among the Mountains, Valleys, and Solitudes of Wales,* Hamilton, Adams, & Co, London, 1860

Condry, W., *Exploring Wales*, Faber & Faber, 1970

Wright, S., *Up the Claerwen*, Cornish Bros, 1948

Quietest under the Sun

Thoresby Jones, P., *Welsh Border Country*, Batsford, 1946

Snowdonia Wanderings

Borrow, G., *Wild Wales*, Collins, 1862

Jones, J., *The Lakes of North Wales*, Wildwood House, 1983

Monkhouse, P., *On Foot in North Wales and the Peak*, Diadem, 1988

Roberts, G., *The Lakes of Eryri*, Carreg Gwalch, 1995

A Great Divide

Bibby, A., *The Pennine Divide*, Frances Lincoln, 2005

Collins, H. C., *The Roof of Lancashire*, Dent, 1950

Dodd, A. E. & E. M., *Peakland Roads and Trackways*, Moorland, 1974

Edwards, K. C., *The Peak District,* Fontana New Naturalist, 1973

Roberts, A. E., & Leach, J. R., *The Coal Mines of Buxton*, Scarthin Books, 1985

Urban Interludes

Darby, G., *West Midlands River Stour*, Home Publishing, 2006

Dilworth, D., *The Tame Mills of Staffordshire*, Phillimore, 1976

Fisher, R., *The Long and the Short of It: Poems 1995–2005*, Bloodaxe, 2005

Pitt, William, *A Topographical History of Staffordshire; Including its Agriculture, Mines and Manufactures. Memoirs of Eminent Natives; Statistical Tables; And Every Species of Information Connected with the Local History of the County. With a Succinct Account of the Rise and Progress of the Staffordshire Potteries,* J. Smith, Newcastle-Under-Lyme, 1817

Wainwright, A., *A Pennine Way Companion*, Westmorland Gazette, 1968

Yorkshire Dales and Moors

Clayton, P., *On High Yorkshire Hills*, Dalesman, 1992

Hartley, M., & Ingilby, J., *The Yorkshire Dales*, Dent, 1963

Houghton, F. W., *Upper Wharfedale*, Dalesman, 1980

Lofthouse, J., *Three Rivers*, Robert Hale, 1949

Morris, D., *The Swale*, William Sessions, 1995

Mitchell, W. R., *Wild Pennines*, Hale, 1976

Pontefract, E., & Hartley, M., *Swaledale*, Dent, 1944

Raistrick, A., *The Pennine Dales*, Arrow, 1972

Raistrick, A., *The Lead Industry of Wensleydale and Swaledale Vol. 1: The Mines*, Moorland, 1975

Raistrick, A., *Malham and Malham Moor*, Dalesman, 1971

Speight, H., *Upper Wharfedale*, Elliot Stock, London, 1900

Speight, H., *The Craven and North-West Yorkshire Highlands*, Smith Settle facsimile edition, 1989

Stephenson, T., *The Pennine Way*, HMSO, 1969

Wainwright, A., *Walks in Limestone Country*, Westmorland Gazette, 1970

Wainwright, A., *Walks on the Howgill Fells*, Westmorland Gazette, 1972

Wright, G. N., *Roads and Trackways of the Yorkshire Dales*, Moorland, 1985

Grouse Moor News, Savills, Summer 2010

Lakeland Diversions

Cooper, W., *The Tarns of Lakeland*, Frank Peters, 3rd edition, 1983

Wainwright, A., *Pictorial Guides to the Lakeland Fells Book 4: The Southern Fells*, Westmorland Gazette, 1960

High Pennines

Bowes, P., *Weardale: Clearing the Forest*, Peter Bowes, 1990

Dibb, A., *England's Highest Peaks*, Mainstream, 2000

Fairbairn, R. A., *Weardale Mines: British Mining No. 56*, Northern Mine Research Society, 1996

Hill, A., *Walking in Northumberland*, Cicerone, 2004

Jonas, J. B., *Walking the North Tyne,* Ramblers' Association, 2005

Ramsden, D. M., *Teesdale*, Museum Press, 1947

Southern Uplands

Banks, F. R., *Scottish Border Country*, Batsford, 1951

Belloc, H., 'On the Sources of Rivers', *First and Last*, Methuen, 1911

House, J., *Portrait of the Clyde*, Hale, 1975

Talbot White, J., *The Scottish Border and Northumberland*, Eyre Methuen, 1973

Highland Springs

Kemp, N., & Wrightham, M. (eds), *Hostile Habitats: Scotland's Mountain Environment*, SMT, 2006

Nelson, G., *Highland Bridges*, Aberdeen University Press, 1990

Price, R. J., *Highland Landforms*, Highlands & Islands Development Board, 1976

Shepherd, N., *The Living Mountain*, Canongate, 2008

Steven, Campbell R., *The Central Highlands: SMC District Guide Books*, SMT, 1972

Storer, R., *The Ultimate Guide to the Munros: Volume 2,* Luath Press, 2009

Strathard News, Issue 13, May 2004

Thomas, C. W., Gillespie, M. R., Jordan, C., and Hall, A. M., *Geological Structure and Landscape of the Cairngorm Mountains,* Scottish Natural Heritage Commissioned Report No. 064, 2004

Turnbull, R. *Walking in the Cairngorms*, Cicerone, 2005

Index

Page numbers in **bold** refer to main entries

Acknowledgments

I would like to thank everyone who has helped with making this book:

My editor at Frances Lincoln, Andrew Dunn, for guidance along the way; Anne Askwith, for much sage and practical advice; and my book designer, Maria Charalambous, for help and inspiration, for keeping my nose to the grindstone and for inviting me to FL's offices, thereby giving me the chance to speculate on the source of the Hampstead Ponds.

Geoff, Paul and other friends who have knowingly or unknowingly been with me on source walks over the years.

Brett for his Scotland weather forecast, Danny for his divining rods, Wheat for *Some Days are Diamonds*, and other musical friends whose tunes in my head have often kept my feet moving.

Mike and Denise for the 'Contour' Road Book and mining historian Simon Hughes for digging out a copy of William Waller's map.

Several webmasters, to whom I am indebted for the use of images from their sites. I can lose hours out of a day simply looking through lovingly collated and strikingly presented local history sites: Paul Townsend, Bristol historian, for permission to use a print of boxer Tom Cribb from his fascinating website bristolpast.co.uk; Alan George and his oldmerthyrtydfil.com website for archive pictures of Taf Fechan and the Storey Arms; Brian Ives at the Nidderdale Museum for the photo of Scar Village; Powys County Archives for permission to use the coloured engraving *Source of the Severn* on the title page, published in London in 1823 by G. & W.B. Whittaker at Ave Maria Lane; Bill Egerton, Sutton Poyntz Village Web Group Leader, for information about the River Jordan.

A couple of photographers who have graciously allowed me to plunder their work: Maria and Pete for the photo of a memorable cruise through London; John Kaye for bringing back childhood memories with his study of Ribble 2492 at Lower Mosley Street, Manchester, 16 May 1959.

And especially Dot, for tolerating a spur-of-the-moment absentee husband and for her ever-valuable counsel.

PICTURE CREDITS